DATE DUE

David Brody's *The Teavangelicals* is a must read for those who want to understand how people of faith are making a monumental difference within the Tea Party. To nobody's surprise, the media doesn't get this phenomenon, but David's book puts them on notice: Teavangelicals are here to stay.

GLENN BECK, #1 *New York Times* bestselling author and founder of GBTV

Always intriguing and raising issues that are under-reported, David Brody provides insight into the movement that was so consequential to the 2010 elections.

JAKE TAPPER, senior White House correspondent for ABC News

The Teavangelicals is a timely reminder that faith and freedom have always been inseparable in America. The rise of the Tea Party and citizen activism from sea to shining sea is the result of people of faith initiating a new and powerful American Awakening.

U.S. SENATOR JIM DEMINT

David Brody has written a captivating and insightful book on the ever-growing Tea Party movement. David's unique insights and expertise makes *The Teavangelicals* a must-read for anyone following the national political scene. Well done.

JAY SEKULOW, Chief Counsel, American Center for Law & Justice

David Brody's *The Teavangelicals* gives readers an intimate look at the inner workings of conservative politics and its operatives. Few writers have the access to decision makers and a free pass to look behind the curtain like David. Whether a religious conservative or someone merely interested in the political process, readers won't be disappointed.

PENNY NANCE, President and CEO of Concerned Women for America

The Teavangelicals

THE INSIDE STORY *of how*

THE EVANGELICALS *and* THE TEA PARTY

are TAKING BACK AMERICA

DAVID BRODY

CHIEF POLITICAL CORRESPONDENT, CBN NEWS

ZONDERVAN.com/
AUTHORTRACKER
follow your favorite authors

ZONDERVAN

The Teavangelicals
Copyright © 2012 by David Brody

This title is also available as a Zondervan ebook.
Visit www.zondervan.com/ebooks.

This title is also available in a Zondervan audio edition.
Visit www.zondervan.fm.

Requests for information should be addressed to:

Zondervan, *Grand Rapids, Michigan 49530*

Library of Congress Cataloging-in-Publication Data

Brody, David, 1965–
    The teavangelicals / David Brody.
      p. cm.
    Includes bibliographical references and index.
    ISBN: 978-0-310-33561-0 (hardcover)
    1. Tea Party movement. 2. Evangelicalism—United States. 3. Christian
conservatism—United States. I. Title.
    JK2391.T43B76   2012
    320.520973—dc23   2012006238

Cover photography: iStockphoto®
Interior design: Beth Shagene

Printed in the United States of America

12 13 14 15 16 17 18 19 /DCI/ 22 21 20 19 18 17 16 15 14 13 12 11 10 9 8 7 6 5 4 3 2 1

This book is dedicated to my wife and best friend, Lisette.
Since high school she has brought
blessing upon blessing into my life
as my personal career counselor, agent,
therapist, prayer warrior, and cheerleader.
Putting Jesus first has always been her top priority,
and it was Lisette who introduced me to the Lord
more than twenty-five years ago.
Not only does she have brains and beauty,
she has a gift from the Lord of making people's lives better,
and that is exactly what she does for me.
So, thank you, Lisette,
for walking with me on this journey we call life
and for riding the roller coaster with me all these years.
(Proverbs 31:10–31)

CONTENTS

FOREWORD

by Mike Huckabee

MANY JOURNALISTS COVERING THIS PARTICULAR PHENOMENON call it everything from "the religious right" to "values voters" to "the Christian right." David Brody, however, is perhaps the one person in American journalism who understands and covers the conservative Christian movement from the inside. With the word *Teavangelicals*, David had coined a term that not only forms the title of the book, but also explains the unique blend of a biblical worldview with the Tea Party emphasis on conservatism and the Constitution. Blend the two, and you have the "Teavangelical."

Not only does Brody's book accurately introduce a moniker for the movement, but his insights help explain the passion and the principles that have given a voice to millions of Americans. As Brody reveals, the Teavangelicals are not so much traditional Republicans as they are traditional Americans. Teavangelicals may feel more comfortable with the Republicans, but they are still a long way from being part of the GOP establishment. Teavangelicals are often misunderstood or miscast as "one-issue activists," but those who make such an assumption reveal deep ignorance of the movement and its manpower.

In his well-researched analysis, David Brody takes the reader behind the scenes of the Teavangelical phenomenon. If you are part of the movement, *Teavangelicals* will be one of the rare books that will treat you with respect. If you aren't part of the movement but just want to understand it better, David Brody will help you gain new appreciation for the sincerity, the substance, and the sensitivity of those who make up the Teavangelical movement.

MIKE HUCKABEE

A NOTE
from the AUTHOR

I DIDN'T WANT TO WRITE THIS BOOK BUT HISTORY FORCED ME TO. I couldn't help the fact that the Tea Party created a new political movement in this country. I couldn't help the fact that evangelical Christians became a significant portion of this crusade. It happened organically, like a YouTube clip spreading virally. There's no stopping it. Just like me at the buffet table.

So there I was, the day after the 2010 midterm elections, sitting bleary eyed at my desk inside the Christian Broadcasting Network's Washington, DC, bureau, when I noticed something interesting. The postelection data showed just how instrumental the Tea Party was in the Republican takeover of the House of Representatives. Those Tea Partiers comprised 41% of Americans who went to the polls on November 2, 2010.[1] But just as interesting was the fact that self-identified evangelicals made up the largest constituency group in the midterm elections. And then came this crossover beauty: more than half of the Tea Partiers also said they were conservative evangelicals.

My mind started to race. My experience on the campaign trail compelled me to acknowledge the fact that evangelical Christians were popping up everywhere at Tea Party rallies around the country. I had always known that evangelicals played a significant role within the Tea Party movement, but now I had the raw data to prove it. I figured there must be a way to sum up this fascinating convergence. How could I best describe this relationship? I needed a name. Tea Party Christian? Too boring. Christian Tea Partier? Too radical. It needed to be catchy yet simple. And then, as I stared at a bagel with cream cheese on my desk, it came to me. To borrow a verse from the Bible (and taken completely out of context!), "The two shall become one." Hence, the birth of the term *Teavangelical*. It made perfect sense!

Still, coming up with the title didn't compel me to write this book. As a matter of fact, since 2008 friends and colleagues have been suggesting I write a campaign-style book. They knew as chief political correspondent for CBN News that I had been blessed to interview the top political and evangelical newsmakers in the country. With multiple appearances on NBC's Meet the Press, CNN, CSPAN, and Fox News, I have gained a reputation as a reliable and fair evangelical political analyst (talk about a niche!). It's humbling and pretty funny too, considering I grew up Jewish (that should be a separate book). But doing a book during the 2008 presidential campaign never felt right. And this time around in the 2012 election cycle, I felt the same way — that is, until a trip to the bus stop changed everything.

In early January 2011, I woke up in a grouchy mood. Maybe I had too much Mexican food the night before. I don't know what it was, but I was just cranky for no particular reason. As I got ready to go off to work on a chilly morning, I noticed there was no car available for my wife to drive me to the Metro station. So I had to walk to the bus stop — with the temperature at about 10 degrees! Ugh! Mumbling and grumbling, I closed the front door behind me, secured my iPod on top of my frigid head, and trudged off to the dreaded bus stop.

On the way there, something happened. I can't explain it other than to say that I felt the presence of God walking with me the entire way. I began praying to him, asking for my crabbiness to go away. I then looked up in the sky and saw the most beautiful full moon I've ever seen, reminding me of God's majesty and creation. And while all of this was happening the song "In Christ Alone" started playing on my iPod. The song spoke to me about how God has blessed our lives more than we will ever know (true!) and how we must put our trust in him alone. Then I heard a lyric that touched my heart like no other: "In every victory, let it be said of me / My source of strength, my source of hope is Christ alone."

At that point I felt a tugging on my heart and soft inner words that said, "Write the book." I figured that had to come from God since it sure wasn't what I wanted to do, considering I was very busy at work and home. Yet God was clearly trying to tell me something —that I may be busy, but I needed to rely on him as my source of strength. Well, my arms are too short to box with God, so here we are. I bring you the story of the Teavangelicals.

As you'll see, Teavangelical organizers and voters come in all shapes and sizes, and you're about to get acquainted with them through their personal stories. In addition, as CBN News Chief Political Correspondent, I've received behind-the-scenes access during this presidential campaign, garnering stories and interviews from the Republican presidential candidates who are navigating the Teavangelical waters.

So sit back and relax. You are about to go on a journey, an excursion through the Teavangelical world. Along the way you'll discover what it means to be a Teavangelical and the main issues that connect evangelicals with the Tea Party movement. You'll even get to take a little quiz to see where you fit on the Teavangelical scale. But beyond all that, you're about to get a real sense of the informal but very real connections and coordination that go on between both evangelical and Tea Party organizers.

A large group of patriotic Americans mobilized themselves in 2010 and changed the conversation inside the Washington, DC, Beltway—not an easy thing to do. Yet that was just Act 1. Act 2 is coming in November 2012. With that said, let's lift the curtain. Now playing on stage: the Teavangelicals!

Chapter 1

THE DNA *of a* TEAVANGELICAL

SITTING ALONE IN HIS APARTMENT WITH AN OPEN BIBLE AND A racing heart, Kellen Guida was thinking seriously about giving his life to Jesus Christ. On a cold Washington, DC, winter night in January 2010, one of the original cofounders of the New York City Tea Party group found himself ready to take the plunge. But would he? After all, growing up Irish Catholic hadn't exposed him to discussions about a personal relationship with the God of the Bible. That sort of chatter was left to evangelicals. Yet after what he had experienced the week before, he knew it was decision time.

Just a few days before this heart-pounding moment, Kellen had sat enthralled at a Tea Party retreat in Jacksonville, Florida. Guida's successful launch of the New York City's Tea Party 365 group had led to his being invited to be a board member of the newly formed powerhouse group the Tea Party Patriots. This Tea Party libertarian joined a dozen others at this exclusive meeting devised to plot Tea Party strategy for the upcoming midterm elections. The meeting turned into more than a strategy session for Kellen.

During this two-day gathering, Kellen met an affluent businessman named Jack (his real name is being withheld for privacy reasons) and a Tea Party leader from the Jacksonville area by the name of Billie Tucker. Both were vocal about their faith. Kellen describes them as "wearing it on their sleeves." While it made some in the room uncomfortable, Kellen was intrigued. Jack, a successful businessman, not only helped Tea Party Patriot board members with adroit tactics, but he also led prayers, asking God for direction and the skill to get through all the upcoming hurdles that the Tea Party members were about to encounter. Jack had discussions with Kellen about how it was God, not himself, who was in control of his life. The fact that this insanely rich businessman was ultimately relying on God and not his own strong skill set was a foreign concept to Kellen, but it got him thinking about this God of the universe. Jack continued to talk to Kellen throughout the next two days, and before Kellen left Jacksonville, Jack gave Kellen a few Bible verses to think about on the way home.

After a few hours on the airplane, Kellen landed at the airport, and under a spell of excitement and confusion, he called Jack and asked, "What the heck is going on?" Thoughts of an omnipotent personal God were consuming his mind. His experience in Jacksonville was feeling more like revival than retreat. He was experiencing the power of God in a way he never had before. Jack encouraged him to open his Bible, and that's exactly what Kellen did on that cold winter night.

A couple of days later, as Kellen sifted through Bible verses with enthusiasm and curiosity, he began to realize that the feelings he was experiencing weren't fleeting ones. "This is real," Kellen told himself. He knew he needed to calm down. The moment was exciting and overwhelming. He slowed down and just talked to God. He then went to his computer and found the Sinner's Prayer of Repentance. And then it happened. From his heart, Kellen Guida recited that prayer by acknowledging that he was a sinner and needed Jesus Christ to be Lord and Savior of his life. Kellen Guida, a Tea Party libertarian in search of God, had embraced Christianity. At that precise moment, he became a born-again Christian. Politically speaking, he became a Teavangelical.

What in the World Is a Teavangelical?

Kellen Guida is just one of millions who call themselves Teavangelicals. So what does that mean? Despite what you might think, a Teavangelical is not an evangelical who likes tea. That person is called a "small group Bible study leader." How can I best describe a Teavangelical? Think of it this way. Pretend you're a Mormon, and you buy into the libertarian movement. You'd be called a "Mormonarian." If you were a Baptist who also happened to be an abolitionist back in the 1860s, you would have been called a "Baptistionist." Or how about an old-time Pentecostal who embraced the disco era in the 1970s? This person would be called an "outcast." Sorry, I digressed there a little bit. But you get the idea, right?

Don't bother looking in *Webster's*. You won't find the definition there. It can only be found here. *Webster's*, take note:

Teavangelical: (noun) a conservative Christian (typically evangelical) who strongly supports the Tea Party agenda or is active in the Tea Party movement (pronounced "TEE-van-GEL-i-cal")

Teavangelicals come in all shapes and sizes. They may be stay-at-home moms or representatives or senators on Capitol Hill. Some may be more active than others. Whatever the form and whatever the level, they are roaming across this land of ours with one purpose: restoring America to greatness.

Now, it's vitally important to understand that Teavangelicals are *not* trying to take over the Tea Party movement or co-opt their agenda. Just because evangelical Christians are heavily involved in the Tea Party movement doesn't mean that they are ready to storm the gates and change the stated goals. If you think that, you're missing the point entirely. These are evangelicals who are breaking bread with the Tea Party. They are part of the Tea Party. Think of Teavangelicals as a large subset of the Tea Party movement. The truth of the matter is that Tea Party libertarians *cannot* win consistently and consequentially without evangelicals by their side. Conversely, evangelicals can't do it alone either.

Are there differences between libertarians and evangelicals? Yes, of course, and we will address the challenges of their coexistence later in this book. For now, though, and for the foreseeable future, they have a common bond and are riding shotgun together in the front seat of American politics. They are partners in this effort to take America back to its founding constitutional principles.

The New Hybrid (and It's Not a Car)

Admit it. You're a little skeptical. You're saying to yourself, "Cute little word. *Teavangelical.* I give you credit for thinking of it, but there's no real movement like this in America. You've been watching too many reruns of *The Brady Bunch.* You've gone a little loopy." Well, you're right. I have watched my fair share of *Brady Bunch* episodes (my favorite one is when they travel to Hawaii and Greg wipes out on his surfboard), but I have not gone loopy. This Teavangelical movement is backed up with cold, hard facts.

When talking about Teavangelicals, it's important to understand their hybrid nature. Just as a hybrid car is powered fully by both gas and electric power, Teavangelicals are fully evangelical yet staunchly Tea Party–esque.

First, let me define what I mean by *evangelical.* The Barna Group, a nationally respected research organization that concentrates on the connection between faith and culture, identifies evangelical Christians as those who have made "a personal commitment to Jesus Christ that is still important in their life today and who also indicated they believe that when they die they will go to Heaven because they had confessed their sins and had accepted Jesus Christ as their savior." They also believe that "they have a personal responsibility to share their religious beliefs about Christ with non-Christians; that Satan exists; that eternal salvation is possible only through grace, not works; that Jesus Christ lived a sinless life on earth; that the Bible is accurate in all that it teaches; and that God is an all-knowing, all-powerful, perfect deity who created the universe and still rules it today. Being classified as an evangelical is not dependent upon church attendance or the denominational affiliation of the church attended."[1]

Now that we have that out of the way, let's make sure we understand exactly what the Tea Party stands for. TEA stands for "Taxed Enough Already" but their core values are as follows:

- fiscal responsibility
- constitutionally limited government
- free markets[2]

With that established, let's start to look at the crossover between these groups.

One of the most respected polling companies in the country is the Pew Research Center's Forum on Religion and Public Life. Their survey, conducted from August 2010 through February 2011, shows the following:

- 69% of registered voters who agreed with the religious right also said they agreed with the Tea Party.

- White evangelical Protestants are roughly five times as likely to agree with the Tea Party movement as to disagree with it (44% versus 8%).

- 64% of Tea Party supporters oppose same-sex marriage.

- 59% of Tea Party supporters say abortion should be illegal in all or most cases.[3]

Before moving on to some other convincing data, let's make an important distinction. Did you notice that the survey above referred to "White evangelical Protestants"? When we refer to a Teavangelical, we are typically (but not always) referring to these types of people. That, however, doesn't mean that Protestants, Catholics, or other religious denominations, races, and ethnicities aren't Teavangelicals. Needless to say, there are many "saved, born-again Christians" that may not identify themselves as evangelical yet still agree with the Tea Party agenda. What about the saved Catholic, Lutheran, Methodist, and so on? Hey, if you follow Jesus Christ and are into the Tea Party movement, you're a Teavangelical! To prove the point, that same Pew research study found that 31% of Protestants agree with the Tea Party agenda (compared to 21% who don't) and 29% of Catholics agree with the Tea Party while 23% don't. So please keep in mind when we talk about Teavangelicals in this book, it really is a simplified term for a broader set of born-again Christians.

Let's move on to more evidence of the overlap. In September 2010, the American Values Survey conducted a survey about how Americans view religion and politics. The Teavangelical trend shows up in spades. Take note:

- Nearly half (47%) of the self-identified Tea Party members say they are part of the religious right or conservative Christian movement.

- 81% identify as Christian within the Tea Party movement and of that number, 57% also consider themselves part of the Christian conservative movement.

- 63% say abortion should be illegal in all or most cases.

- Only 18% support allowing gay and lesbian couples to marry.[4]

The authors of the important study, Robert P. Jones and Daniel Cox, conclude that "on nearly all basic demographic characteristics, there are no significant differences between Americans who identify with the Tea Party and those who identify with the Christian conservative movement."[5]

Poll after poll shows virtually the same stat line on evangelicals. For example, Public Opinion Strategies found that 52% of all self-identified members of the Tea Party movement are conservative evangelicals.[6] Think about that figure for a moment. More than half of Tea Party members are conservative Christians. In other words, more than half are Teavangelicals. What if all the evangelicals inside the Tea Party decided not to participate? What if they took their "Don't Tread on Me" flags and their NIV Study Bibles and said they were done and going home? What would you be left with? Well, let me give you a visual.

Close your eyes, breathe slowly, and picture this. I'm a big New York Mets fan. Every September the baseball team is typically eliminated from playoff contention so they play to just a few thousand fans in a huge fifty-thousand-seat stadium. In other words, it's pretty lonely. There are not many people there. Can you visualize it? A huge stadium with not much of a crowd. Welcome to what the Tea Party would be like without the conservative Christians. They are vitally important. They make the difference between playing to sell-out crowds and advancing to the playoffs or going home with nothing to play for. Tea Party libertarians may be vocal and active, but they simply don't have the numbers if evangelicals stay home. That's the plain hard truth.

The Teavangelical Daily Double

It's time for a game of *Jeopardy*. Are you ready? Here we go (cue the music).

Me: Alex, I'll take Emerging Political Movements for $1,000.

Alex: The answer is: The Daily Double!

Me: I'll bet it all, Alex.

Alex: Good luck, David. You're a gambler. Here goes: This group of voters sees a direct link between fiscal issues and social issues to form the essence of the pro-family movement, an aspect often misunderstood by the mainstream media.

Me: Who are Teavangelicals?

Alex: That's right, David. Have I told you you're the best player ever on *Jeopardy?*

Okay, I got a little carried away, but you got the point, right? Here's the dirty little secret: if you're a social conservative, you're most likely a fiscal conservative. As Ralph Reed told me, "There aren't many social conservative voters who are economic liberals.... I think a society that honors God and honors marriage and family is also unlikely to run up ten trillion dollars in bills on a credit card and hand it to their children and grandchildren."

The Link Between Fiscal and Social Issues

We began by asking, "What in the world is a Teavangelical?" Well, this link between fiscal and social issues is key to understanding the answer to that question. The reason many evangelicals morph into Teavangelicals is because the fiscally conservative message of the Tea Party resonates with them. We often hear about how the Republican Party is made up of social conservatives, fiscal conservatives, and national security conservatives, as if somehow these are three distinct groups. Hogwash! Just like the symbol of the Olympic rings, they are intertwined. This really shouldn't come as a surprise to anyone, yet it does. Just because social conservatives might put more emphasis on social issues doesn't mean they don't care deeply about fiscal issues. To use a food analogy, ice cream may be my favorite dessert, but I like apple pie too!

When former presidential candidate and current Fox News contributor Mike Huckabee walked into our CBN News bureau in the spring of 2011, I knew he'd have an opinion on this topic, considering that he's been scratching his head for years about why regular people with capable brains can't fathom this idea that pro-family conservatives can be passionate about both ice cream and apple pie. "If you really drill into the Tea Party, what you find is that the Tea Party is overwhelmingly dominated by people who are not only fiscally conservative but they are also people who are principally pro-life as well as pro–traditional marriage," Huckabee told me.

The Pew Research Forum once again provides the facts for this convergence of fiscal and social conservatives. Their survey in May 2011 came to the following conclusion:

> The most visible shift in the political landscape since Pew Research's previous political typology in early 2005 is the emergence of a single bloc of across-the-board conservatives. The long-standing divide between economic, pro-business conservatives, and social conservatives has blurred. Today, Staunch Conservatives take extremely conservative positions on nearly all issues — on the size and role of government, on economics, foreign policy, social issues, and moral concerns.[7]

By the way, if you go inside those numbers, Pew says 72% of those staunch conservatives (who have conservative positions on social and economic issues) are Tea Party members, and 57% of these staunch conservatives attend church every week.[8] Sounds like a Teavangelical crowd to me.

This fiscal/social conservative message resonates everywhere, especially in places like Greenville, South Carolina, where a Teavangelical makes this case on the radio airwaves. While I run into Teavangelicals all over the country at rallies, large conferences, and in small homes, I must say I had never before met one in the bathroom. That is, until I met Josh Kimbrell.

Kimbrell is the CEO of the Round Table of South Carolina, a group devoted to bringing economic conservatives and social conservatives together on public policy. He's also the host of the daily radio show *Spiritual Cents*, which airs on Christian Talk 660 in Greenville.[9] I first met Josh when I went to interview him in a downtown hotel on a trip to Greenville in May of 2011. I was supposed to interview him in the lobby. Instead we met prematurely.

"David Brody?" Josh inquired at the bathroom urinal next to me.

"Josh Kimbrell?" I answered.

"Yep," Josh answered. "I recognized your face from TV."

Oy vey! How embarrassing! But with those bathroom pleasantries out of the way, Josh and I moved on to more substantial matters. Kimbrell has built much of his career out of this fiscal issue/social issue connection among people of faith. He studied economics at North Greenville University, and after graduating in 2007 he went on to Gardner Webb University to complete his masters of business degree. He and his wife, Kacy, were part of a group that formed the first Tea Party rally in Greenville back in 2009. The Kimbrells believe that without a Judeo-Christian agenda, America simply will not be successful. In the lobby of that downtown Greenville hotel, Josh told me, "Ultimately a good economic policy and a good social policy are one and the same. There is a direct correlation between our economic crisis and our cultural crisis."

For Kimbrell and other social conservatives, social issues can have disastrous economic consequences, as illustrated in the issue of abortion and Social Security. Presidential candidate Rick Santorum, the former Pennsylvania senator who has been fighting in support of the pro-life cause for decades, says the reason we don't have enough workers to support retirees is pretty simple. He says, "A third of all the young people in America are not in America today because of abortion."[10] Randall K. O'Bannon, director of education and research for the National Right to Life, makes the point that with 53 million babies aborted since Roe v. Wade was legalized in 1973, you can't help the fact that there will be a severe economic impact. O'Bannon says the government has begun "eliminating a significant portion of the tax base that funds government programs like Social Security and Medicare."[11]

Can you now see the link? Teavangelicals see a direct connection between morality and money. The important point to remember is this: if you're a social conservative, you're probably a fiscal conservative. And if that's the case, then you've got some Teavangelical blood.

A Tea Party Great Awakening

Since evangelicals are heavily involved in the Tea Party, it only follows that there is a spiritual component to this movement. In one of the most revealing interviews I've ever done, South Carolina Senator Jim DeMint compared what's happening in America today to what happened a couple hundred years ago. He said, "I think it's very akin to the Great Awakening before the American Revolution. A lot of our founders believed the American Revolution was won before we ever got into a fight with the British. It was a spiritual renewal. I think as this thing [the Tea Party movement] continues to roll you're going to see a parallel spiritual revival that goes along with it."

DeMint continued, "People are realizing that the government is hurting us, and I think they're turning back to [the idea that] God is our salvation and government is not our salvation. In fact, more and more people see government as the problem. Some have been drawn in over the years to a dependency relationship with government, and as the Bible says, you can't have two masters. I think as people pull back from that they look more to God." Teavangelicals, like DeMint, believe that the federal government encroaches so much on the lives of people that Uncle Sam is turning into a godlike figure.

And Teavangelicals fear that as the role of government increases, the influence of religion on society is diminished. The Pew Research Center's Forum on Religion and Public Life found that 79% of white evangelical Protestants believe religion's influence is decreasing in both American society and on government leaders. This figure is up 20 points since 2006.[12] One way Teavangelicals fight that change is through their elected officials. In a separate study, by two respected professors from Harvard and Notre Dame, data showed that people who align with the Tea Party "seek 'deeply religious' elected officials, approve of religious leaders' engaging in politics, and want religion brought into political debates."[13]

This explains part of the motivation for Teavangelicals. They believe government is getting too big and God is getting shoved out of the public square and the public discourse. They won't stand for it and decide to join the Tea Party because that is standing up for the conservative principle of less government. We will discuss the spiritual impact in greater detail in chapter 2 ("Fast and Furious: The Rise of the Tea Party") and chapter 4 ("Teavangelical Rallies").

The Face of the Teavangelical

We've already laid out the factual case to support the Teavangelical theory, but there's nothing like seeing how it plays out in person. It's important to connect faces with the movement. Who are these people? What are they all about? The only way you can really understand a movement is to be familiar with the motives of the citizens who are in it. You have to understand their stories, which are entirely Tea Party and completely evangelical. As I will point out repeatedly, the two go hand in hand. They are not mutually exclusive.

The Chick-fil-A Teavangelical

Take the case of evangelical-Christian-and-Tea-Party-member-turned-Congressman Tim Scott. In 2010 the forty-six-year-old from North Charleston, South Carolina, became the first black Republican ever elected to the House of Representatives from his state. He's also an active member of the Tea Party movement and a born-again Christian.

Scott's life story did not start well. He grew up in poverty in Charleston and was raised by a single mom who worked sixteen hours a day. In ninth grade, he failed four subjects and almost flunked out of high school. At this point, this future Tea Party leader wasn't learning about fiscal discipline. He was learning a different sort of discipline. "My mother was a disciplinarian," Tim Scott told me in an interview during the 2010 midterm election. "She taught me that love comes at the end of a switch, and she was so in love with me she used it consistently!"

Tim Scott's road to becoming a Teavangelical began when he walked into a Chick-fil-A restaurant. As a poor fourteen-year-old working part-time at a movie theater, Scott could only afford french fries at the restaurant. While he was there, he met John Moniz, a born-again Christian who took an interest in young Tim. "John started teaching me the basic principles of conservatism and capitalism, which was amazing because he did it in a spiritual perspective. He led with love," Scott told me. Those conversations led to better grades and a sense of purpose.

The Christian witnessing continued with Scott's friend Roger. "No matter what day it was, he was always happy," Scott recalled.

"And I said, 'Roger, why are you happy?' And Roger was like 'Jesus is Lord.' And I'm like, 'I got it, but what else?'" Scott found the answer to that question at a Fellowship of Christian Athletes meeting in college where he made the personal decision to give his life to Jesus Christ.

From that moment on, Tim Scott would start memorizing different Scriptures. He wanted it to be "grafted into his heart." He also began a political career, where he started to understand and adopt a Tea Party agenda. He was becoming a Teavangelical. Fifteen years ago as a city councilman, Scott tried to put a Ten Commandments plaque outside the council offices, but a circuit court judge stopped that plan. Still Scott says, "It was really giving God an opportunity to be seen and to be heard in the public forum based on the history of our country." Scott was applying the Teavangelical principle of defending and promoting this nation's Judeo-Christian heritage (more on this in chapter 2).

When I showed up at a Tea Party meeting during the 2010 midterm cycle in Myrtle Beach, South Carolina, Scott was on a roll, combining both the Bible and Tea Party neatly into his campaign speeches. He would trot out the following Teavangelical lines:

> "Ethics reform, according to the Book of James, is at a higher level for leaders, and I think it should be."

> On unemployment benefits: "My momma taught me that, according to the Book of Proverbs, if you don't work, you don't eat. It doesn't say if you cannot work. That's a different conversation."

Tim Scott is the prototypical Teavangelical. Combining Scripture and public policy is Teavangelical gold. But for Tim Scott, all the gold in the world doesn't matter. Rather, he's much more concerned with living an upright life before God. "There is nothing special about Tim Scott. I'm an ordinary guy serving an extraordinary God, and that makes the difference."[14]

The Spirit-Filled Teavangelical

It was a snowy night in Cleveland in the dead of winter in 2010. I was jogging briskly through the Holiday Inn parking lot, making my way through the bone-crunching cold and the fluffy white snowflakes. When I got to the door, a middle-aged woman with a big smile greeted me.

"Hi, I'm Tammy Roesch," she said joyfully. She was wearing a T-shirt that read "Coming Soon: The Second American Revolution." Yikes! For a guy who grew up as a liberal Jew in New York City, I looked to see if she was packing heat. She wasn't. Instead, she was one hundred percent Tea Party. But as I began talking to her throughout the evening, I discovered something else. She was a bleeding-heart evangelical too.

Roesch came to the Holiday Inn to take part in an event hosted by Tim Cox, the founder of GOOOH. The acronym stands for "Get Out of Our House," an effort moving forward across the nation to replace all 535 members of Congress (House and Senate) with citizen legislators. Roesch loved the idea so much she signed up to be GOOOH's Ohio state coordinator. But her story starts long before that night at the Holiday Inn.

Tammy and her husband, Al, birthed the Tea Party movement in their hometown of Kingsville, Ohio. The Roesches call themselves "old-fashioned, conservative home-church Seventh-day Adventists."[15] Al writes books, and Tammy's favorite is the one that looks at the character of Jesus. With a home business and five children, Al and Tammy find themselves quite busy, but not too busy to get involved in saving America.

Tammy has always been community oriented, and one day in the spring of 2009, she noticed a flyer from the American Family

Association, a pro-family evangelical organization. On that piece of paper was a call for people around America to organize local Tea Parties. Tammy thought it was a great idea and called her local hometown newspaper in Kingsville Township, Ohio. She wanted to take out an advertisement saying the event would be at the Ashtabula County Courthouse. The paper wanted to know who was organizing it. She was stumped. She quickly responded that she would organize it. The rest is Teavangelical history.

On April 15, 2009, eight hundred people showed up at that little courthouse. A few months later, they had another rally. This time the rally touched on not just the federal deficit but also abortion and returning this country to its Judeo-Christian principles. A year later Tammy Roesch decided to run for state representative in her local district. While she lost that race, her decision to engage in the political process changed her forever and made her a true-blue Teavangelical.

So what makes Tammy Roesch different? It's pretty simple. She decided to prioritize her busy life. It wasn't easy but she did it. People get trapped in the busyness of life, but this Teavangelical wasn't going to be a victim. "I think this is a trap of the devil," Tammy says. "Satan has people so busy and so into what's going on in their personal lives that while they're taking care of that, he is destroying the country. A lot of Christians have this idea that, 'Well, the Lord is in control and we've just got to sit back and he's going to take care of us,'" she said. "That's true. God is in control, but he expects us to do our part. He helps those who help themselves, and if we do nothing then we shouldn't complain when horrible things happen to Christians — and it's going to happen. Our freedoms are being taken away. We're going to be like those communist countries where the government tells you what you can preach and what you can't preach and whom your preacher can be."[16]

Folks, that's called a Teavangelical altar call. The Teavangelical movement is in its infancy; for its ranks to swell, there's going to need to be more Tammy Roesches. While plenty of evangelicals are involved in the Tea Party movement, far more evangelicals are sitting on the sidelines, not yet engaged. Tammy wants to make sure you join up too.

The Filmmaker Teavangelical

"I'm a Christian. I'm saved by grace." Billy Graham did not speak those words. Instead, they belong to Luke Livingston. Livingston is a Baptist homeschool dad who teaches Sunday school at his local church in Woodstock, Georgia. He is also the man behind a critically acclaimed documentary film about the Tea Party. Yes, he's a Teavangelical filmmaker.

Livingston's story is the perfect illustration of how evangelicals are putting their talents to use within the Tea Party. It all started in March of 2009 when his neighbor approached him to put together some videos for the first Tea Party rally taking place the following month at Georgia's state capitol building. His neighbor turned out to be Jenny Beth Martin, the main organizer for the Tea Party Patriots, soon to be one of the largest Tea Party groups in the country.

Livingston thought it would be neat to be part of the inaugural Tea Party rally. Little did he know that this decision would change his life forever. Twenty thousand people showed up at the big event at the state capitol. While there, he ran into many regular, ordinary-looking Americans deeply concerned about this country. Luke wanted to tell their stories, and he did just that. Knowing that the next big gathering would be in Washington, DC, in September, he spent the five months leading up to the rally filming his documentary. "We wanted to tell an entertaining story, we wanted to expose the Tea Party movement, and we wanted to honor God with what we were doing. Those were our three main goals," Livingston told me. "If there were Christians that had a point of view, and they were expressing that, I wasn't going to cover that up, put a bushel on the light. I wanted to make sure this was something family friendly. I didn't want to put together a film that was offensive to anyone. We knew it was going to have to be bathed in prayer because we had such an immense amount of work to do in such a short period of time." A Tea Party documentary bathed in prayer! Does it get any more Teavangelical than that? Can I get an amen?

Tea Party: The Documentary Film was released in December 2009. Now, while Livingston may be evangelical, the film crew was not exclusively Christian. "Our team had a Christian director, a Baptist producer in me. One of our producers was an atheist. It was an interesting dynamic going on, but it didn't keep me from praying or asking God's blessing on our production," Livingston told me. That documentary crew is a microcosm of the Tea Party. You have evangelicals and atheists working together for one cause. Livingston tells me that there's no reason why Christians and nonbelieving libertarians in the Tea Party can't work together since the three main principles of the Tea Party (fiscal responsibility, constitutionally limited government, and free markets) resonate with both groups. "It attracts libertarians and Christians," Livingston told me. "Christians have no problems with those principles. Neither do libertarians. If we can work together and have a broad coalition, then we can have a strong impact."

The challenge of libertarians and evangelicals working together is most assuredly worth exploring. While they may agree on economic policy, social issues are a different matter altogether. Conservative evangelicals are not on board at all with the libertarian belief that the government should stay out of the business of defining marriage or not play a role in regulating abortion. Those are just a few examples of the schism between both sides and it's a legitimate hurdle if these groups are going to be able to work together. Can evangelicals and libertarians check their differences on social issues at the Teavangelical door? It's an open question. There are potential pitfalls ahead, and we'll look at that in the last chapter. For now, though, it's imperative we take a closer look at the reasons why evangelicals saddle up with the Tea Party. In the next chapter, the Teavangelical motivations are revealed, and you get to take a little test to see where you reside on the Teavangelical scale. Don't worry! Your weight will not be factored in!

Chapter 2

FAST *and* FURIOUS:
THE RISE *of the* TEA PARTY

IMAGINE THIS: ONE MOMENT YOU'RE CLEANING HOMES FOR A LIVING. Then, in a blink of an eye, you're one of the top Tea Party leaders in the country. The story sounds remarkable, right? It's also true.

Jenny Beth Martin was living the life. After marrying her college sweetheart in 1992, she eventually landed a job at home as a computer programmer. Her husband started a small-business temp agency. It seemed like the sweet life was just around the corner. Six years into their marriage, they purchased a beautiful five-bedroom home in Woodstock, Georgia, had a few nice cars in the garage, and in 2001, Jenny stopped working so they could raise a family. After going through the emotional ups and downs of fertility treatments, Jenny Beth gave birth to twins in 2003. All seemed well, right? Not quite.

After the 9/11 attacks, her husband's business started to suffer. They took out hundreds of thousands of dollars in loans to keep the company afloat, but by the end of 2008, Lee Martin's company went bankrupt. The Martins blame it on an ailing economy and a bad business deal. The result? The financial roof began to cave in. Their house of eleven years? Gone. They moved into a rental home. The vehicles in the garage? Sold. Jenny Beth and Lee began cleaning homes and repairing computers to make money. So much for the American dream … at least for now.

During this tumultuous time, Jenny Beth decided to get involved with a couple new online groups called Smart Girl Politics and Top Conservatives. Jenny Beth always loved politics. Back in 2004, she was a local county campaign chairwoman for George W. Bush's reelection campaign. So as Jenny Beth spent her time wondering about her family's future while cleaning homes, she managed to hear CNBC anchor Rick Santelli blow a gasket on live television, accusing the Obama administration of promoting "bad behavior" with all these government bailouts. That Santelli rant changed Jenny Beth's life forever.

A light went on inside her head. What Santelli said that fateful day on February 19, 2009, resonated with her, and she began doing what she does best: organizing … and she did it fast! Just eight days later, Jenny Beth and a few other fellow patriots put together the first-ever Atlanta Tea Party rally at the Georgia state capitol. In April, just a month and a half later, came the big Tax Day rally in Atlanta. Jenny Beth led the effort there as well. Eventually, she became one of the national coordinators of the newly formed group Tea Party Patriots, an organization that is now home to more than three thousand local chapters and is considered one of the top Tea Party organizations in the country (more on Jenny Beth and the organization in chapter 3). In 2010, *Time* magazine named Jenny Beth Martin as one of America's most influential people. Not bad for someone who was cleaning homes a year before.

The rapid rise of Jenny Beth Martin mirrors the ascent of the Tea Party movement itself. Like the Vin Diesel movie, both were "fast and furious." So how did people like Jenny Beth and the Tea Party come into prominence so quickly? It's vital to understand the story behind the formation of the Tea Party before delving into why conservative evangelical Christians began to join the movement in droves.

The Makings of a Movement

The casual observer may think that the Tea Party movement started *after* Barack Obama took the oath of office as president in January 2009. Actually, the grumbling of discontent started almost a year earlier in the spring of 2008 during the second term of former President George W. Bush. The Federal Reserve had just come to the financial rescue of the troubled Bear Sterns investment firm, one of the largest in the country. Swooping in to save investment bankers with taxpayer dollars didn't sit well with some. In response, a group of online investors formed a new group called FedUpUSA. They held their first protest in April 2008.

In the latter stages of President Bush's second term the grumbling became even louder as more government money was poured down the drain. In October 2008 he signed into law the Troubled Asset Relief Program (TARP), the program in which the federal government would use taxpayer money to help bail out banks deemed "too big to fail." Two months later, Bush announced that more than seventeen billion dollars of taxpayer money would be used to bail out huge automakers General Motors and Chrysler. Then, in an interview with CNN, came an even greater blunder. President Bush admitted the following: "I've abandoned free-market principles to save the free-market system.... I am sorry we're having to do it."[1] Big mistake.

President Bush's comments and actions mixed with the fact that the more liberal Barack Obama was soon to take over steering the ship ignited the spark of revolution. Within a month or so, various online forums began to pop up, and sporadic protests began to take place around the country. In January 2009, we began having our first Tea Party references. Graham Makohoniuk, a part-time stock trader, was frustrated with the bank bailouts, so he sent out an invitation within a stock market Internet forum titled "Mail a Tea Bag to Congress and to Senate."[2] It started to make some buzz on the Internet. Stephanie Jasky, another online investment blogger, decided to issue a formal "commemorative tea party" invitation for people to show up in Boston on February 1, 2009.[3] Karl Denninger, the founder of Market Ticker, called for a Tea Party protest to take place around the time of Barack Obama's presidential inauguration. All three of these Internet posts went viral.[4]

When President Obama finally took over in January 2009, he told the country that the only way to avoid economic ruin was to pass a massive stimulus bill. Right from the start, the talk of spending more taxpayer dollars in the name of a national crisis wasn't going over well. On February 16, 2009, a day before President Obama signed the massive and controversial stimulus bill into law, Keli Carender, a conservative activist in the Seattle area, organized an anti-stimulus protest. Some call it the first ever Tea Party–style protest. It took her just four days to put it all together, and while only 120 people showed up, something was stirring. About a week later, she organized another protest. The attendance doubled.[5]

From there, it was the media's turn to get involved, and that's when the Tea Party movement really got rolling. In that same month of February 2009 when Obama signed the stimulus bill, Christian financial author and talk show host Dave Ramsey appeared on Fox News waving tea bags, protested the TARP bill, and proclaimed, "It's time for a Tea Party."[6] But by far, the signature event most people point to as the galvanizing moment for the movement came on February 19, 2009. It will be forever known as "The Rant."

Rick Santelli will go down in Tea Party history as an icon. On live national television, the CNBC correspondent was reporting from the floor of the Chicago Board of Trade and vociferously tore apart President Obama's government plan to bail out people who made bad mortgage deals. "This is America!" Santelli exclaimed. "How many of you people want to pay for your neighbor's mortgage that has an extra bathroom and can't pay their bills? Raise their hand." Booing ensued and Santelli wasn't done. "President Obama, are you listening? We're thinking of having a Chicago Tea Party in July. All you capitalists that want to show up to Lake Michigan, I'm gonna start organizing."[7] The boos turned to whistling and cheers, and the Tea Party movement was off and running. National Tea Party leaders will readily admit that Santelli's rant changed the political landscape forever.

On the heels of Santelli, the Tea Party movement got a big boost when TV and radio talk-show host Glenn Beck took to the Fox News airwaves on March 13, 2009, and announced his new 9/12 Project. Beck's effort was an attempt to unite Americans around nine principles and twelve values shared by our Founding Fathers. The idea that this wasn't a partisan effort excited future Tea Party members because they were sick and tired of the same old type of politician. It also excited evangelicals because many of those principles and values were rooted in the Word of God. As a matter of fact, Beck's first two principles read as follows: "America is good," followed by, "I believe in God and He is the center of my life."[8] That sure sounds Teavangelical.

The rest, as they say, is history. Local Tea Party groups began forming all across America. Various rallies began to take place, including the first big one on Tax Day, April 15, 2009. The *New York Times* reported that there were 750 Tea Party rallies across the country on April 15, 2009.[9] If you listen to Tea Party activists, there were a whole lot more, but this was the day the mainstream media gave the Tea Party the first big steroid injection of coverage. From that day forward and over the next year or so came talk of bigger spending and huge federal government programs from President Obama (healthcare reform comes to mind). Obama's expansive views led to even more expansive local rallies, a massive national event on the Mall in Washington, and yes, more April 15 tax-day rallies.

Tea Party–type candidates began to emerge ... and many started winning. Marco Rubio and Rand Paul became Tea Party heroes in 2010 and United States senators. Dozens of other Tea Party members won seats in the US House of Representatives, and in the 2010 mid-term election, thanks to a Tea Party surge (fueled in good measure by pro-family social conservatives, which we will discuss more in chapter 3), the House flipped. Republicans gained control, but more importantly, the Tea Party gained control of the national conversation. The talk was no longer about how much money to *spend* to get America back on track. Rather, it was about how much money to *cut*. The Tea Party had arrived, and America was paying attention.

Breaking Bread with the Tea Party

While we mentioned this in chapter 1, the following bears repeating: the rise and success of the Tea Party simply could not have occurred without socially conservative Christians in the ranks. So why did they sign up? After all, isn't the Tea Party supposed to spout libertarian values focusing exclusively on economic matters? If you read the *New York Times* long enough, you'll start to believe that evangelical Christians ride a two-trick policy pony: abortion and marriage. Not even close. They ride more like a six- or seven-trick pony! The truth of the matter is that evangelicals can actually walk and chew gum at the same time (and listen to Michael W. Smith on their iPods). So let's take a closer look at the main issues that drove the fast-and-furious rise of the Tea Party. As you will see, the following five issues have become places where evangelicals and Tea Party libertarians have begun to break bread together.

TEAVANGELICAL ISSUE #1: *Reclaiming the Country's Judeo-Christian Heritage*

In the Tea Party world, you hear a lot of talk about "American exceptionalism." Herman Cain, a 2012 presidential contender and a beloved Tea Party patriot, says the concept is grounded in the idea that "we are blessed with unparalleled freedoms and boundless prosperity that for generations have inspired an innovative and industrious people."[10] But where do those freedoms come from in the first place?

The fire-breathing Tea Party libertarian will shout from the rooftops that true freedom comes from a rigorous interpretation of the United States Constitution. Any deviation from the Constitution infringes on the liberties set forth in the document. The Tea Party fully recognizes that the principles laid out in the Constitution come from two sources: the Federalist Papers (which were written primarily by James Madison and Alexander Hamilton as a way of explaining the issues surrounding a new US Constitution) and the Declaration of Independence. Libertarians have been complaining for decades that the freedoms and liberties expressed by our Founding Fathers in these documents have been eroding slowly over time. Thus, the Tea Party wants to return to a constitutionally limited government. In evangelical speak, this issue could be phrased another way: a return to Judeo-Christian principles.

While Bible-believing Christians agree with the Tea Party on adherence to a strict interpretation of the Constitution, they tend to focus on a crucial additional layer: all of these founding documents are rooted in a belief in Almighty God. Paul Johnson, the British historian, put it best when he said, "The notion that all of us have something to contribute is God-given and stands at the heart of the Judeo-Christian tradition."[11] The idea here is that this biblically based structure allows for the individual to have true liberty when it comes to their economic freedom. Johnson calls this the "moral basis of capitalism."[12]

The Declaration of Independence states, "All men are created equal, that they are endowed by their Creator with certain unalienable Rights, that among these are Life, Liberty, and the pursuit of Happiness." Evangelicals cherish the idea that the rights provided for Americans in the Declaration of Independence do not come from men. They come from Almighty God.

In the spring of 2011, I visited Karen and Rick Santorum in their northern Virginia home. While Santorum, a 2012 presidential candidate, talked eloquently about the economic and foreign policy issues facing our country, his expressiveness soared to a different level when describing America as a "moral enterprise." Santorum points out that the words "endowed by their Creator" in the Declaration of Independence were put in there for a reason. "I think it's pretty clear what our founders believed from the language they used. We're endowed by our Creator to serve our Creator," Santorum explained to me. "America was the belief in every person being given rights by God, using those rights to serve him and to serve our country."

One member of Congress who is beloved by both the Tea Party and politically active conservative evangelicals is Representative Allen West of Florida. West likes to remind anyone who will listen that this nation's founding is based on Judeo-Christian principles. In a February 2011 keynote speech to the Conservative Political Action Conference in Washington, DC, an influential gathering made up of both Tea Party libertarians and evangelical Christians, he stated, "If we are to have a new dawn in America, it means reclaiming our Judeo-Christian faith heritage. This is not about a separation of church and state, it is about making sure that we do not separate faith from the individual. You must never forget that the American motto is 'In God We Trust.'"[13]

Certain Tea Party groups are making sure Judeo-Christian principles are in their charter. For example, the Greene Tea Party, which is located a couple hours northeast of Indianapolis, proclaim on their website that "Judeo-Christian Principles are the proper and necessary foundation of this free Republic.... We support the moderating influence of Judeo-Christian values in the exercise of governmental power."[14] At the 2010 National Tea Party Convention in Nashville, one workshop was entitled "Why Christians Must Engage." You would also hear plenty of speeches invoking the phrase "Judeo-Christian nation."[15] Here we see yet again the convergence of the Tea Party and evangelicals. In general, they agree that Judeo-Christian principles must play a fundamental role in shaping our society. In some Tea Party circles, you see that played out in a more overtly religious way (pushing more social issues). In other Tea Party venues that may not be as evangelical in nature, you see this carried out under the banner of American exceptionalism. Whatever the case, evangelicals see the Tea Party cause as a way to begin their quest to a return to sacred, time-tested principles articulated in the founding documents and based on Scripture.

TEAVANGELICAL ISSUE #2: *Reducing the Size and Scope of Government*

When you take the time to read the Libertarian Party platform (I highly recommend it and it also doubles as a bedtime story so your young children will fall asleep faster), you completely understand why these Americans believe less government is a big part of the solution to our nation's problems. One of their principles reads that "all individuals have the right to exercise sole dominion over their own lives, and have the right to live in whatever manner they choose, so long as they do not forcibly interfere with the equal right of others to live in whatever manner they choose.... Since governments, when instituted, must not violate individual rights, we oppose all interference by government in the areas of voluntary and contractual relations among individuals."[16] In other words, for the most part the government needs to stay out of the way!

Of course, the wording above that reads, "we oppose all interference by government in the areas of voluntary and contractual relations among individuals" also applies to libertarian views on abortion and marriage and that's a real problem for conservative evangelicals. This is a huge difference, one that cannot be easily overlooked. Protecting traditional marriage and innocent human lives are moral imperatives that are worth fighting for not just at the state level but at the federal level too. Still, since the Tea Party was founded on economic bedrock issues, evangelicals typically will gloss over those differences for the sake of standing in unison to fight a worthy, fiscally disciplined cause. But it should be duly noted that evangelicals will continue to forcefully point out that ultimately it is a solid family moral structure that is integral for society to function effectively.

Tea Party libertarians and evangelicals are in agreement on this idea of limiting the size and scope of government but for slightly different reasons. Conservative Christians recognize that humans are sinful and fallible, thus centralized power can be dangerous. Additionally, if government gets too big, there's an increased chance of dependency. That's scary for evangelicals who believe that people should rely on God, not the government. President Obama's liberal, expansive views of how government should be run became a moral threat to the way evangelicals view the world.

The Dirty Nine-Letter Word: Obamacare

To both evangelicals and libertarians, perhaps no issue exemplifies the overreach of government better than what they see as a dirty nine-letter word: *Obamacare*.

The debate over this controversial new national healthcare program in the fall of 2009 centered primarily on what was seen as blatant government intrusion. On this basis alone, evangelicals, just like Tea Party libertarians, weren't thrilled with it. But conservative Christians became even more engaged because the healthcare plan dealt directly with the issue of abortion. Evangelicals realized that Obamacare would likely include funds for abortion. That was something worth fighting against.

In the summer of 2009, conservative Christian groups held press conferences and sent out press releases nearly every week to make sure their members were engaged on this issue. Conservative Christian Gary Glenn, president of American Family Association in Michigan, hired, trained, and supervised a half dozen Christians in an attempt to take down Obamacare. According to Glenn, these Christian activists went into fifteen Democratic-held congressional districts with a mission to "contact and work closely with local Tea Party groups." One of the men Gary Glenn hired for AFA was Ric Hicks, a born-again Christian who went to school at the Christian-based Regent University. Also a member of the Lake Granbury Tea Party south of Fort Worth, Texas, Hicks organized opposition to candidates in six congressional districts during the 2010 midterm election by teaching people how to do press releases and conduct events, rallies, and protests. One of his main objectives was to make sure the Christians and libertarians in these districts had their congressman's phone number programmed into their phone and on speed dial, making it simple to bombard a congressional office at a moment's notice.

The abortion component within Obamacare played a major part in his effort, and Hicks and his cohorts were able to knock off four of those six members of Congress. So what was the secret to his success? Hicks tells me that the pro-life Christians were forced into action because of Obamacare. "People who would never get out and fight the pro-life cause were fighting the pro-life cause now because

43

of Obamacare." Hicks is convinced that when Obama's plan for national healthcare cropped up, people became engaged, many for the first time. He calls it "a defining moment."

While Hicks was busy fighting Obamacare, the president was repeatedly telling anybody who would listen that his healthcare plan would not fund elective abortions. His administration pointed out that Obama would sign an executive order that would take care of the problem because it would state that no money from the health-care bill would go toward this procedure. Evangelicals knew, how-ever, that an executive order doesn't trump or change an existing law. Pro-family groups like Concerned Women for America, Fam-ily Research Council, American Family Association, and countless others protested vigorously, arguing that the only way to assure no federal monies would go toward paying for abortions would be pass-ing an amendment to the overall healthcare bill.

The Stupak/Pitts Amendment was supposed to be the solution. Democratic Congressman Bart Stupak and Republican Congress-man Joe Pitts brought to the House floor their amendment, which would codify into law the stipulation that no government funds could be used to pay for abortion in the healthcare bill. While that language passed the House, it didn't have a chance in the more Democratic-controlled Senate, hence the supposed compromise of an executive order, which the president did eventually sign.

The healthcare bill became law by a narrow margin. Teavan-gelicals didn't lose this battle due to lack of engagement. Rather, they had fought an uphill battle against a Democratic president, Senate, and House of Representatives—a powerful trifecta that's hard to overcome. The challenge going forward, they realized, was to change Capitol Hill into a land dominated by Teavangelicals.

More Czars Than the Romanovs

If Obamacare weren't enough, evangelicals had another reason to engage with the Tea Party on the growing overreach of government. President Obama appointed close to two dozen high-level, important positions within the federal government who had the power to shape and influence public policy in their specific area. Since they weren't cabinet members, they didn't have to receive congressional approval. While previous presidents also used appointees (President George W. Bush appointed even more than Obama[17]), critics of the president were looking for anything to pounce on so they felt he abused the privilege too. These appointees became known as "czars." Since they don't have an official czar title, it's hard to decipher exactly how many there are but the estimates range from the low teens to the high twenties.[18] Either way, Republican Senator John McCain joked that Barack Obama is appointing "more czars than the Romanovs," a reference to the historical czar dynasty of Russia. He could have said the same thing about President Bush but the czar storyline played into the narrative of the Obama overreach.[19]

One of these czars was a man by the name of Kevin Jennings, and his appointment got evangelicals riled up. Jennings was appointed by the Obama administration to head up the Office of Safe and Drug Free Schools at the Department of Education. He was called the "Safe-Schools Czar," but pro-family groups declared his agenda was anything but safe. Jennings used to run the Gay, Lesbian, and Straight Education Network (GLSEN). They say Jennings' mindset was to aggressively push an extreme gay agenda in the public school system, and they had a body of evidence to substantiate that claim. Evangelicals not only had a problem with his agenda, but they had a problem with the Obama administration's attempt to do an end run around Congress so as not to have him confirmed by the Senate. For someone like Jennings, who would wield quite a bit of influence, especially in shaping policy in our nation's public school system, the czar appointment was causing serious concern. The conservative Traditional Values Coalition spent a considerable amount of time getting out the word about Jennings. The influential American Family Association sent a release out to their 2.6 million members claiming, "This man is not a good role model for the nation's children, nor will he fairly represent all Americans due to his spiteful attitude toward evangelical Christians."[20] It turns out that at the same time evangelicals were raising concerns about Jennings, Tea Party libertarian members were taking issue with other czars, including Van Jones, who was dubbed the radical "Green Jobs Czar." In both cases, Jones and Jennings were forced to resign after pressure from lawmakers, Fox News, the Tea Party, and yes, evangelicals. Evangelicals and Tea Party libertarians focused on different candidates, but constitutional overreach was the main underlying issue driving their actions.

TEAVANGELICAL ISSUE #3: *Returning to Fiscal Responsibility*

We've already established that Tea Party members view the Constitution as a crucial document that limits the power of government. It only follows that if the federal government is limited in influence it would also be limited in how many programs it establishes. Fewer programs means less money spent, which theoretically, at least, would lead to fiscal responsibility. Libertarians can list for you in their sleep the needless alphabet soup of government agencies that need to be jettisoned in the name of saving money (EPA, OSHA, FTC, and so on). Perhaps former Georgia Congressman Bob Barr put it best. In a past run at the presidency, the Libertarian Party member Barr said, "On my first day as president I will freeze federal spending. On day two, I will establish the Commission on Wasteful Government to develop a list of programs with no constitutional basis, which belong at the state or local level, or which don't work. And I will go to Congress with a long list of programs to eliminate."[21]

While libertarians see fiscal responsibility as a way to facilitate a more prosperous nation, evangelicals see the same issue through a biblical lens. The Bible is full of verses that can easily be interpreted as fiscally conservative advice. Evangelicals understand that being a good steward of money is an important biblical tenet. They quote such verses as "A good person leaves an inheritance for their children's children, but a sinner's wealth is stored up for the righteous" (Proverbs 13:22) and "The rich rule over the poor, and the borrower is slave to the lender" (Proverbs 22:7). With a Bible in one hand and a protest sign in the other, evangelicals became well equipped to merge with the Tea Party in the area of fiscal responsibility.

The Debt Ceiling: No Deal

The current dismal state of our nation's economy has made fiscal responsibility a moral crusade for some. That's why you saw many conservative Christians stand side by side with the Tea Party to fight against raising the country's debt ceiling. During that big national debate, Americans were told repeatedly how economic disaster was right around the corner if the debt ceiling wasn't increased. Yet Tea Party members in Congress (many of them conservative Christians) made life exceedingly difficult for the House leadership who were looking to cut a deal. But for the most part, conservative Christian Tea Party representatives on the hill (Rep. Tim Scott, Rep. Tim Huelskamp, and many others) said no way. Why?

It's imperative to understand that evangelical Christians typically see the world in black and white. It's a world of biblical absolutes. With the Bible being very clear on the importance of financial stewardship, you're not going to get much in the way of budging. This is a key trait that both evangelicals and die-hard Tea Party members have. They are principled and won't shift their positions just because it might be easier to do so. Some may call this position stubborn with severe consequences (we will address this in chapter

9), but Teavangelicals will typically stay true to what they believe no matter the consequence.

The Immorality of Debt

One person who fits this description to a tee (pardon the pun) is Rick Santorum, the former senator from Pennsylvania and one of the staunchest social conservatives in the country. He's also a devout Catholic who believes in the saving power of Jesus Christ. He's been speaking out about the immorality of abortion and gay marriage for decades. But as a candidate for president in 2012, it wasn't his pro-life credentials or solid record of defending traditional marriage that he touted in his first campaign advertisement. Instead he pointed out the immorality of the debt. His radio ad exclaimed, "Over half of America now receives some sort of government benefit. And 40 cents of that dollar that they're getting, they're charging their children and grandchildren for the rest of their lives to pay the debt service on the money they're receiving. That is immoral. That is wrong."[22]

The immorality of debt is touted not only in the presidential race but throughout the halls of Congress as well. As a matter of fact, in February 2011, House Speaker John Boehner, also a staunch Catholic, delivered an impassioned plea to thousands of evangelicals at the National Religious Broadcasters Convention in Nashville.

About an hour before he spoke to the crowd, I had a chance to meet with Speaker Boehner. As we began the interview, the speaker looked down at the cuff of my suit pants and then straightened it. How embarrassing! Of course not as embarrassing as a $14 trillion dollar debt, something Boehner was itching to explain to me in moral terms. "This immense debt is a moral hazard," he told me that evening in Nashville. "When you begin to look at the big challenges that face our country both here and the challenges that we see abroad, many people begin to realize that they better start praying as well."[23]

This is a very emotional issue for Speaker Boehner. (Then again he cries at the drop of a hat.) Boehner is passionate about controlling our nation's debt. He also is no dummy. He understands that politically he's going to need a huge swath of evangelical voters with him on this issue if Republicans are to be successful in future elections. Tying the debt to morality helps fuse the bond between the Tea Party and evangelicals. Boehner reminded this NRB audience full of conservative Christians that Beltway politicians have been ignoring the advice laid out in Proverbs ("A good person leaves an inheritance for their children's children," Proverbs 13:22) for too long and implored evangelicals to become engaged on this issue because "What we do now is not about us; it is about them [future generations]. We do not lead for profit or pleasure, but for our posterity. To be able to say we made all we could of the moment God has given us." To Speaker Boehner, a moral fiscal policy is rooted in our founding principles. Evangelicals are hearing that message loud and clear, and it's one of the main reasons they are joining the Tea Party in force.

The Federal Budget: Crafting a Moral Plan

The federal budget is another area where conservative evangelicals pull out their Bibles as a sword in the fight against fiscal irresponsibility. Proverbs 27:12 says, "The prudent see danger and take refuge, but the simple keep going and pay the penalty." Luke 14:28–30 makes the following point: "Suppose one of you wants to build a tower. Won't you first sit down and estimate the cost to see if you have enough money to complete it? For if you lay the foundation and are not able to finish it, everyone who sees it will ridicule you, saying, 'This person began to build and wasn't able to finish.'" This is the mindset of many conservative Christians when it comes to not just the family budget but the federal government's budget as well. They want to vote for lawmakers who take the dangers of doing nothing very seriously, and they believe there is a biblical mandate behind their urgent request.

There is no better example of this than the Republican budget crafted by House Budget Chairman Paul Ryan. With entitlement spending representing nearly 60 percent of the federal budget,[24] this "Roadmap for America's Future" became toxic because it called for significant changes to Medicaid and Medicare. One modification, for example, would be a restructuring of Medicare so that rather than being on the government-run plan you'd get a certain amount of money to purchase health care insurance (those Americans fifty-five and older wouldn't be affected).[25] Change to these programs scares a lot of people and in fact evangelicals are just as concerned about cuts to Medicaid and Medicare as the next guy. However, because of their conservative philosophy and biblical ideas regarding the morality of the budget, they can most likely be more easily persuaded to at least look at what Congressman Ryan is proposing. After all, they are fiscally conservative, so they want substantial cuts (maybe just not from Medicaid and Medicare!).

As a dedicated Roman Catholic, Ryan defends his budget as a moral document. He argues that, based on our country's economic condition, something drastic must be done with entitlement programs or they won't be there at all in the future. In short, doing nothing is immoral. "Ultimately the weakest will be hit three times over: by rising costs, by drastic cuts to programs they rely on, and by the collapse of individual support for charities that help the hungry, the homeless, the sick, refugees and others in need," Ryan said in a letter to Catholic Bishops.[26]

Liberals scoff at Ryan's moral budget talk. They think his "draconian" budget cuts are blatantly immoral. If you listen to the narrative of the progressive community, you might believe that conservative evangelicals don't have a heart for the poor since they want to drastically cut spending. Simply put, they think cuts are very unbiblical and definitely un-Christian. After all, how could a Christian support drastic cuts to social programs, leaving the most vulnerable unprotected?

This book doesn't attempt to settle that argument because it's really more a philosophical disagreement on the role of government. Conservative evangelicals believe it is the role of the church, private groups, and individuals, not the government, to provide compassionate services for the needy, and they back up their beliefs with their giving, typically donating more of their own money than any other church affiliation.[27] While progressives view certain government spending as compassionate, conservatives view that same spending as ineffective, wasteful, and many times without any constitutional basis (though cutting Medicare and Medicaid don't neatly fit into that conservative argument). That's why you won't see evangelical progressives at your neighborhood Tea Party rally.

Defunding Planned Parenthood

When it comes to wasteful spending, the Tea Party can give you a plethora of examples. When you add the moral issue of abortion into the mix, evangelicals join the conversation quickly. Let's look at the case of Planned Parenthood, the nation's largest abortion provider.

The federal budget allocates $363 million dollars every year to this group. The abortion provider receives $293 million through Medicare funding and $70 million a year under the Title X program, which doles out healthcare-related money to community health centers across the country.[28] At every turn, conservative evangelicals are trying to defund Planned Parenthood, making the case that not only should they not receive the money based on moral concerns, but also in this day and age of fiscal austerity those funds are ripe for the chopping block.

Clearly, the timing is now beneficial to the pro-family movement. Prominent evangelical leader Ralph Reed tells me that the defunding of Planned Parenthood is "both a values issue and a fiscal issue but let's be honest about it. The parameters of that debate have now been reframed by the fact that we're basically broke." Reed's counterpart, Gary Marx, who is executive director of the Faith and Freedom Coalition (more on this influential group in chapter 3), imparted to me a piece of advice for Tea Party leaders across the country. "We're saying to them you need to continue to be who you are as Tea Party leaders. At the same time there are areas where we (conservative evangelicals) can work together and be allied like the example of cutting abortion funding for groups like Planned Parenthood."

Federal funding for Planned Parenthood still remains because Barack Obama occupies the White House, but this issue is a perfect example of the crossover between the evangelical pro-family message and the Tea Party mindset. You have a moral concern that is of the utmost importance to evangelicals and instead of arguing it on just moral grounds alone, evangelicals are making the fiscal case as well.

Now, it is true that most national Tea Party leaders stayed away from the defunding Planned Parenthood debate because, in a nod to staying on message, they simply don't want moral issues to creep into any fiscal issue whatsoever. But that really doesn't matter because this isn't about what national Tea Party leaders think. You can't stop an organic bottom-up movement. This issue gives you insight into why conservative evangelicals are joining ranks with the Tea Party. They see both the moral and fiscal dimensions of an issue. In the future, watch for more cultural issues (marriage, abortion, fatherhood, education) to be framed just like this. Morality plus fiscal discipline equals a winning combination for the Teavangelical.

From Spending to Cutting

For evangelicals and libertarians, changing the political conversation in an attempt to regain fiscal discipline hasn't been easy.

There's a lot of work to be done, but they have been very effective at changing the political dialogue in America. Think of President Obama's first term and now picture a football field for a moment. When he first took office, the president had the ball on offense and was driving down the field. He was in a spending and expanding mood. As the quarterback of the team, he was completing passes at an accelerated rate. His air attack included the $787 billion dollar stimulus bill, expanding TARP (Troubled Asset Relief Program) beyond its original deadline, introducing a whopping $3.8 trillion federal budget,[29] and ramming a national healthcare plan through Congress. According to the Congressional Budget Office, all of President Obama's grand plans were expected to more than double the nation's debt to over $17 trillion dollars by 2019.[30]

Barack Obama fumbled the football. In November 2010 Tea Party members, evangelicals, and independent voters flocked to the polls with a message for the president: Enough is enough! They caused a turnover. Now, the Tea Party and their agenda were on the march with an offense dominated by spending cuts.

TEAVANGELICAL ISSUE #4: *Reducing Taxes and Opposing Tax Increases*

We know that the Tea Party feels "Taxed Enough Already," hence the acronym TEA. Libertarians believe that you can create more jobs by cutting taxes and relieving the tax burden on small business owners rather than spending loads more money. They also take the view that tax increases will just give the government more money to waste instead of Americans keeping more of what they make for a living. Sounds simple, doesn't it?

During the debt ceiling debate in the summer of 2011, the Tea Party took quite a bit of heat for holding firm to their conviction of no new taxes of any sort in any congressional bill that came forward. At one point, the Obama administration had a $4 trillion dollar spending cut package on the table, but the Tea Party (and GOP House leadership) said no dice even though the deal wouldn't have included individual tax rates going up. It would have closed certain tax loopholes. But even that wasn't going to fly with the Tea Party. President Obama takes a different view. He believes the wealthy in this country should pay their fair share, and time and time again he's tried to eliminate tax breaks for the rich. While most Americans have received tax breaks under his administration, those same Americans will be hit by a bunch of new taxes that are set to take effect if Obamacare is ruled constitutional.[31]

Why the strong stance? Well, first of all, politically speaking, cutting a deal with the Obama administration isn't appetizing at all. Additionally, the dozens of Tea Party freshmen in the House signed a pledge to not raise taxes under any circumstances.[32] This taxpayer protection pledge has been made famous by the well-known and influential DC Beltway insider Grover Norquist, the president of Americans for Tax Reform. Breaking the pledge and crossing Grover is a political no-no. But most importantly, the Tea Party is tired of the same old Washington game of compromise just for the sake of compromise. Senator Rand Paul, a Tea Party hero, told me, "A solution is more important than a deal, and I don't think anything we did approaches a solution." The Tea Party truly believes that increasing taxes of any kind will send the wrong message to small business job creators in America, not to mention the fact that they believe deficits can decrease by cutting plenty of government programs rather than generating revenue through taxes (which they feel will just be subject to government inefficiency anyhow).

Reducing the Tax Burden for Families

For evangelicals, the tax issue is not about actually paying taxes to the government. Conservative Christians understand that in Matthew 22:21 Jesus says, "Give back to Caesar what is Caesar's, and to God what is God's." Rather, for Teavangelicals the issue is directly related to the health of the family unit. Let's face it: the more the government takes from your wallet, the less money you have to financially support your family.

For years, pro-family Christian organizations have been lobbying lawmakers to make sure the tax burden is made less for families. Groups like the Family Research Council (more on them in chapter 3) and others have been successful in securing higher tax-deduction amounts for items like the child tax credit and the personal deduction allowance. They have also been successful in eliminating the marriage tax, which used to mean couples would pay more taxes if they filed as "married" than as two single filers.[33]

TEAVANGELICAL ISSUE #5: *Restoring Free-Market Principles*

If you're discussing politics with Tea Party members, you can't hang out for too long without hearing the phrase "free markets" invoked repeatedly. Libertarians link free markets directly back to the Constitution. In short, their view is that the Constitution provides for personal liberty. With that freedom comes an economic marketplace of goods and services where people have the right to buy and sell what they want. It's about providing opportunities for people to attain economic success. In this economic venue, Tea Party members see the role of government as one that protects their property rights and makes sure nobody is breaking the law in the free-market system.[34]

Christian economic thought on the subject of free markets concentrates greatly on the providential nature of the system. The idea advanced is that God created us free to make choices. Respected Christian economists Robin Klay and John Lunn argue that God is definitely at work within the free-market system. They pontificate that, "As God hovered over the waters at the time of Creation, perhaps God's spirit also hovers over markets and their participants. His spirit provokes, inspires, and channels millions of free human acts of creation and self-giving, for our good and his glory. Such is the nature of spontaneous orders, like markets, that thrive under the care and preservation of God's providence."[35] Adam Smith, a major, classic philosopher in the area of free markets, referred to this force as the "invisible hand" within the marketplace. While his view of the "invisible hand" is still debated today within economic circles, Smith's writings do suggest that he believed in God's providential role of establishing a moral sense within each individual.[36]

To highlight the convergence of the evangelical and libertarian point of view on free-market economics you have to know a man by the name of Gary North. Years ago North used to work for Tea Party folk hero Ron Paul. The Republican/Libertarian congressman has since gone on to run for president while North has become a respected conservative Christian economist. He's written dozens of books on the subject of biblical economics, and many Christian homeschool students read his books as part of their curriculum.[37] You probably won't find a bigger defender of free-market principles through a biblical perspective than North. He makes the point that the free market is not independent or self-governing in nature. Rather, the principles behind the success of the free market come from the Bible. North says, "The Bible provides the moral foundation of free-market voluntarism. The moral issue is personal responsibility. The Bible places this squarely on the shoulders of the individual decision-maker."[38] This philosophy of personal responsibility resonates with evangelicals. It plays well within the construct of the free-market system, but it also represents the mindset of many conservative Christians when it comes to recognizing that God gives us the gift of free will in our lives.

Teavangelical Test

Now that we've laid out the issues it's time to take a test. Are you a Teavangelical? If so, how passionate are you? For those of you who don't like labels, neither do I. As a boy who grew up Jewish and gave his life to Jesus Christ at age twenty-three, I don't like being labeled as a "Jew for Jesus." I call myself a Bible-believing follower of Christ. Believe me, I understand the danger of labels, so this test below is not an attempt to label people as much as it is a way to gauge your interest and passion in the issues that motivate both the evangelicals and libertarians that make up the Tea Party.

Before we begin, a few ground rules. Obviously, to be a Teavangelical you need to be an evangelical! So look at the three questions below to see if you qualify. If you answer yes to all three, then you pass the evangelical portion of the test and can move on to the next section. A no answer to *any* of the questions below means you don't meet the evangelical criteria. That doesn't mean you don't feel just as passionately about these issues. This is just a fun exercise to see if you would be considered a Teavangelical.

Beliefs

Do you agree with the following three statements?

1. I have made a personal decision to accept Jesus Christ as my Lord and Savior. I believe that salvation is by grace through faith alone.

2. I am pro-life and believe the human fetus is a person and therefore has a right to life.

3. I believe that marriage should be exclusively between a man and a woman.

Did you pass? If so, let's move on.

Policy

Grade yourself on the following Teavangelical issues covered in this chapter. Where do you stand? Grade yourself as follows:

> 1 — I don't care at all about this issue.
> 2 — I do care somewhat about this issue.
> 3 — I do care about this issue.
> 4 — I strongly care about this issue.
> 5 — This issue is crucial to me!

CIRCLE ONE

Reclaiming the country's Judeo-Christian heritage	1 2 3 4 5
Reducing the size and scope of government	1 2 3 4 5
Returning to fiscal responsibility	1 2 3 4 5
Reducing taxes and opposing tax increases	1 2 3 4 5
Restoring free-market principles	1 2 3 4 5

Add up your score.

A *score under 15:* While you may be evangelical, many of these issues don't really resonate with you, so you probably wouldn't be considered a Teavangelical since these issues have to be *very* important to you, and you seem more content to just monitor the situation from the sidelines.

A *score of 15 – 20:* These issues have stoked some interest, and you are on your way to becoming a Teavangelical. You have a desire to engage on these issues and want to know more.

A *score of 20 – 25:* You are thoroughly engaged and interested in the Tea Party agenda and have a hunger to engage on the issues. The question now: are you just intellectually involved or is there passion as well?

Passion

Time to take the passion test. Not that kind of passion. Teavangelical passion! After all, you may care about the issues, but would you actually attend a Tea Party rally or join a local Tea Party group? In other words, would you invest your precious time? Grade yourself as follows:

> 1 — I wouldn't get off the couch for this issue.
> 2 — I might get off the couch for this issue.
> 3 — I probably would get off the couch for this issue.
> 4 — I most likely would get off the couch for this issue.
> 5 — I definitely would get off the couch for this issue.

CIRCLE ONE

Reclaiming the country's Judeo-Christian heritage	1 2 3 4 5
Reducing the size and scope of government	1 2 3 4 5
Returning to fiscal responsibility	1 2 3 4 5
Reducing taxes and opposing tax increases	1 2 3 4 5
Restoring free-market principles	1 2 3 4 5

Add up your score.

A *score under 15:* While you may care about some of these issues, it's not enough to really get you moving and off the couch. You have some desire to keep up on the issues, but you don't long for a spot at the next Tea Party rally. You probably wouldn't be considered a Teavangelical.

A *score of 15 – 20:* You are a rising Teavangelical. In other words, you not only care about these issues, but there is a spark somewhere inside of you. You are willing to engage not only your mind but you also seem to have some passion too.

A *score of 20 – 25:* You're a pretty incredible Teavangelical. You're locked and loaded on the issues, and you're ready to buy the "Don't Tread On Me" mug, T-shirt, flag, and tie!

Conclusion

So what is the bottom line here? Actually, it's pretty simple. You cannot take an issue and attribute it solely to one group of people. The matters outlined in this chapter are not just Tea Party libertarian issues; they are evangelical issues as well.

The media loves to wrap everything neatly in a box and tie it in a bow. You'll hear story after story about how you have your fiscal conservative Tea Party crowd fighting for fiscal responsibility while conservative evangelicals are engaged about the social issues. But that's only part of the story. It's not that simple, and quite frankly, it's intellectually lazy. Evangelicals can actually walk and chew gum at the same time. They can be a hundred percent engaged on the issues of life and traditional marriage and at the same time be a hundred percent engaged in fiscal matters. It's not an either/or proposition, and there is no conflict. Remember, conservative evangelicals see fiscal issues as moral issues.

Does that mean that abortion and traditional marriage issues are a thing of the past? Hardly. It just means the focus for the foreseeable future is on runaway spending. If evangelicals truly mobilize along with the Tea Party libertarians on the issues outlined above, they have a real shot to change the dynamics inside the GOP and make it much more of a constitutionally conservative party. If that happens you may be looking at a president of the United States (and a Congress) who understands the Teavangelical issues and implements them for the good of the country. And if this next president is a constitutionally conservative president who supports fiscally conservative policies, the chances are pretty high that he or she will also champion pro-life causes and traditional marriage. It really is a win-win scenario for Teavangelicals.

Chapter 3

TEAVANGELICAL
ORGANIZATIONS
and LEADERS

I WAS ANXIOUS. VERY ANXIOUS. ON A COLD SPRING EVENING IN Waukee, Iowa, in March 2011, I found myself staring at a white curtain inside a large evangelical church. Frantically, my assertive political instincts began to kick in. How could I get behind that curtain? I knew that if I could get our CBN news crew behind this iron curtain we would enter into a world full of Teavangelicals. For a political junkie like myself, what would transpire there would be better than being backstage with Justin Bieber (though my young daughter may argue with me on that point).

The church in Waukee was playing host to the first major event of the 2012 Republican presidential race: a candidate forum hosted by the Faith and Freedom Coalition. Ralph Reed, the former executive director of the Christian Coalition, runs the operation, and various presidential candidates were gathering behind this white curtain to speak to evangelical and Tea Party activists in his organization. The mainstream media had shown up in droves, and they were all outside the curtain waiting for the official event to begin on stage.

I, on the other hand, had my sights set on getting inside that private, exclusive gathering. No media allowed. Should I just walk in? Should I ask permission? I tried to contact Ralph Reed, who had become a great source of information and perspective for me over the last few years, but as you can imagine, he was pretty busy.

So what did I do? My aggressive nature took over. I decided to just walk in with our camera crew. Ralph Reed spotted me as I made my way past the curtain. I pointed to the camera as if to say I hope this is okay with you. He smiled and nodded his head in agreement. I had entered into Ralph Reed's Teavangelical world.

Inside that iron-curtain meeting, Reed's thank-you message to the troops was plain and simple: the turnout of conservative Christians in the midterm elections of 2010 was critical to not only booting Nancy Pelosi and the Democrats out of power in the House of Representatives, but also in sending a message to the country. "You take time away from business, from hobbies, from family, from personal interests because you love your country and you want to see this country get back on the right track," he told the Teavangelical army.

Later, Newt Gingrich, one of the presidential candidates who attended this meeting, brilliantly summed up the Teavangelical message to these activists: "Are we in fact a country in which your rights come from your Creator and you are personally sovereign and you loan power to the government, or are we a country where the government defies who you are and the government determines your future?"

The Teavangelical Organizations: No Sign Posted

Ralph Reed's group would definitely be considered a Teavangelical organization, but here's the rub: there are no official Teavangelical organizations. It's important to remember that Teavangelicals are evangelicals who are part of the Tea Party movement; therefore, don't start looking for the brick-and-mortar store with the big "Teavangelical" sign in front of it. What we are talking about here are evangelical organizations who engage heavily in Tea Party issues as well as interact with Tea Party groups to see their mission accomplished.

As you set out to read more about the Teavangelical political landscape, here is one critical point you must grasp: any links between the Tea Party and evangelical groups are very informal. Remember, there is no organized or devious collusion going on here between these national organizations. This is more like a loose partnership or collaboration. Since a movement like the Tea Party is so organic, there's no way collusion or even formal organization could happen in the first place. These groups work together on a case-by-case basis on issues that suit the interest of both parties.

Something else to keep in mind: the national evangelical and Tea Party groups listed in this chapter are by no means an exhaustive list of all of the organizations that are loosely partnering together. There are countless others, and quite frankly, there are way too many to name. You will see those organizations pop up from time to time as you read through some of the other chapters. Plus, you will see Tea Party groups and evangelical groups working together at the county, city, and state level as well. The scenes described in this chapter give you a realistic flavor of what truly happens among these groups. You're about to see examples of Christian and libertarian groups working together in common cause with the stated goal of restoring this nation's constitutional principles.

Faith and Freedom Coalition (FFC)

If you went searching for the Teavangelical nerve center, you would head to Duluth, Georgia, just outside Atlanta. There you will find the Faith and Freedom Coalition, a group of roughly ten full-time employees working diligently to influence and reshape the political discourse and landscape in America.

Ralph Reed, the former executive director of the Christian Coalition, is CEO of the Faith and Freedom Coalition (FFC). Reed was instrumental in making the Christian Coalition a force in the 1990s. Now he's back. But this is not your grandfather's Christian Coalition. This is the 2012 Teavangelical version, and it's going gangbusters.

So what is FFC exactly? Reed tells me that his group doesn't claim to be a Tea Party organization but rather "an organizational vehicle for socially conservative Tea Party activists." Essentially, the group is a political grassroots organization that is fusing both the evangelical and Tea Party messages with the goal of getting more Christians to the polls. According to their website, their objective is to "influence public policy and enact legislation that strengthens families, promotes time-honored values, protects the dignity of life and marriage, lowers the tax burden on small business and families, and requires government to tighten its belt and live within its means." Unlike the Tea Party, which prides itself on its laser focus on economic issues, FFC doesn't limit itself to either economic or social issues. They see them as intertwined. What FFC and Tea Party groups do have in common is the belief that government needs to stay out of the way. In other words, the less of Uncle Sam the better.

FFC's Teavangelical message of economic and social conservatism resonated during the midterm elections of 2010. Their congressional scorecards tracked legislative votes in Congress on social issues but also on "$862 billion in new spending for pork-barrel projects, government jobs, and grants to states, paid for with deficit spending."[1] In its attempt to reach out to Christian voters they racked up impressive totals, especially considering the organization is just a couple years old. They were responsible for:

- Building a database of 12.3 million pre-qualified evangelical voters.

- Contacting nearly 6 million voters (within that 12.3 million evangelical database).

- Distributing 16 million voter guides.

- Distributing 8 million pieces of mail.

- Conducting 15 million get-out-the-vote calls.

The result? Victory. Christians flooded to the polls, making the 2010 election the largest turnout ever for evangelicals in a midterm. Not bad for a group that didn't even exist two years ago and doesn't even have a presence yet in all fifty states. As of June 2011, they had roughly 400,000 members and representatives in about half the states in America.[2]

Like every political movement in America, you need dedicated foot soldiers. The Teavangelical movement is no exception. One of those is Gary Marx, the executive director of FFC who has been instrumental in getting FFC off the ground. On a recent visit to their headquarters, Marx emphasized the organization's Teavangelical mindset. "It's not just something where we're saying we can be strong in one region where evangelicals might be more active. No. We're a Teavangelical movement. We've got Tea Party leaders and activists and also evangelicals who are in every single state."

Another man in the Teavangelical trenches is Billy Kirkland, FFC's national field director. During my journey to their Duluth nerve center, Kirkland was quick to point out how FFC helped contribute mightily to the landslide of victories across the country in 2010, but that was only the beginning. "So far what we've seen is it's not losing steam. It's growing. We've got people who are fiscally conservative; they have to balance their checkbooks, but they also attend church regularly. They learn these biblical principles that help create a moral nation."

Indeed, the movement is growing, and 2012 is expected to be a banner year for this quintessential Teavangelical group. The attainable goal is to contact a couple of million more evangelical voters. The media is definitely taking note. FFC's Iowa chapter laid claim to the official kickoff event of the 2012 presidential primary season. Their March 2011 event at Point of Grace Church in Waukee, Iowa, outside Des Moines garnered national media attention, a pilgrimage of presidential candidates, a live C-SPAN broadcast, and an audience of more than 1,500 Iowa conservatives. In September 2011, FFC hosted a pre-debate party in Florida, which all the main presidential candidates attended. Then, a few weeks later in October, they were back at it again at the Iowa State Fairgrounds. Once again, the presidential candidates made the Teavangelical trek, knowing full well it would be imperative that they show up in front of these crucial voters.

While Ralph Reed and his team are major players in presidential politics, this isn't just about defeating President Obama and changing presidents. Clearly that is a nice short-term goal for FFC, but Reed tells me the far more significant long-term view is about the "social and moral renewal" of America. Their national "Conference and Strategy Briefings" in Washington, DC, bring clarity to that vision by attracting high-profile political speakers to educate and train FFC activists from around the country. And we're not just talking social issues. The agenda is a Teavangelical mix with breakout sessions that include "Taming the Federal Spending Beast," "The Future of the Tea Party Movement" (with panelists Jenny Beth Martin and Mark Meckler, the National Coordinators of Tea Party Patriots), "Fighting Anti-Christian Bigotry," and "Obamacare: Repeal, Replace, Reform."[3]

The conferences are a nice way to get volunteers and staff together and make sure everyone is on the same page, but the coordination of actual events between FFC and Tea Party groups is taking place all the time through email communication. Let me give you a few examples.

In November 2011, FFC was asked to speak at the Florida Tea Party Convention. Over one hundred Tea Party groups were represented including the Tri-County Tea Party. In an email to Ralph Reed's assistant, the head of that group writes: "We are seeking the support (sponsorship and/or both) of the Faith & Freedom Coalition and, of course, we would be honored if Dr. Reed would speak to us."

In another instance, Reed is invited to speak at an Atlanta Tea Party rally with Dick Morris. Reed responds: "I'm out of town but would like to figure out a way to have a presence."

These emails are meant to give you just a small taste of the communication that goes on between some evangelical organizations and the Tea Party. Once again, it's not formal. It's all about relationships. "I don't see any formal coordination between Tea Party organizations and pro-family organizations, but I think you can have an awful lot of relationships in which people know each other, trust each other, have worked together on issues," Reed explains.

FFC has used those relationships to set up shop in key battleground swing states like Pennsylvania and Florida. Training seminars and organizational meetings are held, and it turns out quite a few of the FFC volunteers are also Tea Party activists as well. The hybrid nature of the FFC makes them even more potent. Reed declares, "We really view ourselves as a home and a training ground and a deployment center for Tea Party activists who are also socially conservative. We don't want them to turn in their Tea Party passport. We want them carrying two passports. We want them to continue to be actively engaged in the Tea Party movement, but we want Tea Party activists and members who are socially conservative to have a place to be trained, activated, mobilized, and deployed effectively, and we think we are uniquely designed to do that because we are an organization run by people with social conservative pedigrees but by our charter and mission and purpose we work on a broad range of issues."

Ultimately, FFC understands that the success of their organization depends not just on all the hard work, but on the providential hand of God. As Gary Marx prayed at FFC headquarters on the National Day of Prayer: "We pray for your special provision. We know that we don't deserve it. It is by your grace that our country is even here, and we ask all these things in your Son's name. Amen."

American Family Association (AFA)

If the Faith and Freedom Coalition is the Teavangelical nerve center, the American Family Association might claim a title just as important: the Genesis of Organization. If you are a conservative evangelical, you know all about the American Family Association. Pastor Donald Wildmon founded AFA more than thirty years ago. His son, Tim Wildmon, is running things today. To say that they are just another pro-family organization is really an understatement. With over two million online supporters and a website that averages roughly 40,000,000 hits every month, their influence on the culture has been profound.

The AFA defines their mission as an organization that will "inform, equip, and activate individuals to strengthen the moral foundations of American culture."[4] AFA usually gets news headlines when they lead the boycott effort against companies like Ford or McDonald's for supporting the homosexual agenda. They also got media ink for producing and distributing a thirty-minute documentary in support of California's Proposition 8, which changed the state's constitution to protect traditional marriage (though there is an ongoing court battle over its implementation). But you can make the argument that one of their crowning achievements is something that has gone undetected by the mainstream media. It was the American Family Association that became the evangelical engine behind thousands of those original Tea Party rallies back in April of 2009.

We've discussed how the Tea Party movement really got moving after the so-called rant by CNBC reporter Rick Santelli on the floor of the Chicago Board of Trade on February 19, 2009. We think we know the rest of the story. Or do we? The *New York Times* reported that there were 750 Tea Party rallies across the country on April 15, 2009.[5] But as renowned American statistician Nate Silver observes, that figure takes into account mostly rallies in bigger population areas. He surmises that there were in fact many more undetected rallies around the country.[6] How right he·was. It turns out the American Family Association had organized a couple thousand Tea Party rallies by establishing a website called TeaPartyDay.com. Don Cobb, AFA's new-media director, recalls the site going down for seven days due to increased traffic. This was all happening a few weeks before the first big wave of Tea Party rallies in April 2009! AFA continued to busily promote them, telling their online subscribers that America was in "grave danger" and that our "elected officials in Washington are leading us down an unwise path." Then came the AFA Tea Party urgent request: "AFA and other groups have called for a day of TEA (Taxed Enough Already) Party rallies across the U.S. on April 15, including one at noon in front of the city hall in your community. Get with a few friends and go to the rally."[7]

With that simple charge, the AFA organizational adrenaline kicked in. In the weeks that followed, conservative evangelicals across America began to sign up. They volunteered to be local organizers for their Tea Party rallies, complete with contact names and phone numbers, and it was all organized online.[8] When the rallies did take place, event descriptions and photos were shared online days after the reports from the rallies came in.[9] The birth of these Tea Party rallies came not just from influential national groups like Freedom Works, Americans for Prosperity, and others (discussed later in this chapter). There's no doubt that those groups played a significant part in the story of the Tea Party movement, and history will reflect that. But the complete and accurate story is that the AFA, one of the major evangelical pro-family organizations in the country, was instrumental in the genesis of this movement too.

Another note about AFA: they recognized early on that Tea Party sentiment in this country would continue to grow, so they decided to completely change the format of their national radio network. With nearly two hundred radio stations across the country, AFA Radio had been primarily focused on a Christian music format, but with the explosion of the Tea Party that all changed. AFA leaders decided to scrap the music and move to a Christian all-talk configuration. Now, over morning coffee and a muffin, Christians are listening to current-events programming that tackles social and fiscal issues with abandon.

Family Research Council (FRC)

Liberals who follow politics cringe when they hear about the nonprofit 501c3 organization known as the Family Research Council (their legislative arm is FRC Action). They are well aware that this pro-family public policy organization, originally founded by Dr. James Dobson and a few other pastors, has been trumpeting pro-life and traditional marriage values every chance they get since their founding in 1983. There is no doubt that liberals are sick of hearing them spout their Judeo-Christian principles, but conservative Christians clearly want more of it. FRC's numbers don't lie. Since its inception, they've shipped out more than 3,700 different information products, including books, research reports, booklets, brochures, and a whole lot more. In 2010 alone, they sent out 340,000 educational items to Christians across the country. FRC's weekly radio show, devoted to current events, is heard on more than three hundred radio stations across the country. Believe me, they've got more pull than a pulled pork sandwich.

Anyone paying close attention to FRC's agenda will realize that the fragile state of America's economy has always been on their list of top issues. They will talk until they are blue in the face about how conservative social issues are directly linked to economic ones. Has the economic talk increased a notch since the Tea Party's debut in 2009? Absolutely, but the FRC has always been in the business of promoting healthy families through sound economic policy. Tony Perkins, president of FRC, tells me, "If we want to shrink the size of government, which is what the Tea Party is about, we've got to strengthen the family." That philosophy explains why FRC points to a 2008 study showing how US taxpayers are on the hook for $112 billion dollars every year in government programs devoted to unwed births and divorce.[10] The study estimates that if the divorce rate could be cut in half, taxpayers would save roughly $55 billion. When families are fractured, we all suffer.

So what is the result of their organizational viewpoint? Besides putting bulletins and daily email messages out to their 500,000 supporters warning them about the decaying moral fabric of our country, they also deliver "action alerts" concerning the debt to roughly forty thousand pastors around the country. Often these alerts are peppered with biblical language. In one of them, Perkins tells pastors "a Balanced Budget Amendment and a serious statutory spending cap are necessary not only to ensure our current financial survival, but to keep future generations from suffering for the sins of their forbears"[11] (a reference to Jeremiah 11:10).

This rise of the Tea Party has also given FRC an opportunity to really flex its organizational muscle by working with Tea Party members and groups in fiscally conservative areas. One of their national grassroots webcasts featured in the last year titled "The Taxman Cometh" included in-depth interviews with Sarah Field, chief operating officer and general counsel of the Tea Party–focused Liberty Central, and Pete Sepp, executive vice president of the National Taxpayers Union, a group that is active at Tea Party rallies.[12] The cohost of FRC's "Cut, Cap, and Balance" webcast was Colin Hanna, the president of the Let Freedom Ring organization.[13] Hanna's group is influential and heavily involved in organizing Tea Party events across the country.[14] FRC has also written editorials praising the Tea Party[15] and arguing that the movement has brought "renewed attention" to how tax rates are hurting families and businesses.[16]

Of course, some of the evangelical/Tea Party overlap is anecdotal. Officials at FRC remember a time at a Tea Party rally where one of their employees struck up a conversation with a libertarian fellow in the crowd. He mentioned to him that he was from FRC, and the Tea Party libertarian walked over to his car and showed him how he'd been following political events through FRC Action's congressional vote scorecard.[17] He told the Family Research Council employee how much he appreciated their work.

FRC clearly understands that the Tea Party is a civic awakening, but their president, Tony Perkins, is hopeful the country will move to an even bolder next step. "What America needs to follow that civic awakening is a moral awakening, a spiritual awakening that we come back to a sense of our responsibility to honor God in all that we do, to care for our neighbor, and to build a government that honors the family and honors the God who created it."

WallBuilders

Have you ever seen an encyclopedia walk? I have. He's a lanky man from Texas by the name of David Barton. The former vice chairman of the Texas Republican Party is the president of Wall-Builders, an organization dedicated to defending our nation's Judeo-Christian heritage. When Barton speaks, he comes armed for battle with a Bible, a Constitution, and reams of supporting pre–and post–Revolutionary War documents to back up his claims ... and it drives liberals nuts.

The former school educator played an active role in the attempt to make sure Texas high school students were taught God-given principles spelled out in the Declaration of Independence, including the principle that "below God-given rights and moral laws, government is directed by the consent of the governed."[18] Not only does Barton see our history through a Judeo-Christian prism, he also sees the principles of economic policy laid out clearly in the Bible. He regularly teaches how government taxes on capital gains (Matthew 25:14–30) or on someone's inheritance (Proverbs 13:22) are unbiblical.[19]

The reason WallBuilders can be considered a Teavangelical organization is because Barton is not just speaking to the church circuit. In Tea Party circles, the evangelical Barton is a rock star with a message that is in demand and popular. "Finding a Tea Party group that is faith hostile is extremely difficult to do," Barton tells me. WallBuilders receives so many invitations from Tea Party groups for him to speak that he ends up having to turn down quite a few.

So what does Barton speak about specifically? He's relaying a very evangelical message to these Tea Party groups, including informative talks about the faith of the founders, the intended role of faith in government, and even a thirty-minute presentation on the forgotten Christian heroes of America's founding. And what is Barton's take on Tea Party groups? "I see the Tea Party being filled with people of faith, of making faith very practical. They're taking principles of faith into areas where those principles of faith have not been introduced in fifty to sixty years. The Tea Party, whether all of them recognize it or not, [is] espousing biblical views of economics."

The name WallBuilders comes from the prophet Nehemiah who led a movement to rebuild the walls of Jerusalem. This Old Testament story tells not only of rebuilt walls but also of a rebuilt people, as the community moved from despair to a new relationship with God. In the same way, the Tea Party sees a nation in despair with the "walls" of our nation needing to be rebuilt. David Barton and his team are picking up their hammer, nails, and Bible ... and the Tea Party is listening intently.

Concerned Women for America

Penny Nance is someone you'd like to have tea with. She's classy, intelligent, and seems like loads of fun. But while she may enjoy a cup of tea, she's a tad bit busy these days running the biggest public-policy women's organization in America. Beverly LaHaye, a well-known, long-time Christian conservative activist, founded Concerned Women for America in 1979. Since that time, they've taken pride in the effort to merge biblical principles with legislation on Capitol Hill and in all fifty states.

While many groups can lay claim to merging evangelical and fiscal issues into their message, not too many have the clout of CWA. Penny Nance and her team have up-close and personal contact with political leaders in this country. She's invited to private meetings and events with presidential candidates, and the organization is extremely well respected in the nation's capitol. That access, plus an active and voluminous base of support, gives CWA the Teavangelical wallop to make a difference.

The national media like to call on CWA for their analysis on women's issues, especially abortion. But these concerned women of America do not limit themselves to women's issues. They are actually on the front lines fighting with the Tea Party to restore this country to sound constitutional principles and fiscally conservative economic policy. When Congressman Paul Ryan came under attack for his budget plan, CWA defended him, saying, "Elected officials should be willing to do something, rather than burden our children and grandchildren with a mountain of debt and destroy the financial future of the nation."[20] The group also cohosted a "Spending Revolt" bus tour with the influential Tea Party organizing group Americans for Prosperity.[21] Among CWA's thirty-six state directors and six hundred chapters across the country are a bountiful group of Tea Party warriors. These conservative moms are churchgoers *and* Tea Party attendees. Penny Nance tells me that when she speaks at CWA leadership conferences around America, she always asks the following question: "Do you attend Tea Party rallies?" Almost without exception, Nance watches virtually every hand go up in a room filled with over one hundred Christian activists.

One of those raised hands belongs to Bobbi Radeck. She is CWA's state chapter leader in Ohio and is also extremely active inside the Ohio Tea Party scene. She is a regular with the Cincinnati Tea Party and the nearby group in Westchester, Ohio. When she's not hard at work for CWA, Bobbi and her Tea Party friends try to get Americans in position to become voting precinct captains or poll watchers. While Bobbi Radeck wears both a CWA hat and a Tea Party cap, her main goal is to be an effective witness for Christ anywhere she goes. "This is a missions ground for me," she says.

Janne Myrdal is another one of CWA's state directors who is just as comfortable talking about abortion as she is about the federal budget. This Norwegian native made her way to the United States in the early 1980s. She became a US citizen in 2005, and while she's always had an insatiable appetite for politics, it exploded even more so when the Tea Party came on the scene. When that happened in 2009, she got involved right away and now sits on the executive committee for the North Dakota Tea Party Caucus, home to at least four hundred members (Janne points out that's pretty big by North Dakota standards). Three years before joining the Tea Party effort in North Dakota, she had already been CWA's state chapter director, responsible for coordinating local legislation efforts, so the Tea Party movement fit in nicely with Janne's desire to be active.

Since Janne Myrdal wears her deep pro-life convictions on her sleeve, she's not afraid to bring up the subject with Tea Party libertarians in North Dakota. She'll ask them point blank whether they really want their taxpayer dollars going to fund someone else's abortion. Their answer? Of course not. Janne just played the Teavangelical card. However, even though North Dakota Tea Party members know her as the pro-life CWA woman, she makes sure to tell everyone at those events, "I'm here as a concerned citizen." Janne says she will leave the rest to God. "You can't bring church to the Tea Party, but you *can* bring your faith and testimony."

Tea Party Organizations: No Labels Please

Now that we've looked at some of the main evangelical organizations that work with the Tea Party, it's time to quickly look at some of the main national Tea Party groups. Now, the actual phrase "Tea Party organization" is a little misleading. The organic Tea Party movement is proud of its natural roots, and any national group that tries to claim that it's speaking for or taking credit for the Tea Party will be routinely dismissed as an imposter. The national organizations I will list would all agree that they *do not* speak for the collective Tea Party. It's impossible. Rather, they see themselves as vessels of coordination within the myriad of local groups and the patriot citizens that make up the movement. Of course to be successful you need structure, and these organizations have done a great job at synchronizing the effort as best they can. Remember, this is still a young movement and will be a continual work in progress.

Highlighted here are brief summaries of four main national Tea Party groups, although there are others like Liberty Central (founded by Virginia Thomas, the wife of Supreme Court Justice Clarence Thomas) and Tea Party America who are important to the national dialogue as well.

Tea Party Express

The story of Tea Party Express does not start out in a living room or at a kitchen table. It actually started with a couple of guys who know politics pretty well. In 2008, Sal Russo, a longtime Republican political consultant, and Howard Kaloogian, a former state assemblyman in California, started a political action committee called Our Country Deserves Better. They were annoyed that 2008 presidential candidate John McCain was not doing enough to take on Obama. When the Tea Party rallies began to take shape in April of 2009, Russo, Kaloogian, and the PAC staff came up with the idea of a two-week bus tour across the country designed to put the pressure on Capitol Hill politicians who had a fondness for spending taxpayer money. The bus tour became a hit, and the rest is history.

With donations coming in and hundreds of thousands of grassroots activists signing up to get involved, the Tea Party Express phenomenon grew. More bus tours ensued, and PAC money was spent with the goal of selectively targeting (and removing) anti–Tea Party politicians from office. In their view, there was no room for wishy-washy, moderate politicians, and they were looking to financially back constitutionally conservative candidates. In 2010, Tea Party Express helped Mike Lee knock off Utah's longtime incumbent Senator Bob Bennett. In Massachusetts, they helped pull off a major upset when Scott Brown got elected to the seat formerly held by Democratic icon Ted Kennedy. And in Delaware, they backed the winning Christine O'Donnell in the primary against moderate Mike Castle. The media took notice. In the fall of 2011, the organization cosponsored the first-ever Tea Party debate in conjunction with CNN.

While Tea Party Express does not highlight social issues at all (and these national groups are adamant about staying away from the hotbed social issues), that doesn't mean there isn't evangelical crossover. Their chairwoman, Amy Kremer, is a Christian who is friendly with evangelical leaders including Penny Nance, the president of Concerned Women for America. Kremer has also taken part in plenty of Tea Party panels sponsored by evangelical Christian organizations, including the Values Voters Summit hosted by the Family Research Council in 2010.[22] FRC returned the favor that same year when Tom McClusky, vice president for government affairs, spoke about mandatory taxpayer funding in Obamacare at a Tea Party Express event held on Capitol Hill.[23]

Tea Party Patriots

Tea Party Patriots may ring a bell with you. In chapter 2, we introduced you to its founder, Jenny Beth Martin. She and cofounder Mark Meckler coordinated the first Tea Party rallies in the Atlanta area, and after their big rally in April of 2009, she officially established the group as Tea Party Patriots (TPP). Unlike Tea Party Express, which endorses candidates, TPP does not. Their focus is on organizing, training, and educating over one thousand local Tea Party groups around America in the effort to elect constitutionally conservative candidates.[24] They have a very specific goal of making sure they go into every state in the country at least twice to conduct training so local groups can turn voters out in November.

Jenny Beth Martin knows a thing or two about voter mobilization from her association with the Teavangelical Ralph Reed. During 2004 both of them worked on the Bush campaign. Martin and Reed have a good relationship, which has led to crossover appearances at each other's events. Jenny Beth has appeared on panels at Reed's Faith and Freedom Coalition conferences,[25] and Ralph Reed has returned the favor by speaking at big Tea Party Patriots events.[26] It was through Reed that Martin really began to understand what it takes to put a political organization together.

Americans for Prosperity

Americans for Prosperity (AFP) is influential — so influential that it got the attention of President Obama during the 2010 midterm election cycle. AFP was causing havoc for Democrats with all their campaign ads and grassroots organizing. Finally Obama got fed up and told Democrats in Austin, Texas, "All around this country there are groups with harmless-sounding names like Americans for Prosperity, who are running millions of dollars of ads against Democratic candidates.... And they don't have to say who exactly the Americans for Prosperity are. You don't know if it's a foreign-controlled corporation. You don't know if it's a big oil company, or a big bank."[27] Actually, all President Obama needs to know is that Americans for Prosperity is his worst nightmare.

AFP came into being in 2004. Its founders, Charles and David Koch (pronounced "coke"), are billionaire brothers who for decades have been dolling out money to conservative and libertarian projects, causes, and think tanks.[28] Millions of dollars have gone to conservative organizations like the Heritage Foundation and the American Enterprise Institute along with the libertarian CATO Institute. (One of the brothers, David, was actually the Libertarian Party candidate for vice president of the United States in 1980.) In 1984, the Koch brothers established Citizens for a Sound Economy, a think tank devoted to less government interference. In 2004 the organization decided to restructure into two separate entities: Americans for Prosperity and Freedom Works.

AFP describes its mission as "educating citizens about economic policy and mobilizing those citizens as advocates in the public policy process."[29] They take pride in their ability to organize at the local, state, and federal grassroots level, and they've done a bang-up job. The organization has thirty-two state chapters and 1.7 million activists in all fifty states. In 2009, they held over three hundred anti-Obamacare rallies, while the next year they coordinated over five hundred Tea Party–related events.[30] Obviously AFP is a dominant player in the Tea Party movement.

So where's the Teavangelical connection? Let me introduce you to Tim Phillips, the president of Americans for Prosperity. Before joining AFP, Phillips helped establish the powerful Century Strategies Public Relations firm with ... wait for it ... Ralph Reed. That's right. Reed and Phillips are good friends. They're also evangelical Christians who love God and embrace Tea Party values. Reed's FFC organization and Phillip's AFP group work together where appropriate, including an instance where FFC cohosted a 2010 AFP conference in Georgia called "Defending the American Dream."[31] AFP has also worked with other evangelical organizations, including participating in live video webcasts hosted by the Family Research Council[32] and cosponsoring bus tours with Concerned Women for America. The Teavangelical cooperation and networks are everywhere you look.

FreedomWorks

To the casual observer, FreedomWorks might appear like your typical, inside-the-beltway, Washington, DC, conservative organization. The chairman of the board is former Republican House majority leader Dick Armey, and its vice chairman is billionaire publisher Steve Forbes, the former GOP presidential candidate. While those high-powered names give the organization decades of experience to draw on and instant credibility with the media, the real magic comes from a hardworking, top-notch staff that has created ways to train and connect Tea Party members across America.

The man waving the wand is Matt Kibbe, the president and CEO of FreedomWorks. Kibbe has a unique style: with his long sideburns, glasses, and a sixties-retro look, some in the media describe

Kibbe as if actor "Billy Bob Thornton cleaned up for a job interview."[33] *Newsweek* calls Kibbe "one of the masterminds" of Tea Party politics.[34]

Kibbe is not a showman. He's an economist who knows public policy like the back of his hand. Kibbe's tenure dates back fifteen years to when FreedomWorks was called Citizens of a Sound Economy. In his fight for less government and lower taxes, Kibbe and the staff enlist volunteer activists all around the country and then begin to teach and inform them in the ways of the Tea Party.

While FreedomWorks does play an important role by endorsing candidates through their political action committee, they spend a bunch of their time with those on the front lines of the Tea Party. They bring activists into their Washington, DC, headquarters on a regular basis, and they're not there to sip tea. They show up ready to work hard in what is called "Boot Camp," a three-day exhaustion fest where hundreds of activists from dozens of states gather to learn everything from the hot public policy issues and strategies for repealing Obamacare to techniques for handling the media in their local districts.[35] The organization has also started something called FreedomConnector, a website where you plug in your zip code and you can find a Tea Party near you.[36] As for overt evangelical connections, you won't find as many at FreedomWorks, but the organization has participated in various coalition meetings with the Family Research Council in the last couple years, trying to defeat President Obama's healthcare plan.

It's pretty clear to see that whether it is FreedomWorks, Americans for Prosperity, Tea Party Patriots, or Tea Party Express, the activity never stops. Changing the course of America is a 24/7 operation, and evangelical organizations are teaming with all of the Tea Party players in a campaign of a lifetime.

Chapter 4

TEAVANGELICAL RALLIES

HE HAD BLOOD ALL OVER HIS FACE AND WAS ABOUT TO TAKE HIS last breath. As he lay dying in the gravel on the side of a lonely Iowa road in the middle of nowhere, Stacie and Carrie Stoelting came rushing over to the gruesome scene. The college-age sisters were on their way to Grandma Hilda's house for Mother's Day festivities when they saw the horrific crash unfold: a helmetless motorcyclist flying through the air after hitting a car that had just entered the highway intersection. Now, Stacie and Carrie found themselves up-close and personal watching a life slip away. They called 911 but felt helpless knowing there was nothing they could do to save his life.

So what did these two sisters do? They got down on the ground and prayed with this man to accept Jesus. Before losing consciousness, he heard their comforting words and through hand signals communicated that he wanted to give his life to Christ.

The incident on that Iowa highway four years ago changed the Stoelting sisters, crystallizing their understanding that life is short and you never know when that last breath will come. So these evangelical sisters created a political and social online magazine called Unite the USA as a way to encourage positive patriotism among the millennial generation (those thirty and younger). "We don't want to be the generation that dropped the ball," Stacie Stoelting tells me. Their website asks young potential voters to not just talk but act by attending town hall meetings and educating themselves about the Constitution and the issues of the day.

Ultimately, that Tea Party–type message started getting noticed by Christian media outlets and Fox News too. The increased visibility led to invitations by Tea Party groups. But when they go, they don't speak. They sing! The two of them also happen to be gospel singers who possess a vocal range of three octaves. They've recorded albums called *Heavenly* and *In God We Still Trust* in honor of veterans and patriotic Americans.[1] Now they sing patriotic songs at many Tea Party rallies across the country.

Whether they're singing at Tea Party rallies or helping a dying man find Jesus Christ on a desolate Iowa road, Stacie and Carrie Stoelting are Americans who are making a difference in a uniquely Teavangelical way.

The Rally Demographics

Conservative Christians are good at a few things. They can quote Scripture pretty well, they put together delicious potluck dinners, and they also play a mean game of Bible Trivial Pursuit. You know what else they do very well? They show up at Tea Party rallies. The Stoelting sisters are two prime examples of Teavangelical Tea Party rally supporters, and the demographics prove it.

We hear a lot from national Tea Party organizers that these rallies are made up of disgruntled Republicans, frustrated Democrats, and action-minded independents. That is a hundred percent true. But when you get inside the rally numbers, you see a distinct Christian flavor.

One of the largest and most substantial polls done on the Tea Party so far comes from the Diane D. Blair Center of Southern

Politics and Society in conjunction with the Winthrop Rockefeller Institute. Their survey was conducted pretty soon after the 2010 midterm elections. What they found is what we've been describing in this book and what has been my experience throughout the young history of the Tea Party. The report showed that 10.6% of people surveyed defined themselves as Tea Party members. Among that group, the average Tea Party rally attendees are "predominantly white, middle class, educated, Christian males over the age of 45." They break it down even further:

- 91.4% are white
- 57.8% are men
- 42.2% are female
- 63.2% are over the age of forty-five
- 85% are Christian
- 37.4% believe that the "Bible is the actual Word of God and is to be taken literally, word for word" (this figure is 29.7% for non–Tea Party members)
- 7% believe that the "Bible is inspired by men"[2]

I think you can see now why so many of these Tea Party events are strongly influenced by Christians. It really is a pure numbers game. When you have 85% of the audience believing that Jesus Christ is God, then what do you expect? What's been most impressive is the fact that these events have been able to take on a Christian flavor yet at the same time not alienate Tea Party libertarians. Think about that for a moment. You have a bottom-up political movement that isn't controlled by any one organization or person, and yet you don't see the 85% of Christians clamoring to take over the Tea Party rallies with a message dominated by social issues. Leigh-Ann Bellew heads up a conservative mother's group in New

Jersey, and she admits it's not the easiest thing in the world to hold back your traditional positions on marriage and abortion. She knows there are many likeminded people with her at the Tea Party rallies. "I wish they'd be more vocal about it, but I think they're afraid that might divide up the movement," she says.[3]

Praying to Jesus

Let me clue you in to a little secret. If you've never been to a Tea Party rally, guess what they do. They pray. That's right. I said it. I went there. They actually pray. I'm not suggesting that if you show up at a Tea Party rally you will experience a full-fledged altar call. You're not going to see local Tea Party leaders asking people to repent of their sins and give their lives to Jesus Christ. Rather, you'll see speakers opening up most rallies with a prayer to God or prayers for divine intervention.

This heavenly intercession was explained to me in the small southeastern town of Ottumwa, Iowa. The township is relatively plain looking and is divided in half by the Des Moines River. Its politics are also divided in half. The city votes half Democrat and half Republican, and that's why this small city has received visits from the likes of Teddy Roosevelt, Richard Nixon, and Barack Obama. Add the folks on board the Tea Party bus tour to that list of visitors.

On a summer day in June 2011 when our television crew was in Ottumwa, we met April Linder, the communication director for the Iowa Tea Party. This group arranged a nineteen-city tour of Iowa with the goal of drumming up Tea Party support, training activists, and mobilizing people at the rallies. As we made our way to interview April outside the Ottumwa Library, I couldn't help but notice the Tea Party–flavored music playing in the background. The song, "Keep the Change," by country music singer Daryl Worley, possessed lyrics that were perfectly Teavangelical, especially when he says, "Gonna keep our God, our freedom, and a little money in the bank!"

It was the perfect musical interlude as we conducted our interview with April. She revealed to me that every morning the participants on the Iowa Tea Party bus pray. Linder and the organizers of the tour needed divine intervention because event planning would often change at the last moment, which meant a good possibility for low turnout. In actuality, often more people than expected showed up at these events. "God wants these people there or they wouldn't have turned out," Linder told me. "We would get on the bus and go; God obviously has a purpose because things fell into place even when we had no control over them whatsoever.... God's hand has been in everything that I've been able to be involved in and he's going to keep leading us."

While they're praying on the bus and seeing God's hand during their Tea Party rallies, the event outside also begins with prayer. At the Ottumwa rally, organizers made sure to thank God first before getting on to Tea Party business. The prayer was simple and to the point: "Heavenly Father, we just want to thank you for the ... courage that you gave those original founders of the Declaration of Independence that gave us our freedom."

All around America the Bible is out and heads are lowered in prayer at these rallies. The prayers are a mix of evangelical language and Tea Party manifesto. In short, it's a Teavangelical prayer. At an event in Salina, Kansas, in April 2011, the Reverend Kerry Basinger of Salina Heights Christian Church spoke at a Tea Party rally, thanking God for "a land built on sacrifice and hard work, not government programs and free rides.... In the name of the One who changed my life, Jesus Christ. Amen."[4] In Santa Fe, New Mexico, Tea Party leader John Onstad stepped to the microphone and prayed, "Help us to recall and celebrate the devoted patriots who founded this great nation some two hundred short years ago. Let us stand today arm and arm with the founders of this great republic, resolute against the continuing and ever-present powers of tyrants, both foreign and domestic." The crowd followed with a resounding, "Amen!" followed by a woman shouting, "Free in Christ, you're free indeed!"[5]

The Americans who are praying at these rallies are not doing it for show. It's the real deal. Their love and passion for God and country is with equal zest. While fiscal issues dominate the conversation at these rallies, they don't check their faith at the door. Senator Jim DeMint, one of the de facto Tea Party leaders, once told me, "'I'm praying for you' comes up more than anything else in these crowds, so I know there's a spiritual component out there."[6]

All of this talk of prayer and spirituality related to the Tea Party movement might spook some people. It definitely may send the separation-of-church-and-state people reaching for their heart medication. But not only does prayer work, it also fits in perfectly at Tea Party rallies. Believe it or not, you can actually be a Spirit-filled, praying member of the Tea Party. That's not to say all of the participants are like this, but make no mistake that if you attend a Tea Party rally, you will likely hear a stirring invocation and a heartfelt benediction.

Many of those who attend Tea Party rallies know what to expect. They understand that a distinct God-infused flavor is part of the drill. Playing up America's Christian heritage is one of the main attractions used to persuade people to go to Tea Party events. The Texas Tea Party actually has a page on their website devoted to promoting the Christian legacy of this country complete with quotes that declare that "this great nation was founded not by religionists but by Christians, not on religions but on the gospel of Jesus Christ." They make clear that these Tea Party rallies are imperative because "if we don't get a hold of the fact we have all but lost our Christian heritage, and get activated to take it back, and quickly, what kind of a future will we be leaving our children?"[7]

Signs and Pamphlets

I have to admit that I like catchy phrases on bumper stickers, especially Christian-style bumper stickers. One of my favorites is "In Case of Rapture, This Car Will Be Unmanned." Then there are the Teavangelical types of bumper stickers that say, "Jesus Saves/Obama Spends." But when you go to a Tea Party rally, be prepared to see plenty of signs of divinity. Some of the ones I like include "In God We Trust, Not Congress,"[8] "God Only Asks for 10 Percent," "Give Me Freedom, Not Taxes,"[9] "Thou Shalt Not Change the Constitution,"[10] "Evil Triumphs When Good Men Do Nothing,"[11] and "Save the USA: Restore God, Prayer, and the Constitution."[12]

But the signs are just the outer layer. What lies beneath is a much deeper effort by conservative Christians who are showing up at Tea Party rallies to promote their platform in a number of areas. At Tea Party rallies and events around the country, the pamphlets displayed on tables by certain groups reflect the issues they care about.

For example, a group called Frontline Ministries was distributing pamphlets titled "Salt and Light: The Great Commission and Who's Responsible for Educating Your Children." This Christian organization believes that public schools indoctrinate children, and they implore parents to not send their kids to an institution that's run by the state or government. They make clear in the pamphlet that "the state or government has usurped the role of the family and church in operating K–12 public schools." The school-choice issue intersects both the antigovernment view of the Tea Party and the pro-Judeo-Christian perspective of evangelicals.

The Greenville Tea Party Creed, which is handed out to participants as they enter the event, invokes the most important documents sacred to evangelicals and the Tea Party. It reads: "We the members of the Greenville Tea Party are guided in our actions by four fundamental documents which we venerate. They are the Ten Commandments, the Declaration of Independence, the Constitution of the United States, and the platform of the Republican Party." These types of pamphlets and programs are par for the course at many Tea Party events.

The Christian Flavor

Do you like cookies-and-cream ice cream? Well, what if I told you I was going to take the cookies out of the recipe? You'd be left with an ice cream flavor called "cream." Pretty standard. Leave it to me to make yet another food analogy in an attempt to explain what it would be like at these Tea Party rallies without evangelicals. In short, the evangelicals are the cookies inside the cream. When I asked evangelical South Carolina radio talk-show host Josh Kimbrell to explain to me what you would be left with if evangelicals were not part of the Tea Party rallies, he answered matter-of-factly, "A handful of people who won't be consequential." This is not to be disrespectful to Tea Party libertarians, because evangelicals within the Tea Party movement wouldn't be consequential either if the libertarians didn't show up. It's simply to make the point that because evangelicals are showing up to these rallies and events in droves it just makes the crowds larger and the feeling part pep rally and part Christian retreat.

At the first national Tea Party convention held in Nashville, Tennessee, in February 2010, the liberal group Media Matters sent an undercover reporter named Melinda Warner to the event. She says her experience at times was like attending a church camp complete with "music, a sermon, a large group prayer (on our knees), followed by small group prayers (hand holding), and then a movie. That schedule could have easily been opening night at a retreat, if only there had been a call to the altar." She attended a workshop called "Why Christians Must Engage" hosted by well-known evangelical pastor Rick Scarborough. She even overheard participants saying "We have God on our side" and that "Twenty percent of the Ten Commandments is economics."[13] That liberal reporter got clued in to something that Tea Party regulars know very well. You simply cannot separate God from the Tea Party.

In Columbia, South Carolina, Chad Connelly, the founder and president of the Christian-based group Foundation for American Restoration, speaks at dozens of Tea Party events. He pontificates about American Christian history and its connection to a vibrant free-market society. "My talks have been extremely Christ-centered and God-themed ... and I know that those events that I've been to focused on the big picture, and God is the cornerstone of America and God is one of the major reasons our country has been successful," Connelly told me one afternoon in steamy Columbia.

Then there is the story of William and Selena Owens, Christian political activists whose faith-based appearances have become a staple at Tea Party rallies. When they take the podium, the crowd is in for a Teavangelical treat. It becomes a mini-pulpit where they not only advocate Tea Party principles but also inject God into the equation. One of their eleven books is called *The Power within a Conservative Woman — Engaging America for God, Family, and Country*. When pitching their spiritual message and their book, Selena Owens makes the point that the book "stems from a Christian premise. It will tell you about the power of God within you to help circumvent this and how to engage."[14]

Everywhere you look you find a Christian element at these rallies. Granted, the Christian influence may be greater at some events than others. You'll see more of an evangelical influence in Southern states than those up in the blue state Northeast, but the overall message remains the same: while the Tea Party's focus is on getting our economic house in order, God's Word is ever-present, crucial to the message, and won't take a backseat to anything.

The Real Tea Party Housewives of Atlanta

Jenny Beth Martin

We've taken you inside these Tea Party rallies, but they don't just happen by chance. A lot of careful planning and meticulous effort happens behind the scenes. Two women have played a distinct role in the birth of these Tea Party rallies. They probably would not identify themselves as Teavangelicals per se, but don't think for a minute that God doesn't play a very significant role in their lives.

Earlier in this book, we introduced you to Jenny Beth Martin and Amy Kremer, two of the key players in the Tea Party movement. If the Bravo network were to make a television show about them, they might just call it *The Real Tea Party Housewives of Atlanta*. Martin and Kremer live less than thirty minutes apart in the suburbs of Atlanta, Georgia. They have a lot in common. Both used to be stay-at-home moms, both love God, and both have taken the Tea Party to new heights.

Before founding Tea Party Patriots, Martin was struggling after her husband's business went belly up and her family went through bankruptcy. When CNBC anchor Rick Santelli went on his Tea Party rant in February 2009, Martin was living in a rental property. But she got busy doing what she does best: coordinating. The organizational skills she learned as a mom came in handy when putting together those first Tea Party rallies. "A lot of what I do is coordinating, and at home that's what I was doing. I love making spreadsheets and making lists," Martin told me when I visited her in Woodstock, Georgia.[15] Little did she know that the Tea Party movement in April 2009 would change her life, and Martin would end up in 2010 as one of *Time* magazine's most influential people.

Martin is quick to point out that these Tea Party rallies around the country need to stay focused on promoting the three core values of fiscal responsibility, constitutionally limited government, and free markets. Everyone is welcome at these rallies so long as they stick to those issues. You will find that socially conservative evangelicals, for the most part, don't disagree with that mindset at all. It's not that Martin is against any sort of social conservative agenda. As a matter of fact, she believes that "one of the most basic social values or social issues is the ability to provide food on the table for your family." Once again, we see how Tea Party Christians see the intersection of economics and the strength of the family.

Martin considers herself a God-fearing Christian. She grew up in the Methodist Church and her dad was a Methodist minister. Her brother went to seminary. "Church and God have always been a part of my life," Martin tells me. While she may not consider herself a Teavangelical, she is on the same page with evangelicals when it comes to protecting and preserving the Judeo-Christian heritage of this country. "Our founders pointed to our freedom. It wasn't granted by the government. These are God-given rights," Martin says. "One verse that always stands out for me is 'Trust the Lord with all your heart, and lean not on your own understanding; in all your ways acknowledge him, and he'll make your paths straight,'" Martin recalls (Proverbs 3:5 – 6, NIV 1984). She admits that her dependence on God is behind her ultimate success. "Sometimes I don't know exactly what I'm doing, and I just reach down and have that faith in God that if I rely on God I'm going to figure out the right thing to do."

Amy Kremer

Amy Kremer doesn't mess around. As chairwoman of Tea Party Express, she's flying high as one of the most influential members of the Tea Party movement. Amy knows a thing or two about flying since she used to be a former Delta Airlines flight attendant. Now she travels around the country three weeks out of the month. "I travel more now than when I was a flight attendant," Kremer told me at her home in the Atlanta suburbs.

When Kremer is home, her nerve center is an upstairs office decorated with a plethora of "Live Free or Die" decorations. For the first two years of the Tea Party movement, however, she was planning rallies from her kitchen table. "For a lot of women, the kitchen is the heart of the home, so that's where we're most comfortable. And everything revolves in and around the kitchen, so it was only natural that it should be here." Kremer is fully aware that the rallies are a huge part of the Tea Party's success, but she also acknowledges, "We can have rallies until the end of time, but in order to truly effect change we need to change the players." She's trying to do that by rallying against moderate senators like Olympia Snowe, Richard Lugar, and Debbie Stabenow.

Kremer knows that the rallies she organizes and attends in an attempt to change the political landscape are made up of plenty of evangelicals. "You see the common thread of God and faith continuously throughout this movement," Kremer observes. But this Tea Party mom, who grew up Methodist and attended church twice every week, realizes that there is a delicate balancing act out there at these rallies because not everybody is evangelical. "Some people don't have those same beliefs, and I don't want to alienate them." Therefore, her goal is to stay focused on the fiscal issues and not let the hot-button social issues detract from the message. You won't see Amy Kremer wearing her faith on her sleeve at these rallies, but "he [God] is very much a part of my life."

God is such a big part of her life that she relied on him greatly when her organization partnered with CNN to host the first-ever Tea Party debate. Her high-profile role led to a speaking slot on the debate stage in front of a national audience. Amy was so nervous backstage that she gathered two of her Tea Party friends together. They all prayed that God would calm her nerves and give her the right words to say. Amy proceeded to head out on stage and delivered an eloquent speech. Whom do you think she credits?

Amy Kremer will be the first one to admit that she's nobody special. She's your typical mom who decided to get off the couch and begin doing something, and she wants to see other patriotic, disgruntled, and busy moms show up at rallies too. "You don't have to allow it to consume your life," Kremer said. "If you truly want to get involved, start a small book group or a Constitution study group or something just with some other moms." And why is she doing all this? "I'm not doing it to be in the history books. I'm really doing it for my child and my eventual grandchildren, I hope," Kremer explained. But as I left her house that day I knew that Kremer was entirely mindful of the position God has placed her in. "He has a hand in my life," Kremer said with a smile.

Racism at the Rallies?

Jenny Beth Martin and Amy Kremer agree on Tea Party policy matters, but they also are united on the issue of combating the media myth of the supposed strain of racism seen at Tea Party rallies. Is the Tea Party movement racist? No, it is not. Are there some racists who show up at rallies? Absolutely, but anyone trying to brand the Tea Party as racist is just plain wrong. While I have been to dozens of Tea Party rallies without seeing a hint of racism, that doesn't mean my anecdotal experience tells the whole story. The truth is we just cannot dismiss some of these derogatory signs that show up at rallies. When some show up with posters that read, "Obama's plan: White Slavery," or, "American taxpayers are the Jews for Obama's ovens," it bears further exploring.

Since the overwhelming majority of Tea Party members are

white, cries of racism come with the territory. Indeed, a Blair Rockefeller poll details the fact that 84.5% of white Tea Party members
do not believe it's the responsibility of the federal government to
make sure that minorities have job equality with whites even if it
means you will have to pay more taxes. Moreover, more than 60% of
this same group believes America has gone too far in pushing equal
rights.[16] A CBS News/New York Times Poll shows that the majority of Tea Party followers (52 percent) think that too much is being
made about the problems black people face.[17] However, to make the
leap from those positions to accusations of racism is quite a stretch.
So let me get this straight: if you don't believe in affirmative action
policies, you're racist? Of course not.

The truth is that some racists have shown up at Tea Party rallies
even though that sort of hatred does not represent the Tea Party in
any way, shape, or fashion. The Institute for Research and Education on Human Rights (admittedly a liberal-leaning organization)
documented instances where indeed white nationalists would show
up and speak at some Tea Party organized events and hand out
literature too.[18] One state chairman of a white nationalist group
even admits that, "The Tea Parties are fertile ground for our activists." Mark Meckler, the national cochairman of Tea Party Patriots
has been outraged at these reports and says they would ban any of
these groups if they found out they were doing this. "We have a 100
percent zero-tolerance policy towards this type of group," Meckler
says. "This type of activity has no place in the legitimate Tea Party
movement."[19]

That's a message that black Tea Party conservatives like Brandon
Brice have been trying to raise since the movement began. Brice has
been active in the Tea Party movement, but he's also been involved
in governmental politics as the Director of Education Affairs inside
the Office of the New Jersey Governor Chris Christie. Brice has a
pretty decent megaphone too since he's been a regular guest con-

tributor on Fox News. As a guy who has been to the rallies he's making sure that the Tea Party movement doesn't just blow off some of these racist happenings in an attempt to simply say it doesn't exist. "The tea party leaders should apologize on behalf of the irresponsible comments that were made, but they should also stand very firm on where we stood and where they stood in 2009."[20] Evangelicals may want to heed that advice. The Tea Party needs evangelicals not just from a numbers perspective to affect change but the movement would be well served if evangelicals rose to the occasion to state unequivocally that any hint of racism will not be tolerated at these rallies or otherwise. Granted, evangelicals can't play hall monitor at all these rallies, but the hint of racism speaks to the larger need of evangelicals using their moderating influence to help shoo away the extreme elements of certain Tea Party members.

Despite these examples of racism, it is truly hard to make the argument that the Tea Party movement is racist in nature. Even the liberal leaning authors who wrote the Tea Party report on racism from the Institute for Research and Education on Human Rights admit that. "It would be a mistake to claim that all Tea Partiers are nativist vigilantes or racists of one stripe or another, and this report manifestly does not make that claim."[21] Plus, some of the movement's most popular and influential leaders are black, namely, presidential candidate Herman Cain and Congressmen Allen West and Tim Scott. If this movement was truly racist, do you think these three Christian men would put up with that? Ron Miller—a Tea Party, African-American conservative and the author of the book *Sellout*—puts it this way. "If the Tea Party movement, fragmented as it is, had an opportunity to select the one man that they'd want as president of the United States right now, it would be Allen West, followed closely by Herman Cain."[22] Of course, running for president didn't exactly work out for "The Hermanator," even though he treated America to a wild ride while it lasted.

Ultimately, the real long-lasting issue here isn't whether the Tea Party is racist. We know that, by and large, it isn't. The bigger concept to wrestle with is how does the Tea Party plan to expand a base that is nearly all white? The economic (and social) message coming out of the Tea Party is all about fiscal constraint and tied to individual responsibility. Those are conservative values that can and should apply to blacks and whites alike. If that's the case, how does the Tea Party spread that message effectively into the inner city communities and elsewhere? Whether from the bottom up (which is how the Tea Party formed to begin with) or with the help of national Tea Party leaders who have the media megaphones, that message is one that can bolster the ranks, protect the Tea Party from cries of racism and ultimately provide a moral and just mission that true Bible-believing evangelicals would gladly sign up for.

Glenn Beck's Rallying Cry

It's extremely difficult to do a chapter on Tea Party rallies without paying special attention to one of the biggest rallies of all: Glenn Beck's "Restoring Honor" rally on the National Mall in Washington, DC, in August 2010. Hundreds of thousands of patriotic, Tea Party, God-fearing Americans showed up for a gathering that felt more like a spiritual revival. Beck brought over two hundred pastors on stage with him as they prayed for the country. "Something that is beyond man is happening," Beck told the crowd. "America today begins to turn back to God."[23]

Now, if Billy Graham were leading this humongous Tea Party rally, then it would become a pretty straightforward tale of the power of Christianity within the Tea Party. Alas, it wasn't Graham. It was Beck, an iconic conservative media mogul and a Mormon. While polls show that evangelicals like what Beck has to say more than the average American, most of them have a problem with his

Mormon theology.[24] So while Beck is up there talking about God, technically it wouldn't be accurate to call him a Teavangelical. Yet this is where an asterisk is needed and where labels in certain situations may not tell the entire story.

When Beck began invoking God's name at nearly every turn during the nationally televised rally, some evangelicals got queasy. Some raised the red flag, arguing that the apostle Paul warned Christians "against uniting with unbelievers in spiritual endeavors."[25] Beck's evangelical supporters came to his defense, saying that "Christians concerned about Glenn's faith should judge the tree by its fruits, not its labels."[26]

While both sides can make a theologically solid argument, there is a larger factor to consider here. Glenn Beck was there not to advance Mormonism but to advocate a Tea Party message based on faith. In essence, he was preaching a Teavangelical message. What Glenn Beck did was to inject God squarely and forcefully into the Tea Party equation. He used his powerful megaphone to give God the glory, and faith has now become part of the national discourse within the context of the Tea Party.

"That moment [Glenn Beck's rally] marked a turning point in the relationship between religious conservatives and the Tea Party," according to Bryan Fischer of the American Family Association. Without a doubt it was refreshing to see someone with real influence stand up in public and not hide God in the closet.

We will never be able to measure this quantitatively, but if I had to venture a guess it wouldn't surprise me that Beck's summer rally got more people inquiring about who God really is. Maybe more are searching today. Glenn Beck deserves credit for that. We know as Christians that God can and will use anybody for his glory. So you never know how it's going to play out. What we do know is that if someone approaches us and asks us about Jesus we had better be ready with an answer. Who knows? That encounter may happen at a Tea Party rally.

Conclusion

Throughout the years, conservative evangelicals have powered important movements like the Moral Majority and the Christian Coalition. Tea Party rallies are the next wave in that revolution. John Green, a political scientist at the University of Akron, sums it up well: "There was an opening on the right for organizations and candidates and groups that could appeal to different elements of the religious coalition.... In many ways the Tea Party has filled that niche."[27] The result is evangelicals and libertarians plugging away together across America at these rallies. The fruit of their labors may not materialize overnight, but who ever said this would be easy? With a fight ahead to make sure America adheres to constitutionally conservative principles, maybe the Teavangelicals should take their cue from liberal Democrat Adlai Stevenson, who once said, "Patriotism is not a short and frenzied outburst of emotion but the tranquil and steady dedication of a lifetime."[28]

Chapter 5

THE TEAVANGELICAL
FLAVOR *of the* MONTH

IT WAS JANUARY 19, THE DAY OF THE BIG GOP PRESIDENTIAL DEBATE in Charleston, South Carolina, and Newt Gingrich was approached by a supporter who handed him a note. The short message encouraged him to read a particular Bible verse. Later that day, less than two hours before the debate, Gingrich sent an email to a couple trusted advisors. The subject line read as follows: "Can one of you send me this." The body of his email simply said, "Isaiah 54:17."

The Bible verse states, "'No weapon forged against you will prevail, and you will refute every tongue that accuses you. This is the heritage of the servants of the LORD, and this is their vindication from me,' declares the LORD." It sure was an appropriate line considering all the incoming fire Gingrich was receiving at the time from presidential candidate Mitt Romney, his chief nemesis. A few days later Gingrich would win the South Carolina primary with major help from evangelicals and the Tea Party. How could the former Speaker of the House, who had been married three times and committed adultery twice, be a favorite of evangelicals? How could a significant portion of the Tea Party (in South Carolina and Georgia at least) embrace a man who at one time backed an individual health-care mandate and spent decades inside Washington as a politician?

Those questions are just a few of many perplexing conundrums, all culminating in a wild ride that saw many of the Republican presidential candidates filling the bill as "the Teavangelical Flavor of the Month." Why did Rick Perry and Michele Bachmann, two candidates who are classic Teavangelicals, not make it to the finish line? Why did Rick Santorum do so well? How did Mitt Romney persevere despite not paying much attention to the Tea Party and evangelical crowds? Most important of all, what are the lessons learned if a Teavangelical is to become the nominee of the Republican Party? All of the answers are clear, but they require a little digging and a few back stories to reach a logical conclusion.

In just five months, from August 2011 through January 2012, we saw five different candidates rise to become the Teavangelical flavor of the month. As we sift through this period chronologically, we find that the perfect candidate never existed for both the Tea Party and evangelicals, and that presented a host of challenges for voters and the candidates alike. But it wasn't just that. There were also so *many* Teavangelical-style candidates to choose from that they ended up splitting the Teavangelical vote, and that was good news for Mitt Romney. It's a fascinating storyline for a primary season that can only be described as one of the more memorable in American history.

July/August: Michele Bachmann

If you're going to be a strong Teavangelical candidate, you need a few things in your corner. First, you need to be a Bible-believing evangelical, and it helps if you wear it on your sleeve. You also need to have credibility with the Tea Party. Michele Bachmann had both. She even declared to me during her campaign that she was proud to call herself a Teavangelical: "I absolutely am, because I believe that we are taxed enough already. Government shouldn't spend more money than what it takes in. We should follow the Constitution, and I'm a believer in Jesus Christ, so I think that makes me a Teavangelical."[1] In June, when she announced her candidacy for president in Waterloo, Iowa, she declared that the GOP is made up of "social conservatives, and I'm one of them. It's the Tea Party movement and I'm one of them." Bachmann felt just as much at ease talking about her Christian faith as she did the deficit.

Michele Bachmann, with her ability to combine fiery rhetoric with folksy syntax, connected with a Teavangelical crowd looking for a passionate candidate to defeat President Obama. Her oratory and communication skills were a major plus, and as the only female in the race, her campaign looked different and felt fresh. All of this excitement and newness, combined with spending lots of money, culminated in a victory in the much-ballyhooed Ames Straw Poll in Iowa. But Bachmann's presidential run showed that having two key constituencies doesn't automatically translate into a GOP presidential nomination coronation. Some problems were lurking beneath the surface.

Texas-Sized Problem

One of the first difficulties came immediately after she won the Ames Straw Poll. Texas Governor Rick Perry got into the race on the same day as her victory. Like Bachmann, he too was a Teavangelical, but he had the executive experience that she didn't, and the media saw him as a real contender. Essentially, he cut into her audience and ruined her victory lap. "He took her bump away, and she didn't get to drive it in the weeks afterward and that really hurt," Bachmann's campaign manager Keith Nahigian told me. But it was more than that.[2]

The day after the straw poll, Perry decided to head to Bachmann's hometown of Waterloo, Iowa, to speak to the Blackhawk County Republican Party. While Perry spent plenty of time schmoozing with the crowd beforehand, a decision was made to keep Bachmann on her bus. She would make a grand entrance and not compete with Perry for attention. She didn't work the crowd beforehand and had to be introduced a second time before finally entering the room. "She kept us waiting, she was not here mixing," said one of the Iowans at the event.[3] The media coverage coming out of the event was negative, and the campaign knew it.

"That night was a disaster for us," said Bachmann senior advisor Bob Heckman. "Staying on the bus was a big mistake. That story of Waterloo was all over the state in twenty-four hours." Heckman said it was unfortunate because even though the incident made Bachmann look like a diva, she is anything but. Everyone on the campaign had nice things to say about her. "She's not a diva and pretty easy to deal with. She's easy to talk to, but we made her look like she was a diva candidate," Heckman concluded.

The Messaging

The Waterloo incident was problematic, but a larger issue was messaging. Some on the team felt that Bachmann needed to run primarily as a Teavangelical. They wanted to see her as the unconventional, renegade Tea Party champion going around in a pickup truck and being a woman of the people. She had the credentials to do so since she was chairman of the Tea Party Caucus on Capitol Hill and loved to talk about her faith. "I thought she had to run as the outside-out-of-the-box Tea Party evangelical candidate, someone who says the system is broken and we need to bust up the china to fix it," Bob Heckman told me. "She was the leader of the Tea Party movement, and she needed to run as the leader of the Tea Party movement." Peter Waldron, who ran the campaign's outreach to evangelicals and Tea Party groups, agreed. "One would have thought that she would be the natural evangelical social conservative candidate. However, whoever made the decisions at the top miscalculated. They tried to make her into a conventional Republican conservative."

But senior members of the Bachmann team were between a rock and a hard place. It may have seemed natural to run the candidate in the direction of her natural tendencies, but the campaign also had another hurdle. She was a woman running for president with no executive experience and a relatively short stint as a member of the House of Representatives. "We were trying to help her get over the commander-in-chief hurdle," her campaign manager Keith Nahigian told me. "With a woman candidate it was a bigger hurdle." So the campaign needed to show that Bachmann was a serious player. Early on she would go to events and highlight her command and knowledge of complex financial laws like Sarbanes-Oxley and Dodd-Frank. At one town hall event in Sioux City, Waldron and a campaign associate turned out evangelical voters, but the message centered mostly on Sarbanes-Oxley, Dodd-Frank, and how she voted against the debt ceiling. "We invited oranges there and the messaging was talking apples," Waldron said. Nahigian begged to disagree. "I think they're making too much noise because of our underperformance in their area."

In October, campaign operatives met in Des Moines to discuss the messaging. The Iowa team wanted more control of the candidate when she came to the state and requested that there be more of a harder evangelical turn and less focus on her Washington, DC, experience. It was an opportunity for some of the staff to air their grievances. There were some changes made, but still not enough to satisfy certain members of the team.

There's a lesson in all of this. A Teavangelical presidential candidate must be a ringmaster by simultaneously winning the Tea Party crowd, the evangelical crowd, *and* the mainstream media. It's a tricky balancing act and a major challenge.

Distractions and Complications

While messaging was the main concern from some within the campaign, other distractions and complications were present too. One night before a December debate in Sioux City, three members of the Bachmann team decided to quit. Guy Short, Kent Sorenson, and Bob Heckman were tired of how they were being treated. According to Heckman, they were told earlier in the week that they would be given press passes to go backstage and visit with Michele Bachmann before the debate and be in the media spin room afterward. But they were denied access. Sorenson and Short had had enough and left the debate before it started and headed to a local eatery. Heckman caught up with them afterward, and they all agreed to quit. Later, Bachmann's husband, Marcus, showed up with a senior advisor, and after all was said and done, they convinced all three of them not to resign. While this incident may seem petty, it revealed hints of dissension within the campaign.

While none of them quit that evening, Kent Sorenson did leave the campaign two weeks later in a most unusual way. He was Bachmann's campaign chairman in Iowa and had been introducing her at events during the week before the Iowa caucuses. But at an afternoon event in Indianola he stayed silent, saying that he had just come from the dentist office and didn't feel comfortable speaking. Then the shocker—a few hours later he showed up at a Ron Paul event and endorsed her rival! Nahigian, Bachmann's campaign manager, said they found out about it on Twitter. "It was gigantic. It came as a real shocker. I've never seen anybody do that."

The incident was significant because it happened at a critical time—just days before the Iowa caucus when undecided voters were making up their mind. While Bachmann's poll numbers were trending upward at the time, the Sorenson fiasco took the campaign off message because it became a big news-media story for a couple of days. "Our message wasn't *why* to vote for us. It was about talking about other stuff," Nahigian said.

Another complication was the fact that, as a woman, Bachmann had to overcome some built-in biases in Iowa. In the homeschool community you would have thought Bachmann would be a gigantic hit, considering she homeschooled her children. But when Nahigian asked their homeschool coordinator what the campaign could do to energize that community, he was told that a lot of the homeschoolers do not believe a woman should be president.

Looking Back and Looking Forward

While nobody in the Bachmann campaign has a desire to play Monday-morning quarterback, Nahigian had at least one idea for an improvement were Bachmann to run again. "We probably would have been better with an exploratory committee. We started so fast. You can't go a long way with that lack of mooring," he told me. The exploratory committee would have given her the opportunity to build more of a fundraising base beneath the campaign. Bachmann had a hard time competing with the top-tier players because she didn't have substantial cash to go up on Iowa television in the crucial month of December.

Still, Bachmann has the potential to do very well next time around. It's always hard to win your first time out, and Nahigian believes we haven't seen the last of her. "She broke a lot of ground," he said. "I think she will be a player in years to come."

August/September: Rick Perry

When Rick Perry announced his candidacy in mid-August, he was immediately considered a serious challenger. He had it all — a governor from the big state of Texas, a large personality, superior retail-politicking skills, and an evangelical faith that he loved to talk about. How could this guy go wrong? The media dubbed him a top-tier candidate, and his early fundraising numbers were impressive. Yet while Perry had relatively solid Tea Party and evangelical credentials, two policy positions he took while he was governor of Texas came back to haunt him.

Tea Party members disagreed with his stance on allowing children of illegal immigrants in Texas to receive tuition discounts to attend colleges in the state. He dug his grave even deeper when he said that if you oppose that policy, then "I don't think you have a heart."[4] On the evangelical side, Perry came under criticism when he signed an executive order (later overturned) that would have mandated teenage girls in Texas to be immunized against human papillomavirus, the most common sexually transmitted disease. Perry reasoned that it made sense because it was known to cause cervical cancer, but evangelicals (and many others too) felt it was none of the government's business to tell a family what they should do. To be fair, Perry's executive order had an opt-out for parents, and he even admitted he had made a mistake, but it was too little too late. His Republican presidential rivals blasted him in debates for the whole county to see.[5] These issues didn't help Perry with Teavangelicals, but it was his performances in the presidential debates that had conservatives everywhere exclaiming, *"Oy gevalt!"*

The Oops Moment

Rick Perry had just said the *oops* word live on national television. He simply couldn't remember the name of the third government agency he wanted to abolish. We've all had those times where we lose our train of thought, but when you're running for president those moments are crushing. Perry walked off stage, looked at his campaign team, and (as one of his senior advisors relayed to me) said, "Where is the room? Where do I have to go?" That room is called "the spin room," normally reserved for campaign operatives to spin the post-debate analysis to the media. Presidential candidates don't normally go to "the room." But Perry knew he had to after one of the clumsiest moments in presidential debate history.

After visiting with the media, Perry told campaign aides, "I know I'm going to have to do a lot of media tomorrow, so just let me know." Perry was resigned to the fact that he had to somehow dig himself out of a political grave. His campaign went into damage-control mode. They canceled a fundraiser scheduled for the next day, and they proceeded to book him on every national media outlet they could, including late-night talk shows like David Letterman. Instead of shrinking back and blaming others, Perry took full responsibility. "It takes a pretty special person to pull it off," this senior campaign advisor told me. In the same breath he also acknowledged the political reality of Perry's campaign. "We had some unfortunate choice of words and stumbles in key debates on national television, and it stung."

You would think Texas Governor Rick Perry would be the perfect Teavangelical candidate. And on paper he was. He spoke like a Tea Party member, had a record to match, and had even attended Tea Party rallies before they were fashionable. As a born-again evangelical, he wore his faith on his sleeve, and talking about the Holy Spirit came naturally. There was no act with Rick Perry. He was the real deal. So what happened?

As mentioned above, the debates happened. With so many of them it led to quite a few shaky performances. Perry had not debated much when running for governor. The campaign tried to fix the problem by changing the way he prepared for the debates. "In the beginning we did mock debates but then figured it was better to sit around the table and ask questions and give answers to make it feel more comfortable," one of Perry's senior advisors told me.

But it wasn't just the debates. The Perry campaign acknowledged that jumping in relatively late (the day of the Iowa caucuses) hurt him. Chalk it up to a lesson learned. "The constrained amount of time to sustain that place in the atmosphere, trying to be able to do the politics, fundraising, and to be able to do all the things you need to do was challenging," the Perry advisor said. All of this led to Perry being seen by voters (and yes, Teavangelicals too) as a less-than-stellar candidate.

The Almost Big Endorsement

Perry's fortunes were slipping away as he headed into December, but there was still hope that he could land a big endorsement from the Family Leader, the socially and fiscally conservative pro-family organization, and its leader, Bob Vander Plaats. "Our board was really close to endorsing Rick Perry," Vander Plaats told me. Indeed, just a few days before all of them agreed that Santorum was the majority choice, the board was leaning toward Perry. Vander Plaats asked them to take the weekend to think and pray about it.

When they reconvened on a Monday conference call over the lunch hour, the board members had a change of mind. "Each one basically felt like we needed to go with Rick Santorum," Vander Plaats told me. So why the switch from Perry? Vander Plaats has a strong idea. "There was some concern expressed at the board meeting that when Perry was on top it was at that time Perry didn't need us. He was not responding to our invitations to be part of our Thanksgiving Forum, our presidential lecture series, and our marriage-vow pledge. Everything was about jobs and the economy when he was on top. After he dropped in the polls, then he signed the marriage vow, then he participated in the Thanksgiving Forum, and then he began running commercials that he was a man of faith." Once again, Perry came close, but close only counts in horseshoes, right?

A Smelly Night in Iowa

In December 2011, Rick Perry cranked up the campaign bus and traveled around Iowa for a few weeks in a last-ditch effort to spark interest among voters. When our CBN News television crew made our way into Denison, Iowa, to interview him on his bus, I remember thinking that the smell of the town was something fierce. The people are nice, but the town smells like a mix of cow, skunk, and the New Jersey Turnpike. Then I thought, wait a minute. What stunk more? Denison or Rick Perry's bungled attempt to win the Republican nomination?

Perry was in good spirits when we spoke to him on his bus, but you could tell that he had become a second-tier candidate. The crowds were smaller, the entourage was tinier, and the applause was softer. If you were a fan of Perry's, the whole nomination process had to be deflating. Hopes were so high for Perry when he got into the race in August 2011. It was his nomination to lose, and unfortunately for him he did a pretty good job of doing just that. He was an experienced governor of one of the largest states in the country, hyperventilating over the Tenth Amendment and proclaiming Jesus every chance he got. If there was ever a model Teavangelical, Rick Perry was it. But there's a Teavangelical lesson in Perry's failed quest for the nomination. It's not just about having a message that resonates, because Perry had that. What he didn't have was the ability to communicate it effectively. What he needed was Michele Bachmann's public speaking skills (and by the way, Bachmann could have used Perry's depth of governmental experience). Combine the two and voila — a Teavangelical candidate who can definitely win the nomination. Put another way, a "Rick Bachmann" or "Michele Perry" would have fared much better. But alas, it wasn't mean to be. Perry's senior advisor summed it up best when he said, "The Tea Party and evangelicals wanted to be for Rick Perry, but we didn't give them a good reason to."

September/October: Herman Cain

Herman Cain was standing by the printer in his Atlanta office on September 27, 2011. Cain's secretary picked up what had just come off the copier and said to him, "That's for you." She handed him the best piece of news he'd seen since his presidential campaign began. A new national Zogby poll had just been released that showed him leading the presidential field.[6] Just a few days earlier Cain had surprised everyone by winning an important straw poll among Florida voters. Herman Cain told me that once he saw the printed copy of the Zogby poll he walked into his office, sat down, said a prayer, and then exclaimed, "Lord, this could really happen!" Herman Cain had just officially become the Teavangelical Flavor of the Month.

You can easily make the argument that Herman Cain electrified the conservative base of the Republican Party more than any other candidate. His public speaking skills captivated his audience every time out. His humorous and no-nonsense politically incorrect rhetoric was an insatiable match for a base looking for a candidate to shake things up. They loved it when he said, "Stupid people are running America!"[7] His Teavangelical stripes were on display constantly. He not only spoke the Tea Party creed but he lived it too by being one of the first to speak at Tea Party rallies. And from an evangelical perspective, this associate minister loved talking about Jesus and credited him with saving his life after being diagnosed with stage 4 cancer.[8] During his short-lived flavor-of-the-month status during the months of October and into November, polls showed that evangelicals supported him more than any other candidate.[9]

As a minister, Cain went hand in hand with the church. As a matter of fact, Cain recalled one time during the campaign season he was serving communion at Antioch Baptist, his home church in Atlanta, when the pastor stood up and said, "There isn't another church in America where a presidential candidate helps to serve communion!" Half of the congregation stood up and applauded—not bad considering most of the church probably votes Democratic.

Many parishioners told Cain how they'd started to reassess some of their opinions about the Republican Party because they'd been listening to what he had to say. "They got past the label of Republican. They got past the label of conservative," Cain told me. "Did I convert all of them? No. Did a large percentage start to reevaluate? Yes." Cain has a way of making people listen and take notice. Remember his 9–9–9 tax plan? Catchy, right? Enough said.

When people started to take more notice, however, the glare of the media got much brighter too. His missteps were magnified, including when he got a bit tongue-tied on an answer about abortion, which led some conservative evangelicals to question where he stood on the issue[10] (he's firmly pro-life). He also stumbled and struggled for words in an interview with the *Milwaukee Journal Sentinel*, which questioned him about President Obama's response in Libya[11] (the Cain team said he was exhausted). But clearly the biggest problem was the allegations of sexual harassment and misconduct leveled at Cain. One woman claimed to have had a thirteen-year affair with him and provided text and cell phone records as evidence. Mainstream media outlets around the country went into 24/7 coverage mode. Cain says the media overreacted to the unproven allegations. "What does a text message prove? Nothing. What does a phone call prove? Nothing. What does a signed autograph book prove? Nothing."

To this day, Cain is convinced that the timing of these stories was no coincidence since they broke on a Monday or a Tuesday three weeks in a row. "The only reason I am out of this race is because of gutter politics and a deliberate and coordinated attack on my character. Period," Cain explained to me. "Someone wanted me out of the race because I was being overly successful." He wouldn't elaborate on who he thinks is responsible, but he's determined to find out.

As time dragged on during this torturous time, Cain knew he had a decision to make. Despite his popularity with the base, the allegations were taking a toll on his poll numbers, which began to decrease rapidly. His evangelical support was drying up too, but most importantly, his wife was feeling frustrated. After the third story of sexual misconduct, he recalled her saying, "I hate to turn on the TV on Monday morning because every Monday a different one broke." His die-hard supporters also got discouraged after the third story broke. Finally, on December 1 in a hotel room in New Hampshire, Herman Cain had a frank discussion with a close friend and supporter. Together they pondered the future of the campaign. Finally, Cain made the decision to quit. As he told his close friend, "They're not going to stop the attacks, and I'm not going to put my wife through this."

On Friday morning, Cain called his wife, Gloria, on the phone before returning home and said: "I'm ending this because I'm determined to not put you through this crap." When he got home to his Atlanta home Friday evening, Gloria and Herman sat down and had a nice meal. She asked plenty of questions. "I answered all of her questions and then some," Cain said and then added quickly, "She didn't believe any of this stuff."

Herman Cain had the personality and communication skills to become the GOP nominee. There's no question about that. But there's a stubborn little rule in Teavangelical politics. If you're a Teavangelical candidate and you're running for president of the United States, any hint of improper sexual misconduct discovered during your presidential run (real or perceived) becomes too much to overcome.

There's another rule if you're a Teavangelical: the liberal media is not your friend. They can build you up, but they can also tear you down in an instant. They will milk a story for weeks if it's sexy enough and pulls in ratings. Just ask Herman Cain. He may have ended up as a flavor of the month, but conservatives around the country will always have a sweet spot for the man known as "The Hermanator."

November/December: Newt Gingrich

Unlike Michele Bachmann or Rick Perry, former Speaker of the House Newt Gingrich is not a classic Teavangelical. He doesn't wear his faith on his sleeve, and you would think that decades inside Washington or the fact that he was being paid handsomely by government mortgage giants Fannie Mae and Freddie Mac would make the anti-GOP establishment Tea Party skeptical. But sometimes it's not about the actual vessel itself. Gingrich defied all expectations to become a candidate who effectively articulated the Teavangelical message with gusto and in the process managed to bring large swaths of both groups into the fold. He would not have gotten as far as he did without the support of Teavangelicals in addition to his boffo performances in all those presidential debates.

Newt Gingrich was brash in his rhetoric, and that was a perfect match for the Tea Party, especially in the Tea Party–heavy states of Georgia and South Carolina. His rants against the GOP establishment and the media solidified his Tea Party standing. In addition, Gingrich's appeal to many in the Tea Party was his ability to tap into their mistrust of the GOP establishment. When Gingrich declared that his campaign was "a mortal threat to their grip on the establishment, because we intend to change Washington, not accommodate it,"[12] many in the Tea Party fell in love. Furthermore, the Tea Party was getting tired of the media and the GOP establishment telling them that Romney would be the eventual nominee. Sarah Palin, who voted for Gingrich in the Alaska Caucus, summed it up neatly when she proclaimed, "Newt is an imperfect vessel for Tea Party support, but in South Carolina the Tea Party chose to get behind him instead of the old guard's choice."[13] When all was said and done, two-thirds of South Carolinians who voted were Tea Party supporters, and nearly half of them voted for Gingrich.[14] In Georgia, his performance was even better, winning more than half of Tea Partiers. Around the country, hundreds of Tea Party groups endorsed his campaign,[15] and he won a Tea Party Patriots Florida Straw Poll.[16]

Gingrich had "street cred" right from the beginning of the Tea Party movement. He and his staff at American Solutions for Winning the Future were on some of the first Tea Party conference calls back in 2009. He spoke out forcefully at early rallies about President Obama's unpopular healthcare plan.[17] When I spoke to him in January of 2011 on his campaign bus, he explained to me that he was talking about the Tea Party before there was a Tea Party. "In 1994, when we were doing the Contract with America, I convinced a very good friend of mine, Sharon Cooper, to write a book called *Taxpayers Tea Party* ... and we actually went to Boston, and did a tea party. So when the Tea Party movement started I was totally simpatico because I had been actively trying to launch a tea party concept some fourteen, fifteen years earlier."

Newt and Evangelicals: A Match Made in Heaven?

The mainstream media is still scratching their heads trying to figure out how in the world Newt Gingrich could do so well with evangelical voters. While Rick Santorum also did well with evangelical voters, Gingrich won the evangelical vote in big primary states like South Carolina and Georgia. In South Carolina a whopping 40 percent of them voted for Gingrich.[18] In Georgia it was roughly 50 percent. There are many reasons Gingrich was attractive to evangelicals. Obviously having three marriages and committing adultery twice didn't make the list! But it seemed for most evangelicals, the positives outweighed that one giant negative.

One of the big plusses in Gingrich's corner was his defense of America as a Judeo-Christian nation. Every turn he got, he would point out how Christianity is under attack in this country. In Iowa, Gingrich put it very simply. "Our Judeo-Christian civilization is under attack from two fronts. On one front, you have a secular, atheist, elitism. And on the other front, you have radical Islamists. And both groups would like to eliminate our civilization if they could. For different reasons, but with equal passion."[19] But Gingrich, who has written books about America's Christian heritage and has spent years speaking to pastors about engaging more on pressing social and political issues from the pulpit, told me another reason he thinks evangelicals supported his campaign: "I understand that there's a war against religion, and that I am prepared ... to actually fight back for the first time in our lifetime, and take on the judiciary when it is overreaching, and when it's trying to drive God out of life."[20]

The other big reason evangelicals liked him is because Gingrich couldn't care less about political correctness. Newt is over the top with his bombastic style, and many evangelicals like it that someone has the courage to say something that other candidates won't. At the Thanksgiving presidential forum in Des Moines, in front of a couple thousand evangelicals, Gingrich received the loudest applause of the night when he said to the government of Iran, "You have a short time to solve this [nuclear weapon issue] on your own, and if you don't, we will solve it for you. And we frankly couldn't care less what the rest of the world thinks."

Newt's Evangelical Army

During the 2012 campaign, Gingrich was supported by some pretty heavy hitters in the evangelical world (Don Wildmon, George

Barna, Mat Staver, Chuck Norris), but the support from Beverly and Tim LaHaye is an interesting story.

Mrs. LaHaye is the founder of Concerned Women for America. Mr. LaHaye founded the influential socially conservative networking group Council for National Policy back in 1981 and has since gone on to even greater fame, cowriting the popular evangelical Left Behind book series. He's known Newt for roughly thirty-five years. Right after the midterm elections the LaHayes had breakfast with Gingrich in California. During that time LaHaye probed deeply to find out about Newt's relationship with God. "He assured me that he truly repented of his sin," LaHaye told me. He felt satisfied that Gingrich owned up to his past marital failures. After all, "We Christians are forgiving people," said LaHaye. As the campaign went on, Newt's intellect and proclivity for taking on the press sealed the deal for LaHaye. "When he had the guts to take on the press I knew he was a man who could stand up for the right things." After praying about it together, the LaHayes endorsed Gingrich about a week before the South Carolina primary.

Dr. Jim Garlow, senior pastor at Skyline Wesleyan Church in San Diego, is another evangelical leader who came on board for Newt. Garlow has known Gingrich since 2009 and has always been amazed at the man's intellect and, as he describes it, his "Churchillian fortitude." But things got personal at a private meeting in 2010 when Garlow pressed him on his not-so-glowing marital past. Garlow came away impressed by Gingrich, who he says was remarkably transparent, surprisingly tender, had a teachable spirit, and maybe most important of all didn't do any blame shifting. During the early part of this campaign Garlow brought Gingrich in to meet with pastors in the area. He remembers Gingrich saying to them, "I have so much regret for how much grief I have caused so many." After that a few pastors came up to Gingrich and began to pray for him and lay their hands on him. "I felt there was a break in the heavenliness at that point," Garlow recalled.

One of Newt Gingrich's closest evangelical advisors is David Lane, described by some as an evangelical "mastermind"[21] or a "stealth weapon for the right."[22] Lane goes around the country organizing pastor conferences where they hear from prominent evangelical politicians, pray with each other, and get valuable information about key political issues going on within their state. Later on, Lane works with many of those same pastors to make sure their churches are set up to register Christians to vote and hand out voter guides. All of this is done below the radar; Lane doesn't seek media headlines. He's interested in making a difference within churches, which he believes will translate to political success at the local, state, and national levels.

Lane worked in Texas for years and became good friends with Rick Perry. He stayed close with Perry through the beginning of his presidential campaign and continues to have deep ties with his Texas team, but eventually he moved on to bring spiritual guidance and counsel to Gingrich. He met Gingrich in 2006, and Gingrich has attended dozens of Lane's pastors events over the years. In one of them held in Iowa in December 2011, Lane asked Gingrich and his wife, Callista, to come up to the podium so the four hundred pastors in the room could pray for them.

For Lane, though, his communication with Gingrich comes often through email exchanges and it's spiritual, not political. After Gingrich lost the Florida primary, Lane wrote to him, "Pray about where you are, ask the Lord to confirm to you His direction. Once you hear Him say, 'This is my will for you,' double down and move forward." Newt responded: "Thank you. I actually feel liberated. You will love the next phase of this campaign." On that same day after the Florida loss, Lane sent another email to sixty or so evangelical pastors in which he wrote, "Raise up Newt to confront the false gods of multiculturalism, political correctness, and secularism. Give Newt an ounce of faith to allow you to fight Your battle through him, and the faith to stand and believe God for the impossible. Help Newt to stand and not lose his nerve like Saul." And in an email at the end of November, Lane had this encouragement and charge for Gingrich. "What you're doing is spiritual, the by-product is political … keep it in that order, representing His interest and you'll soar. Keep pushing. Read your Bible and pray." Newt's simple response: "I am very grateful for your courage, persistence, and prayerfulness.

Newt's Teavangelical Lesson

Newt Gingrich did surprisingly better than many people thought in the 2012 presidential race. A little more money in Iowa and Florida to combat Mitt Romney's ferocious assault on his character and record would definitely have helped him, not to mention a little less Rick Santorum, who managed to significantly cut into Gingrich's Teavangelical base. Ultimately, though, Gingrich provided a valuable Teavangelical lesson in presidential politics. You don't necessarily have to be a perfect vessel with a morally impeccable past to be successful. I know this may come as a shock to liberals, but evangelicals are able to forgive, and many forgave Newt for his past transgressions. Not all, mind you, and clearly having less baggage will probably help get you farther along, but Gingrich proved it's not a death knell either. Ultimately, the Tea Party and evangelicals are looking for someone to shake the establishment up, speak his mind forcefully and unapologetically, and articulate constitutionally conservative values and principles. Gingrich went farther than anyone thought because of his ability to do exactly that.

December/January: Rick Santorum

It was early fall in 2010 and Rick Santorum sat in his Northern Virginia home, seriously contemplating running for president. Around his kitchen table and living room sat his wife, Karen, former Senate Chief-of-Staff Mark Rogers, and trusted friends and media advisors John Brabender and Virginia Davis. The discussion centered not just on whether he would run for president but what his message would be. They all believed the problems facing America needed to be seen through a moral lens. Then they asked a simple yet pertinent question: If not Rick, then who exactly? No suitable answer followed, and thus a campaign was born. "The campaign was literally birthed in his kitchen and his living room," Mark Rogers told me.

Since that birth, Santorum has had plenty of growing pains. His campaign lay relatively dormant month after month as he polled in the low single digits despite spending more time in Iowa than any other candidate. When I asked him in October 2011 about all these other Teavangelical flavors of the month, he simply responded, "I'll wait until December, thank you very much." You know what? He was dead on. The other Teavangelical candidates' weaknesses were exposed and Santorum bided his time. He became the reliable alternative for Iowa voters looking for someone other than Romney. "Almost overnight the money starting coming in," senior advisor John Brabender told me. They knew Santorum's message was finally catching on, but a key endorsement helped grease the skids.

An Iowa Blessing

At 8:00 p.m. on a cold winter night in the middle of December, Rick Santorum settled into the Stoney Creek Inn in Urbandale, Iowa, for an important meeting. No campaign aides were present—just Rick and a very important guest. As he walked into a private room off the lobby, Bob Vander Plaats, president and CEO of the Family

Leader, met him. An endorsement by the board of this influential pro-family organization would be vital if Santorum were to have any chance of catching fire in Iowa.

Vander Plaats, who twice ran for governor and served as Mike Huckabee's state chairman in 2008, is deeply respected by Iowa evangelicals. He and Santorum had known each other for a long time and had bonded over the fact they are both fathers to special-needs children. Earlier in the campaign, after the Ames Straw Poll in August, Vander Plaats had called Santorum to encourage him to stay in the race despite measly poll numbers.

Now at this one-on-one meeting, Vander Plaats told Santorum that he had real worries about endorsing him because he questioned whether Santorum's campaign team had the money and organization to trumpet the endorsement effectively. "I was frankly concerned that he just didn't have resources. I did not want to have an empty endorsement," Vander Plaats told me. News reports at the time quote multiple sources saying Vander Plaats wanted up to one million dollars to publicize the endorsement to Iowa voters.[23] Vander Plaats flatly denied this. "There was never any ask for money by the Family Leader to candidate Santorum or the Santorum campaign, and there was never an ask for money by Bob Vander Plaats to candidate Santorum or the Santorum campaign. My endorsement was never for sale," Vander Plaats explains to me.

While the Family Leader board did unanimously support Santorum, they ultimately stayed away from endorsing any candidate. The board felt that it would be wise to stick to issues and not endorse candidates. However, Vander Plaats and Chuck Hurley, another top official at the Family Leader, decided to give their blessing to Santorum as private citizens. For Vander Plaats, Santorum's long record of fighting for the conservative pro-family agenda as a senator was crucial. "Santorum led on these issues and had success on these issues." While Michele Bachmann had championed many of the same causes as Santorum, Vander Plaats had a little apprehension. "We did have some concerns about Michele Bachmann's campaign apparatus."

The endorsement by Vander Plaats and Hurley came exactly two weeks before the Iowa caucuses. What transpired next was pretty remarkable. Rick Santorum sat at a paltry 7 percent in the polls,[24] but then Vander Plaats set up a Political Action Committee (PAC) to help advertise Santorum's candidacy to Christian conservatives. The PAC dropped $100,000 dollars in those two weeks. Meanwhile, Newt Gingrich, who had peaked in early December, was getting blasted apart on the airwaves by Mitt Romney and his poll numbers were taking a dive. At the same time, Michele Bachmann and Rick Perry weren't getting much attention from the media. That left Rick Santorum, a candidate who had built a solid network of organizers in the state and who kept plugging away as the first candidate to visit all ninety-nine Iowa counties. He became the guy at the prom that nobody had danced with yet but was available all evening. While it was initially thought that Romney had won Iowa by eight votes, ultimately Santorum prevailed by a mere thirty-four votes. The undecided broke hard for Santorum, and he became the Teavangelical flavor of the most important month of all: December in Iowa!

Teavangelicals Flock to Santorum

Santorum's success in Iowa showed that evangelicals within the Tea Party movement clearly powered his rise. It sure wasn't the Libertarians. Santorum has a disdain for their approach to government, saying that he will "fight very strongly against Libertarian influence in the Republican Party and the conservative movement."[25] Unlike Libertarians, Santorum does believe there is a proper role for the federal government to play, especially when it comes to shaping the moral fabric of American society. Obviously the Libertarians in the

Tea Party have problems with Santorum's approach, so why does he still poll so well?

It's a complicated answer with a logical conclusion. You can definitely make the argument that his Tea Party record is mixed. His fiscal record, while definitely conservative, is not Tea Party pure. He defends the millions of earmarks he asked for as a US senator; he voted for No Child Left Behind, Medicare Part D, and the Highway Bill; and he voted to increase the debt ceiling several times.[26] On the other side of the equation he was against the bank and auto bailouts; he never supported an individual healthcare mandate in his political career; was against cap-and-trade proposals; and voted to cut taxes again and again. There is a case to be made on both sides, but here's the tie breaker that put him over the top with the Tea Party: when Santorum talks about matters of faith and this nation's Judeo-Christian principles, it resonates with many in the Tea Party because as we've been documenting all along, evangelicals are a big part of what drives the movement in the first place. Remember, conservative Christians make up more than half the Tea Party, and nearly 60 percent of the movement identifies as social conservatives.[27] Bringing up social issues at Tea Party events and weaving his message of how faith and the constitution are completely intertwined has done Santorum a great deal of good. Libertarians might not like his overtly faith-based message, but Teavangelicals delight in it.

Let's be honest here. If Santorum did not have the support of Teavangelicals he would have never gotten as far as he did. When the field was narrowed down to the final four candidates, it was Santorum who nearly doubled up Romney in the polls from support among Tea Party Republicans and white evangelical Republican voters.[28] His ability to connect the prospects for a prosperous economy with a moral code rooted in a belief in the Almighty also played very well with blue-collar workers who value both hard work and pro-family values.[29] In essence, his lunch-bucket message to the heartland of the country was that this is a fight for the soul of America and that the United States is a "moral enterprise."[30] That message resonated in different parts of the country, as evidenced by his Super Tuesday wins in North Dakota, Oklahoma, and Tennessee. His theme also resonated deeply in the key rustbelt state of Ohio. His razor thin loss there on Super Tuesday wasn't because of his message. It was because he was outspent by the better-funded Mitt Romney. Santorum's message combined with Romney-type money would have surely led to an Ohio victory and probably would have given the 2012 race another dramatic turn. While Mitt Romney positioned himself as the best candidate to create jobs and fix the economy, Santorum senior advisor John Brabender told me, "This country is about more than just the latest labor statistics." Santorum's message caught on because it wasn't defined so much by results as it was by a sweeping, loftier vision for America. Romney left that message space available, and Santorum, despite not having deep coffers did all he could do to make the GOP primary extremely competitive.

Authenticity and Faith

There was another factor in Rick Santorum's corner when going up against Mitt Romney: authenticity. While Romney lacked that trait among the conservative base, Santorum had it oozing out of his pores. Unlike most presidential campaigns that employ a pollster, Santorum never had one. "He doesn't want someone telling him what to believe," Brabender said. Part of Santorum's charm with voters was this knack for just being himself and not straying from his core.

Brabender said the campaign received phone calls from well-intentioned supporters who thought he should tone it down on social issues and the faith-based talk, but Brabender said, "He was not going to be afraid of mentioning God in public." As a matter of fact, on the day of the presidential debate in Mesa, Arizona, Rick went to Catholic Mass early in the morning, and because it was Ash Wednesday, he did not shy away from putting ashes on his forehead even though he had a couple of campaign events later that day. Some candidates may have struggled with this dilemma of what to do since the visual of ashes on a forehead could turn off some potential voters. Santorum didn't care. He was going to practice his beliefs regardless of the outcome.

Of course, Santorum's authenticity has a flip side. Because he doesn't back down from talking about social issues or his faith, the media has a ready-made storyline. For example, the media trotted out the story of how back in 2008 Santorum told an audience at the Catholic Ave Maria University in Florida that "Satan has his sights on the United States of America."[31] Santorum has a long history of making remarks that don't comport with a liberal worldview, so while that story didn't bother Teavangelicals (they already know all about the spiritual fight between good and evil), it did end up being cable news fodder for days. Compounding the issue (politically at least) is that Santorum doesn't back down from his remarks. Because of his authenticity he always tries to answer questions forthright and honestly. He engages, defends, and explains rather than quickly dismissing and moving on to what he wants to talk about. A Santorum advisor admires the authenticity but knows the media will run with a narrative that Santorum is loony. "It's a palpable concern for us."

Those are the risks you take when you're willing to just be who you are. Voters warmed to Santorum for exactly that reason. They liked his inner moral compass and his passion for this country. Glenn Beck probably summed it up best when he said, "If there is one guy out there that is the next George Washington, the only guy that I could think of is Rick Santorum."[32] We sure don't know if Santorum will be another George Washington, but what we do know is that Santorum did his own version of crossing the Delaware River in the dead of winter. His campaign was a long, cold slog to achieve victory, but it was well worth it every step of the way.

The Non-Teavangelical Flavors of the Month

Mitt Romney

We know a few things about Mitt Romney. He has great hair, loads of campaign cash, a great organizational structure, and a family that looks like the modern-day version of *Leave It to Beaver*. But there's one thing he doesn't have but desperately needs: the trust of conservative voters. Because he doesn't have it, the Romney campaign has had a much more difficult time in their attempt to secure the GOP nomination than they expected. The Tea Party's list of concerns about Romney is long, including how he pushed through an individual healthcare mandate when he was governor of Massachusetts and how he defended the big bank bailouts in 2008–2009. Evangelicals were skeptical because Romney flip-flopped on abortion (he's now pro-life) and seemed more open to gay rights issues when he was governor of Massachusetts.

Technically, Romney's Mormon faith would clearly disqualify him from being a Teavangelical, but concerns about him from both the Tea Party and evangelicals led to minimal outward effort toward these factions from the campaign. He did do a couple evangelical-based events with the Faith and Freedom Coalition and the Family Research Council and showed up for a couple Tea Party events, but by and large Romney positioned himself as the businessman candidate who could best fix the economy, create jobs, and beat President Obama. There were opportunities for him to do a myriad of pro-family and pro-life forums with the other presidential candidates, but he chose not to. Some evangelical leaders told me how they would invite Romney to their event but they never even received a response.

"Romney has an evangelical problem and it's not what some may believe," Reverend Sammy Rodriguez explained to me. "It's not that evangelicals have a problem with Romney. It may very well be that Romney has a problem with evangelicals. His outreach to the evangelical community is almost nonexistent." Romney, however, unlike all of the other candidates except Ron Paul, had run for president once already and courted evangelical groups back in 2008 when he focused more on social issues. In 2012 he positioned himself differently and adjusted his campaign schedule accordingly to run more of a national, broader campaign.

Because he made virtually no attempt to court the Tea Party and evangelicals, the results became predictable. After all the early primary states had voted in January, Romney was getting beat solidly by Rick Santorum in these two key Republican Party demographics. The Pew Research Center concluded, "Romney has struggled at times in winning over the conservative elements of the Republican electorate — Tea Party supporters, conservatives, and white evangelical Republicans."[33] Throughout the early primaries, the Romney campaign calculated that their strongest hand could be played to Independent voters and economic-minded conservatives and figured that the Tea Party and evangelicals would eventually be receptive to Romney's "Mr. Fix It" message. But in the process they inadvertently left a void to be filled by a candidate who could weave together a sweeping moral vision for America that combined both social issues and economic matters. Enter Rick Santorum in the role of the anti-Romney.

While Romney might not be the top pick of evangelicals or the Tea Party, that doesn't mean he didn't try to court some important figures. Behind the scenes there is actually plenty of good will. Some of his attempts go as far back as 2006 when he was still governor of Massachusetts. In a private meeting at his home in the Boston suburbs, Ann and Mitt Romney visited with more than a dozen evangelical leaders including Franklin Graham, the late Jerry Falwell, Richard Land, Jay Sekulow, Frank Wright, and Gary Bauer. They sat in a circle and ate sandwiches while discussing topics like the fight against radical Islam, stem cell research, and Romney's Mormon faith. It was by all accounts a pleasant meeting. About a month later, all the evangelical attendees received a giant box. Inside was a chair with a brass plate on the back of it. Inscribed on the plate was Romney's signature with the words, "There will always be a seat for you at our table."

In 2009, about a year after Romney's failed presidential bid, he met with a group of influential pastors in the Atlanta area. Romney's evangelical campaign advisor Mark DeMoss, who works as an important liaison between evangelical leaders and the Romney campaign, arranged the meeting. Attendees included Andy Stanley (North Point Community Church), Louie Giglio (Passion City Church), Randy Pope (Perimeter Presbyterian), and Richard Lee (First Redeemer Church).

During the 2012 presidential campaign, Romney met privately with top executives from Focus on the Family, one of the leading pro-family evangelical organizations in the country. The one-hour meeting took place at their headquarters in Colorado Springs in September 2011. Present at the meeting were Jim Daly, the CEO and president; Tom Minnery, the head of the government and public policy division; Tim Goeglein, a vice president; and Mark DeMoss, Romney's evangelical advisor. Romney was asked about topics like a federal marriage amendment and a human life amendment, but the conversation also shifted to the areas of immigration and the Arab Spring. Afterward, Goeglein told DeMoss that the meeting went very well.

DeMoss himself went to present Romney's case to more than a hundred evangelical leaders in Texas in January 2012. The meeting was called to see if these evangelical figures could coalesce around one presidential candidate. DeMoss knew Romney wasn't going to be their guy (Santorum won the majority of support), but in his private remarks during the meeting he took all of them to task for not speaking up when Romney's faith was criticized by a couple speakers at the Values Voters Summit a few months earlier. "As much as I assume all of us take fundamental exception to Mormon doctrine or theology, I would hope we could agree that anti-Mormon bigotry or mean-spirited behavior is not only inappropriate in the context of choosing a president, it is a poor testimony as followers of Christ in *any* context. I was embarrassed when such rhetoric was on full display, ironically at the *Values* Voter Summit last fall; and to my knowledge, the only evangelical to publicly reject it was Chuck Colson."

Yet no matter how much Romney reached out to evangelical leaders, he always had an uphill climb with evangelical voters. You would think that being pro-life, pro-traditional marriage, pro-strict constructionist judges, and a wholesome family man would be the ideal candidate for evangelicals, but there seemed to always be that lack of trust.

Some say that evangelicals just won't vote for a Mormon, but only 15 percent of white evangelical Protestants feel that way. A whopping 91 percent of them would vote for him in a general election.[34] This statistic reveals something very important. As much as there was a steady chorus of "anybody but Romney," there was an even louder chorus that screamed, "Anybody but Obama." That worked in Romney's favor, and so in some cases he was able to win Tea Party and evangelical votes just on the basis of electability alone. This, combined with concern over jobs and the economy in the 2012 race, made Romney attractive even to some Teavangelicals.

Early in the 2012 campaign, as Teavangelical candidates rose and fell, Romney played the role of the consistent frontrunner to a T. He didn't need to use any organizational muscle on candidates Herman Cain and Michele Bachmann. They went away on their own. When Rick Perry challenged him, Romney got tough with him in the debates, extinguishing that threat. When Newt Gingrich came along, Romney's campaign took him very seriously and unloaded millions of dollars in negative campaign ads against him, derailing Gingrich.

But when Rick Santorum entered the equation a problem arose. Romney's campaign didn't take him seriously enough after Iowa. They were busy worrying about Gingrich. They hardly fought back against Santorum with campaign ads or opposition research. Only when the former Pennsylvania senator started racking up a few wins in some Midwestern states did they fully engage. But by then Santorum's national poll numbers had him neck and neck with Romney. In essence, they underestimated Santorum. Yet despite all of that, money matters, and Romney lowered the boom in the crucial state of Ohio. He spent millions of dollars more than Santorum, and his negative campaign ads against Santorum gave Romney a narrow win and averted true disaster. His well-oiled organizational machine also proved to be a huge difference on Super Tuesday because, while Santorum's campaign wasn't able to get on the ballot in the state of Virginia, Romney coasted to victory. Still, as the former governor of Massachusetts, Romney couldn't seal the deal on Super Tuesday because he couldn't win in Deep South states like Tennessee. It revealed his vulnerability with the GOP base (Teavangelicals). Compounding the issue for him was that despite trying to cast himself as a Washington outsider, voters were able to see that he was really playing the role of the presumptive nominee chosen by the GOP establishment. That role was always a hard fit for a feisty, aggressive conservative Teavangelical electorate who had a mistrust of GOP kingmakers in the first place. All of this caused the campaign a few headaches along the way, to say the least, but organizational muscle and a campaign drawer full of cash can solve a lot of problems.

Ron Paul

Dr. Ron Paul never became a Teavangelical of the month. Unlike the other flavorful candidates who had never run for president before, the seventy-seven-year old Texas congressman had already journeyed into presidential politics. He has a loyal following that never wavers and that garners him solid poll numbers. Yet while that consistent support may sound good on the surface it has never translated into frontrunner status. Not being able to win caucus states like North Dakota and Alaska on Super Tuesday continued to frame the narrative that he's a candidate with important things to say but no victories to show for it. Nevertheless, Ron Paul's journey isn't necessarily about winning the White House. You get the sense that he's more interested in a commanding message than being commander-in-chief.

Libertarians and scores of young voters who see politicians as corrupt view Dr. Paul as incorruptible, and they power much of his message. While Libertarians sing his praises, however, so do a surprising number of conservative evangelical Christians. Doug Wead, a senior advisor for the campaign who heads up much of the evangelical outreach, remembers walking into Dr. Paul's main headquarters in Virginia and being taken aback. "When I came in I saw the place overflowing with born-again Christians." So what is the attraction, exactly?

Let's first look at the data. Ron Paul won a presidential straw poll at the conservative evangelical Values Voter Summit in the fall of 2011. In the Iowa Caucuses, he won 18 percent of the evangelical vote, second only to Rick Santorum.[35] Sydney Hay is one of the reasons why. Hay used to be the campaign manager for Duncan Hunter during his 2008 presidential run. She was also involved in Pat Robertson's 1988 quest for the presidency and Alan Keyes's presidential campaigns in 1996 and 2000. As one of Paul's top evangelical organizers, she traveled around Iowa frequently and hand-delivered a letter from Dr. Paul to nearly a hundred pastors (she emailed out hundreds more).

The letter contained these striking words from the Libertarian-leaning presidential candidate: "I have accepted Jesus Christ as my personal Savior and strive each day to follow His teachings in all I do, both personally and politically." Later in the letter, Paul struck a perfect Teavangelical note when describing the role of government in people's lives. "In 1 Samuel Chapter 8, Samuel warned the Israelites against placing a King between themselves and God," Paul wrote. "Have we, as a people, allowed our government to replace God, to become as a King?" His idea that the federal government needs to stay out of people's lives was the sort of message that resonated with conservative evangelicals.

Once Sydney Hay delivered those letters, many of those same Iowa pastors sent letters to other pastors encouraging them to take a serious look at Dr. Paul. Highlighted in the pastor-to-pastor letter were the candidate's strong pro-life views. "Surely the blood of those children murdered in abortion mills within moments of being delivered full-term cries out to our Holy God," the letter states. "Dr. Ron Paul has delivered 4,000 babies. He has written an entire book on the subject of abortion. He has authored bills declaring that human life begins at conception. He holds life to be sacred. It is non-negotiable."

Despite the evangelical outreach in Iowa and other states, Paul's message to evangelicals had limited bandwidth. His message has more appeal to Libertarian-leaning Christians than typical conservative evangelicals because of Paul's stance on foreign affairs. Ron Paul wants to cut off all aid to Israel, and that doesn't sit well with most evangelicals, who are Israel's strongest supporters. Even though Dr. Paul would eliminate all aid to her enemies too, it was still a tough sell. "Israel was something I had to confront in every conversation I had," Hay said when recalling her meetings with evangelical pastors. In addition, Ron Paul's noninterventionist foreign-policy positions (like not being pro-active against a dangerous and nuclear Iran) cost him evangelical votes too, not to mention some support within the broader Tea Party movement. Another challenge for Paul was the fact that unlike Michele Bachmann and Rick Perry, who love to talk about Jesus in public, candidate Paul is much more reserved. He was raised in a Lutheran household (he's now Baptist) and considered becoming a pastor back in his youth. Two of his brothers did become ministers, but he's more old school, believing you keep your faith private. The truth is that if he were more open about his faith he'd probably be able to attract more evangelicals. Doug Wead remembered being with him in a hotel room in Des Moines at a pastor's conference pleading with him to talk to them about his deep faith. "It drives me up the wall, but he won't call any attention to it," Wead told me.

Privately it's different for Ron Paul. He knows the Bible backward and forward and once told Wead backstage at a debate in Spartanburg, South Carolina that his whole philosophy (civil liberties, foreign policy, the economy) boiled down to one thing. "It's all biblical. The Ayn Rand libertarians can't figure me out," Wead remembered Paul telling him. Sydney Hay recalled when Dr. Paul called her in the fall of 2010 asking her if she'd help with the campaign if he decided to run for president. She said he told her that, "His faith was going to drive his decision. It would be driven by if he and Carol [Paul's wife] thought it was what God wanted them to do."

Ron Paul will go down in American history as a man whose

ideas challenged the status quo and changed the conversation in this country. He's considered the godfather of the Tea Party, and his trendsetting economic message of fiscal responsibility ushered in Teavangelical support.

But don't miss these crucial points: His foreign policy positions were a major problem for the Teavangelical audience despite a certain anti-war mindset among some Libertarians and evangelicals. A major part of the Tea Party had a problem with his noninterventionist views, as documented in a Pew Research poll that showed that 60 percent of Tea Party members are for peace through military strength,[36] not exactly what Ron Paul is preaching. Equally concerning was the fact that Tea Party straw polls would consistently show that, while they liked Ron Paul's overall message, they didn't think he could actually win the nomination.[37] Both of these factors contributed to his limited appeal.

But thanks to his strong, unyielding, common-sense economic message, his appeal grew more in 2012 than it did in 2008, and that leaves Ron Paul and his supporters hoping that he'll be in a position to have a major say in the Republican Party platform at the GOP convention. Either way, Ron Paul set out to get people's attention and change the conversation in this country, and in many ways he has done exactly that.

So what does it all mean? In the end, why did some Teavangelical candidates like Rick Santorum go farther than others? It's relatively simple. To be a successful Teavangelical candidate you need a message that resonates and the ability to communicate it, a limited amount of flubs and past political baggage, a strong command of the issues and a wealth of experience. You have to have *all* of these to put yourself in a position for success. Santorum had all of these, and the other candidates had at least one missing ingredient. Of course, it also helps if you actually have a head start on money, organization, and campaign infrastructure right from the beginning of the race rather than trying to build as you go. Rick Santorum found that out the hard way when he was essentially battling Romney one-on-one in the key states of Michigan and Ohio. Mitt Romney proved that sometimes it's not just about the message. If you want to be serious and viable throughout, it helps to have a campaign ATM machine dispensing lots of cash.

Chapter 6

TEAVANGELICAL
POLITICAL
POWERHOUSES

IT WAS SOMEWHAT OF A SURREAL EXPERIENCE. AS OUR CBN NEWS team was getting ready to set up for our exclusive interview with Sarah Palin in Santa Barbara, California, I walked into what I expected to be an empty room. I was wrong. There was a young woman sitting on a chair looking down at her Blackberry. As I looked more closely, I noticed this wasn't just any young woman. This was Bristol Palin, Sarah's daughter and someone I'd read about in *People* magazine. (Yes, I admit it, I read it.) I wasn't quite sure what to say so I just blurted out, "Hey, Bristol, what's up?" Bristol smiled and gave a polite hello. We chatted about her upcoming flight back to Alaska and her role in *Dancing with the Stars*. Finally, after thirty minutes or so, Sarah Palin walked through the door. Bristol's "Mama Grizzly" had arrived, and so had an American Teavangelical powerhouse.

Sarah Palin

Say what you want about Sarah Palin (and many of her critics sure have taken the opportunity to say a few choice words), but the former governor of Alaska is one of the most influential politicians alive today … and she oozes Teavangelical traits. She is a born-again believer who has no problem walking the walk and talking the talk when it comes to her devotion to Jesus. During the interview in Santa Barbara she told me that she's "reminded so often of 2 Timothy 1:7, knowing that God does not give us a spirit of timidity or of fear, but he gives us a spirit of power and love and a sound mind, a sound mind so that we can keep things in perspective. We can stay grounded. We can know what is real. We can know truth. So just calling on that verse, reminding myself over and over again what God promises, that gets me through the tough times."

She sure had her rough periods as a vice-presidential candidate in 2008. Despite a love affair with voters on the campaign trail, the media did their best to make her a human punching bag. In 2012, the media wasn't going to get another chance at her because Palin decided not to run for president of the United States. To the casual observer, that move may be seen as a reduction in her political power, but actually it makes her more valuable to the Teavangelical movement. While it goes without saying that winning the White House would be a crucial step to advancing a Teavangelical agenda, it is equally important to have a United States Senate and a US House of Representatives full of constitutional conservatives. This is where Palin comes in, as she is intent upon changing the political makeup of the Republican Party.

There's a reason Sarah Palin is known as "Sarah Barracuda," because just like a barracuda, she has no fear. She displayed that fearless nature during the 2010 midterm elections, especially during the GOP primaries when she decided to wade into contests and go with the upstart constitutional conservative candidate rather than the establishment pick. Anytime she showed up at a rally to endorse a candidate, national and local media would follow. This translated into headlines and increased focus and attention on that particular race.

In South Carolina, she showed up during a key GOP primary to endorse Republican gubernatorial candidate Nikki Haley, who was in a dogfight for the Republican nomination. In Delaware, her support for Christine O'Donnell a week before the GOP primary helped lead to an upset over established moderate Republican Mike Castle. In Kentucky, she backed Tea Party upstart Rand Paul in his Senate race against mainstream Republican candidate Trey Grayson. In New Hampshire, she got involved too, backing eventual GOP primary winner Kelly Ayotte, who went on to become a United States Senator. And in Nevada, Palin threw her support behind Sharron Angle instead of Sue Lowden, the GOP-handpicked candidate.

In all of these cases, Palin displayed her most important attribute: the ability to shape the Republican Party with candidates who fit a constitutional conservative mold, not a standard Republican pattern. Granted not all of her GOP primary candidates won (Angle and O'Donnell), but this had more to do with flawed candidates than with Palin. And while her general election record wasn't perfect, the majority of candidates she backed in gubernatorial, House, and Senate races did win.[1] As Senator Jim DeMint says, "What happened in 2010 had a lot to do with Sarah Palin. If she continues to do that, I think we're going to have an even bigger victory in 2012."[2]

Palin has given herself the mission of finding the best and brightest candidates out there and then putting her neck on the line for them. And her Teavangelical pedigree really shines through when it comes to deciding which candidates to back. Typically, she chooses those who espouse Tea Party values and are pro-life. Hence, she is choosing many Teavangelical candidates.

In 2010, every female candidate Palin chose was pro-life, and nearly all of them were backed by the Susan B. Anthony List (SBA List), a pro-life organization that Palin has embraced. As a matter of fact, it was at an SBA List event where Palin coined the famous term "Mama Grizzlies," a reference to conservative, pro-life women candidates.[3] Translation: a female Teavangelical. By the way, the SBA List had a banner year in 2010. They dropped eleven million dollars on ninety races. They won two-thirds of those, including a 70% increase in pro-life women in the US House of Representatives.[4] Not too shabby, and with Sarah Palin's voice a crucial part of the effort, there's no telling what's in store for the future.

What we do know about Sarah Palin is that she has a huge base of support. Her television platform on Fox News gives her the ability to reach millions in a single telecast. Her Facebook and Twitter accounts are filled with millions of dedicated followers. Her political action committee, Sarah PAC, is an offensive juggernaut able to contribute some cold, hard cash to needy Teavangelical candidates. Most of all, she is the rare individual who is able to juggle a giant megaphone in one hand and the Bible and the Constitution in the other. The power she wields is uniquely Teavangelical, something she communicated to me that evening in Santa Barbara. "I do believe, David, that there are more commonsense conservative Americans on our side on the issues that we stand for than there are those who oppose the idea of individualism and God-given liberty," Palin says. "They're engaged, they're very much in opposition to big government, this liberal overreach, overtaxation, overregulation of this administration [and] what they are doing to us. Because there are so many of us I feel that there is just this army of Davids willing to take on the Goliath of big government." Sarah Palin is ready to lead that "army of Davids" onto the political battlefield in 2012 and beyond.

Palin loves movies where the underdog prevails. One of her favorite pictures is *Rudy*, the true story of a young man overcoming the odds and achieving his dream to play football at Notre Dame. Palin is a lot like Rudy in that she enjoys a tough challenge. As she puts it, "They don't give up, they keep plugging away, they work. They work harder than the other guy, so they get farther than the other guy."

Sarah Palin's work is just beginning, and she'll be asking for God's help every step of the way. "He says we can ask for favor. I ask for favor in situations so that I can continue down the path. And it's the most important thing in my life, my faith, so I prioritize to make sure that I'm spending the time that I need to stay all geared up." Game on.

Mike Pence

If you don't follow politics closely, you probably haven't heard of Mike Pence, but let me be clear about this: the US congressman could very well be the next governor of Indiana and has a pretty decent shot of being the first Teavangelical president of the United States.

As the teenagers might say, "He's got it goin' on." Pence is an evangelical Christian who is beloved by both the conservative pro-family movement and fiscally conservative organizations. He is well respected by national-security conservatives, and the conservative intellectual community (Bill Kristol, Charles Krauthammer, the *Wall Street Journal*, and *National Review*) admire his body of work. The media respects him too, with the *Washington Post* labeling him "a new face on conservatism" who has "delivered conservative opinions with the even tones and polite demeanor of his Midwest upbringing."[5] Anytime the liberal media describes an evangelical Christian in that way you know you have achieved a measure of respect. In addition, Pence connects with the average voter. As a former radio broadcaster he likes to call himself "Rush Limbaugh on decaf."[6] In theory at least, Mike Pence appears to have the full package.

Pence considered running for president in 2012 but decided against it, saying his heart was in Indiana.[7] The six-term congressman is making a run to become governor of Indiana instead. The move may be a good one for Pence since being governor is sometimes a logical and necessary step to becoming president. In his early fifties, the congressman probably has a window of opportunity until 2024 to run for the presidency. If he does take the plunge, you can be sure he's going to emphasize his Midwestern roots. When I asked him about running for the highest office in the land, he told me, "One of the great things about America is that anybody can be anybody, even a small-town kid from southern Indiana who grew up with a cornfield in his backyard can dream."[8] If Pence ever becomes president, it may well be a Teavangelical dream come true.

Pence's résumé is chock-full of Teavangelical prerequisites. For two years during his time in Congress he was head of the Republican Study Committee, a group of more than 170 of the most conservative House members. Their objective was to push the Republican Party in the direction of adopting both social and fiscal conservative policies. He's also been an important member of the Values Action Team on Capitol Hill. VAT, as it is known, is a smaller group of lawmakers who meet regularly with many conservative Christian public-policy groups (Family Research Council, Focus on the Family, Concerned Women for America) to coordinate legislative activity on Capitol Hill with grassroots support among the groups. Lawmakers press the groups to either circulate letters of support for an issue or organize phone-call blasts to Capitol Hill operators. This cluster of conservative Christians is on the frontlines of the culture war in America, and Mike Pence is right there with them. In the process he has built major "street cred" with the pro-family movement.

As for Pence's Tea Party credentials, the best place to start is in the numbers. Club for Growth, one of the most influential conservative economic public-policy groups in the country, gave Mike

Pence a 100% rating on their legislative scorecard in 2010. His life-time rating is 99%.

When it comes to Tea Party rallies, he's a regular fixture. And one of the major Tea Party leaders in the country has really fallen for Pence. Dick Armey, chairman of FreedomWorks, would have loved to see Pence run for president, convinced that he could have brought social and fiscal constitutional conservatives together. He says, "I always thought I'd only get one Ronald Reagan in my life-time.... Maybe Mike Pence could be that second one."[9]

While Tea Party leaders love Pence, so do social conservative voters who follow politics. In a September 2010 presidential straw poll conducted by the Family Research Council, Pence beat the field, which included plenty of big-name Teavangelicals like Sarah Palin and Mike Huckabee. The results led FRC President Tony Perkins to declare, "Those who are truly conservative, fiscally and socially, are enthusiastically supported by voters."[10]

It would make sense that Pence is popular with both evangelicals and the Tea Party. He's able to weave a moral component into the fiscally conservative message of the Tea Party. At rally after rally he doesn't shy away from emphasizing biblically sound principles, yet he doesn't come across as a "Bible thumper" either. That's just not his style. He's pretty laid-back, so lines that may sound like "Religious Right" talk don't go down as such coming from his lips. At a gathering of conservatives in June 2010, Pence said, "What's animating this authentic American movement [the Tea Party] is that our present crisis is not just economic and fiscal. It's moral in nature.... Our leaders need to recognize that public policy alone will not cure what ails this country. It's going to take public virtue and a return to the institutions that nourish the character of the nation and reaffirm our commitment to the sanctity of life, the sanctity of traditional marriage, and the importance of religion in everyday life."[11] Spoken like a true Teavangelical who could one day speak those same words during a presidential inauguration speech on the west steps of the US Capitol.

Mike Huckabee

If you could only hire one person to sell the Teavangelical message, you would be hard-pressed to pick anybody other than Mike Huckabee. The former governor of Arkansas and Fox News analyst has a knack for explaining complicated issues in a simple, often humorous way. Huckabee is fond of saying, "I'm a conservative; I'm just not mad about it,"[12] and that pretty much sums him up. His likability factor is off the charts, and his Southern demeanor gives him a disarming quality. Even if he were to deliver bad news, you can see Huckabee doing it in such a way that it doesn't seem so bad after all. He reminds me of those folks in the South who say, "Oh, you look a little heavy in that dress, bless your heart!" He's very "Reaganesque" in his demeanor, and you're either born with that talent or not. His likability is what makes Mike Huckabee a Teavangelical powerhouse.

If Huckabee had run for president in 2012 as he did in 2008, he would have been the clear frontrunner. National polls showed him to be popular with high name recognition. Alas, he did not run and instead positioned himself as a TV Teavangelical who shows up on the mighty Fox News airwaves pushing Tea Party principles and socially conservative policies to an audience of millions.

Huckabee is also involved in the effort to elect more conservative politicians across the country. His political action committee, Huck PAC, is dedicated to the issues of life, traditional marriage, and fiscal sanity and will be very active in the 2012 election.[13] In the 2010 election cycle his PAC spent around $1.8 million dollars.[14] It may not be as much as Sarah Palin's PAC, which raised nearly triple that number,[15] but reading the numbers misses the overall point.

Sarah Palin may outdraw Mike Huckabee when it comes to PAC money, big rallies, and full-fledged media exposure, but there's simply nobody better at communicating the message effectively than Mike Huckabee.

Huckabee is a great example of how you need the right messenger for the right message. Politicians can be saying all the right things, but if you don't connect with people and touch their hearts, it probably won't amount to a hill of beans. It's also important to have credibility with the mainstream media, because, like it or not, they still shape the narrative in American politics and can have a major effect on how Americans view politicians. (Just ask Sarah Palin.) Huckabee has this credibility, having gone through an extensive media vetting process in 2008 and coming out on the other end as a media darling (unlike Sarah Palin). This is why Huckabee has the capacity to be very potent in the future.

The reason Huckabee resonates with ordinary Tea Party Americans is because at his core he's really one of them. He's a God-fearing, patriotic American who espouses social and fiscal conservative values. They have something else in common too. Just like the Tea Party folks, Huckabee also is a regular guy who talks like a regular guy, not a politician. He summed it up best when he told me once, "I think the greatest thing that's happening in regards to the Tea Party is that it's reminding the rest of America that ordinary people can make a dramatic difference in this country."[16] Huckabee is just an ordinary guy who through God's grace has been able to do extraordinary things.

Marco Rubio

Out of all the Teavangelical powerhouses mentioned in this chapter, Senator Marco Rubio of Florida clearly has the most upward momentum. At just forty years old, this rising GOP star has already been mentioned as a possible vice-presidential choice and a future president of the United States. "I certainly can't allow it to convince me that I'm better than I really am because the political process is full of people that were once rising stars and now aren't," Rubio told me during a conversation in his Capitol Hill office in the fall of 2011. While being humble is a noble trait, this son of Cuban immigrants has a world of potential. The question is, how will he use it?

Rubio's story could be a chapter from a book on the American dream. Born in the early 1970s to parents who left Cuba before Fidel Castro's regime, Marco grew up in both the Miami and Las Vegas areas. His father was a bartender and his mother was a hotel housekeeper and a stock clerk at Kmart — truly humble beginnings. Growing up in a working-class, first-generation immigrant family taught Rubio the valuable lessons of hard work, which he eventually parlayed into a law degree from the University of Miami. Just four short years later, he became a member of the Florida House of Representatives. In 2006, he became speaker of that body. Not too shabby considering he wasn't even thirty years old yet.

In 2009, he decided to run for the United States Senate against political heavyweight and current governor Charlie Crist. It was a monumental challenge considering Rubio was far down in the polls, had little name recognition, and even less money. What Rubio did not lack was perspiration and the ability to communicate a message. Just as Rubio was getting started, so was the Tea Party. His message of fiscal conservatism versus Governor Crist's more moderate views (including supporting President Obama's stimulus bill) gave Rubio an opening and the Tea Party a hero. The word began to spread about the dynamic Rubio, and big endorsements followed from Senator Jim DeMint and Mike Huckabee. Dick Armey, one of the big national Tea Party leaders and the former Republican House majority leader, endorsed him early in 2009, calling him, "an inspiring leader for the next generation of the conservative movement."[17] This is a Teavangelical trifecta of an endorsement. The rest, as they say, is political history. His poll numbers began to rise, and so did the financial donations into his campaign. He won the Florida Senate race handily, became a media darling, and the Tea Party viewed him as one of their major success stories during the 2010 midterm elections.

For the most part, Rubio did not overtly inject his Christian faith into his Senate campaign. That's not Rubio's style. As a Roman Catholic, Rubio has a more reserved approach, but that hasn't stopped him from giving God the credit everywhere he goes. During our visit on Capitol Hill he told me his life would be "empty" without God and then expanded further. "If you look at our society, people are trying to fill this need and they fill it with all kinds of things, whether it's drugs or other things. You have this gaping void in your life that life doesn't make sense without God."

While Rubio does attend Catholic Mass, he has also spent the last number of years attending Christ Fellowship Church, one of the largest evangelical Protestant churches in the country. He likes it there because "they do a great job of teaching the Word of God and they've brought a lot people to salvation." He enjoys it so much that he's putting his money where his mouth is, donating more than $60,000 to the church in an eight-year span.[18]

When discussing God in private and in public, Rubio focuses a lot of his message on Teavangelical principle number one: reclaiming the country's Judeo-Christian heritage. He believes the Declaration of Independence was "as much based on spiritual concepts as it was on political ones." It's not lost on Rubio that "our rights as people come from God. They don't come from our president or from the Supreme Court or even from Congress. Government doesn't give us our rights. God gives us our rights. Government protects our rights."

The sky's the limit for Marco Rubio. While the future may seem rosy, we never know how it will ultimately play out. In the meantime, Marco Rubio plows away, working diligently at his day job as a United States senator. But he lives for Thursday evenings when he leaves Washington, DC, to return home to his wife and four children. Rubio is a family man at heart. "I'll make much more of a difference in this world as a father ... that's why it's important I do a good job of that," Rubio tells me.

He could make a huge difference as a future president of the United States too, and if he ever makes it to 1600 Pennsylvania Avenue, he'll have his priorities straight. He aspires to live a life that is God-centric, because when that happens, "your worldview is that of eternity, not that of the next fifty years that we have left, and you judge things a little bit differently, and you have a peace that comes from that.... None of us are promised prosperity, none of us are promised happiness, none of us are promised a problem-free life. What my faith promises you is that if you trust in God no matter what comes your way, he will give you the strength and the peace to handle it." Rubio would be well served to take his own advice if and when his big moment on the stage arrives.

Jim DeMint

With his modest demeanor, Senator Jim DeMint of South Carolina reminds me of a small-group Bible-study leader. To be sure, DeMint has been involved in his fair share of Bible studies, but this humble United States senator is not just sipping tea as he flips through the pages of the four Gospels. He's been drinking political tea since the Tea Party began in 2009. This born-again believer is a beloved hero of the Tea Party movement.

DeMint is not your typical politician. He was in the business community for a decade and a half before entering politics in 1999. After serving six years in the House of Representatives, he became a senator in 2005 and has since established himself as one of the most conservative members of the Senate.[19] However, he won't be around for long, since he has decided to not seek a third term in 2016.[20] This makes sense considering DeMint is a proponent of term limits, which falls nicely in line with the Tea Party mindset.

Before he hangs up his Senate cleats, DeMint has some work to do. He's in the process of giving the Republican Party an extreme makeover. He tells me that he wants some "new Republicans"[21] to join him on Capitol Hill. These are code words for a new batch of constitutional conservatives.

DeMint has set up a very powerful political action committee called the Senate Conservatives Fund. This PAC spent over eight million dollars[22] in its quest to elect these "new Republicans." DeMint's PAC backed some winning candidates (Marco Rubio, Rand Paul, Mike Lee) and some losing ones (Christine O'Donnell, Sharron Angle, Joe Miller), but DeMint's true impact isn't in the number of wins and losses. Instead, his power lies in his boldly standing up to the Republican Party leadership by backing insurgent constitutional conservative candidates rather than traditional GOP establishment picks.

DeMint is working to restructure the Republican Party by getting actively involved on the front end in the primary process. His endorsement and the money that follows are critical not just to the candidate, but also to the potential to change the makeup of Republicans on the Hill. Senator DeMint explains it to me this way: "The problem here in the Republican Party is not that our base has gone to the right. The problem in the Republican Party is that the leadership has gone to the left, and the Tea Parties and the Republicans out across the country are right there where American principles have always been, and I'm trying to pull the party back to the mainstream of where America really is."[23]

DeMint is also a force on the presidential campaign trail even though he's not on it. In the run-up to the infamous debt-ceiling vote in Washington during the summer of 2011, he circulated a

"Cut, Cap, and Balance" pledge, calling for reductions in deficit spending, limits on federal spending, and passage of a balanced budget amendment by Congress. It became so popular that national mainstream media news outlets were doing stories about it, and GOP presidential contenders were lining up to sign it.[24]

On Labor Day 2011, DeMint hosted a one-of-a-kind presidential forum devoted to the role of government and how candidates view the Constitution. CNN described the forum as a chance for the candidates to "kiss the ring of Tea Party kingmaker Jim DeMint."[25] Leave it to the media to embellish the situation, but there was some underlying truth to that line. DeMint's endorsement carries with it significant weight because it gives a candidate cover and credibility with the Tea Party and evangelicals.

Senator DeMint's brand of conservatism is classic Teavangelical. He's a diehard social conservative who has been outspoken on the issues of homosexuality, school prayer, and abortion. At the same time, he's received the love of Tea Party members by preaching fiscal conservatism until he's blue in the face. DeMint has been extremely artful in conjoining both messages into one.

DeMint isn't doing any of this for political gain. Rather he truly believes that the Tea Party is a spiritual awakening in this country. The way he sees it, our relationship with the Almighty and the prospect of an almighty government are directly related. "It's no coincidence that socialist Europe is post-Christian, because the bigger the government gets the smaller God gets and vice versa. The bigger God gets, the smaller people want their government, because they're yearning for freedom."[26]

Allen West

There's a reason I have saved Florida Congressman Allen West for the end of this chapter. Just like a Broadway musical, you want to end the show with lots of pizzazz and energy. Allen West won't be starring on Broadway anytime soon, but he's a constitutionally conservative Christian crowd pleaser everywhere he goes. For you basketball fans out there, you may understand it better this way: Allen West takes it "strong to the rack." And the Tea Party loves him for it.

Unlike the genial demeanors of Teavangelical powerhouses like Mike Huckabee and Jim DeMint, the first-term congressman brings intensity to his Teavangelical status, which comes no doubt from his military background. He's a former lieutenant colonel in the United States Army who was born into a family with a deep military background. He served more than two decades and has been honored with many awards including the Bronze Star, the fourth-highest combat award in the US Armed Forces. His stints include high-level positions during Operation Desert Storm, and Operation Iraqi Freedom.[27]

West's intensity has gotten him into trouble before, effectively ending his service in the military when he was fined for using improper interrogation methods during the questioning of an Iraqi police officer in 2003.[28] West admits to allowing two 4th Infantry Division Battalion soldiers under his command to beat up the police officer after he wouldn't give them necessary information. West also admits to firing a pistol near the man's hand and threatening to kill him. The Iraqi officer did eventually give them the information they needed, leading to two key arrests. At his hearing he was asked if he would do it again. West replied, "If it's about the lives of my men and their safety, I'd go through hell with a gasoline can."[29] You might be able to see why the Tea Party loves to have this guy on their side. He plays for keeps, and he does not back down. Sounds like the Tea Party, doesn't it?

While others may choose their words more carefully, you will usually find West throwing caution to the wind. He has no problem mixing it up and has no time to play the political correctness game. Democratic Florida Congresswoman Debbie Wasserman Schultz found that out firsthand.

West and Wasserman Schultz have a long and nasty history between them. They both represent districts in Broward County, Florida, and West was none too happy when Wasserman Schultz organized a protest outside his headquarters over the fact that West was a columnist for a biker magazine that had quite a few sexist references to women. West demanded an apology. He never got one.[30] Fast forward to the fall of 2011. Wassermann Schultz went to the floor of the House of Representatives and said that West's support of the GOP Cut, Cap and Balance approach to the budget would lead to increased costs for people who receive Medicare in Florida (that's a lot of people and a lot of West's constituents). West was not there to defend himself during the speech, but after hearing about her comments, the Florida congressman fired off a derisive email to her: "You are the most vile, unprofessional, and despicable member of the U.S. House of Representatives. If you have something to say to me, stop being a coward and say it to my face, otherwise, shut the heck up."[31] You simply don't want to mess with Allen West. As he put it in a radio interview after that incident, "As a Christian man I will turn the other cheek, but when I start to get a crick in my neck, I'm going to take care of business."[32]

It's that type of attitude that has endeared him to Tea Party members across America. One of the big speeches that brought him major recognition among the Tea Party took place in Fort Lauderdale in 2009. As a congressional candidate he pounced onto the stage and charged the crowd to "get your musket" and "fix your bayonet."[33] This compelling video eventually went viral and has over two and a half million YouTube hits.[34] Some of his critics have tried to paint him as a nut job, but West says, "Trying to portray me as an extremist, a radical, and a dangerous person is just plain wrong.... I have a passion for my country."[35] The people who dismiss Allen West's remarks as radical don't understand his appeal to a very important and growing section of voters in this country.

You may be wondering why in the world evangelicals would embrace someone like this. After all, evangelicals are reserved and nice, and all that bombastic language by West would turn them off, right? Not really. Sure, for some evangelicals he may not be their cup of tea (excuse the pun), but don't forget that evangelicals operate in a world of biblical absolutes. In other words, their world is colored in blacks and whites and not many shades of grey. This is the world in which Allen West finds himself.

Specifically, evangelicals will be attracted to his strong defense of Israel and his absolute obliteration of radical Islam. Be forewarned: if you try to defend radical Islam through the Koran at a town hall meeting you had better be prepared to get a mouthful from West. An employee for the Council on American-Islamic Relations (CAIR) showed up at a Pompano Beach, Florida, event asking him to point to a spot in the Koran where it tells Muslims to kill Americans. West swatted the question away, telling him that it wouldn't say that because America wasn't even around when the Koran existed. But that wasn't the end of it ... not by a long shot. West continued to point out a series of Muslim aggressive acts over the centuries and concluded by telling the questioner, "Don't come up here and try to criticize me! Put the microphone down and go home!" Maybe most evangelicals wouldn't be as confrontational as West, but deep down there is a level of respect for the man because in their minds he is telling the truth.[36]

West is a mighty defender of Judeo-Christian principles too. Growing up in the Atlanta area, he attended Methodist church every week, and the principles of God's rich blessing on America were engraved into him at a very young age. His parents also instilled in him a love of God and country. Today, as he travels around America, he boldly proclaims, "This is a Judeo-Christian country. We must be proud to say that. We must never back down from it."[37] Don't underestimate the words he speaks. It takes political guts to say that knowing full well the media headlines that follow will paint him as a fundamentalist nut job. Of course, when the media does this, it just gives West even more credibility in the evangelical world, since many conservative Christians are painted the same way.

You know you're a Teavangelical when you start to take your message and head into church and start delivering patriotic-sounding sermons from the pulpit. From time to time, West will be invited to speak to church congregations. He told parishioners at Ebenezer Baptist Church in Boca Raton, Florida, how sad it is that the country has become so secular nowadays that we shy away from talking about spiritual things. Leave it to West to change that mindset by linking spiritual truth with public policy. "If we return back to God our economy will be strengthened. If we return back to God we will have our borders secure," West told the congregation.[38]

Allen West is not a perfect man. He doesn't claim to be, and after reading this section on him you can see why. I'm sure he'll be the first to admit he could probably say things a little gentler, but his boldness and brashness is in truth a breath of fresh air in today's politically correct environment. The congressman from Florida has a world of potential to go far in national politics and bring the Teavangelical message center stage. Whether or not that happens is really up to how West navigates the uncharted political waters ahead. Will he be able to tone down his rhetoric while still being true to who he is? We don't know the answer to that, but what we do know is that one of his daily prayers comes from 1 Chronicles 4:10 where Jabez cried out to God saying, "Oh, that you would bless me and enlarge my territory! Let your hand be with me, and keep me from harm so that I will be free from pain." And God granted his request.

So what do all of these Teavangelical powerhouses have in common? First, they boldly proclaim their faith and don't shrink from it. Additionally, all of them have some sort of political power structure in place, whether it is a political action committee, a Senate seat, or simply the attention of the mainstream media. Finally, the heart of their message is a return to Judeo-Christian principles. It is from this belief that springs all of their public-policy solutions. Those answers for America appeal directly to both the Tea Party and evangelicals, hence the perfect confluence of the Teavangelical message.

Chapter 7

SPREADING
the GOOD NEWS:
TEAVANGELICALS
and THE CHURCH

IS THERE SOMETHING YOU DO VIRTUALLY EVERY SATURDAY? MAYBE go to Walmart, mow the lawn, or watch a sporting event on television? Danita Kilcullen stands on a street corner.

At 1:00 every Saturday afternoon since February of 2009, she has planted herself at the same spot, the northeast corner of Oakland Park Boulevard and Federal Highway in Fort Lauderdale, Florida. If it's raining, she goes. If the humidity level is at 99 percent, no sweat. She's there. Kilcullen is the founder of Tea Party Fort Lauderdale, which bills itself as "America's longest-running Tea Party," established nine days after the famous rant by CNBC's Rick Santelli.[1] Danita and sixty or so of her Tea Party friends are out in the Florida sunshine every week for two hours, waving their banners and holding an outdoor rally complete with guest speakers, including some big fish like Florida Congressman Allen West.

Kilcullen tells me she is a "natural-born Tea Party girl," and that is no lie. She's also a Teavangelical. Many of her fellow Tea Party comrades are evangelicals, and Danita readily admits that without God the movement wouldn't be working out too well. "We can't do anything without God. We do march with God."

Danita has always felt that churches need to address the political issues of the day, but fifteen years ago, she felt her church wasn't engaging the issues as much as she would have liked. "Pastors need to not have a 'turn the other cheek attitude.' People in the pews are sitting there, ready to get out there, but they need to hear it from the pulpit." After a great deal of thought, Kilcullen decided to leave that church and wound up at the Worldwide Christian Center with a pastor who's full not just of the Holy Spirit but of political passion too.

Kilcullen's pastor is Rev. O'Neal Dozier, an African American and a former NFL football player, champion bodybuilder, and Vietnam veteran. To say Dozier knows something about a fight is an understatement! He also knows how to fight in the political arena as he helped the reelection efforts of President George W. Bush and Florida Governor Jeb Bush.[2] Throughout the years, Reverend Dozier has made a habit of being politically active and speaking out on the issues. Clearly Kilcullen found a kindred spirit in him.

The bond is so tight that Dozier often winds up on that same street corner in Fort Lauderdale with Danita. They set up Tea Party protests together, and if you think the pastor holds back when he speaks, think again. After a few African-American Democratic Congressmen charged the Tea Party with racism, Reverend Dozier shot back, "The Tea Party is a godly ordained party."[3] Dozier isn't just proving it in word, but in deed too. In February 2011, Reverend Dozier opened the church doors to celebrate Tea Party Fort Lauderdale, honoring them with a plaque in front of the whole congregation. I believe that would officially be considered a "Teavangelical Sunday service."

Danita Kilcullen and Reverend Dozier represent an interesting dynamic taking place across the country. Pastors and church members are coming together to spread the Teavangelical message both inside and outside the walls of the church.

Women Impacting the Nation: A "Winning" Hand

In the 1980s, the stock brokerage firm E. F. Hutton came up with the famous advertising slogan: "When E. F. Hutton talks, people listen." Well, Sue Trombino is the Teavangelical E. F. Hutton. When she speaks at churches, women rise from the audience and want to be a part of what she's started.

Trombino will be the first to admit that she's just an ordinary churchgoing mom in southern Florida, but this Teavangelical also happened to form a group called Women Impacting the Nation (WIN). Simply put, these are study groups of about a dozen women each who meet twice a month to read the Constitution and study books that help them to defend their Judeo-Christian belief system. Some of the books they have read are *Take Back America* by Matt Staver, *America's Godly Heritage* by David Barton, and *Bible Positions on Political Issues* by John Hagee. "We have become a nation of nonthinkers," Trombino tells me. She's out to change that ... one woman at a time.

From her childhood experience of living all over the world, Sue Trombino came to appreciate just how great America is. But she also realized that many Americans are apathetic, disinterested, and ill informed about our country's religious history and constitutional principles. Her WIN talk groups were established to change that, and they're based on Teavangelical value number one, reclaiming our country's Judeo-Christian heritage. These meetings are rooted in biblical Christianity as they always start out with a prayer, the Pledge of Allegiance, and a hymn. But to be clear, the meetings are nonpartisan. "It is not about the elephant or the donkey. It's about the lamb," Sue declares.

These WIN talk groups started in 2008, with a couple of dozen churchgoers in Florida, but now they're spreading into places like Montana, New York, and California. Why are they increasing? Obviously, the increased visibility and blossoming of the Tea Party movement has something to do with it, but Trombino has also taken her message into churches around the country as part of a much bigger movement.

The Awakening

If you look up the definition of the word *awake*, it says, "to stop sleeping." That's the exact message some major evangelical organizations are trying to get across to churches in America. In 2009, a coalition of dozens of faith-based evangelical Christian groups (made up of well-known groups like the American Family Association, Family Research Council, and others) formed the Freedom Federation as a way to advance their "shared core values."[4] A year later, they began a series of national conferences called "The Awakening," designed to mobilize church attendees into action by mixing Christian faith with public policy. The breakout sessions included topics ranging from social issues to ones titled "How to Avert a Monetary Collapse."[5] Liberty University, one of the most notable evangelical Christian universities in the country, played host to the big event attended by national politicians.

The national Awakening conferences paved the way for individual state "Awake" events held in churches around the country. WallBuilders founder David Barton and Matt Staver, founder and chairman of Liberty Counsel, became two of the main evangelical figures that began traveling to churches around the country. Sue Trombino, who had developed a close working relationship with

Staver through the years, went with them to these churches too. When people fill the pews for Awake, they are treated to a two-hour event complete with information about the founding of America, what pastors can and can't say from the pulpit, how to vote your values, and how you can register to vote.[6] The event is also simulcast on the Internet to thousands of other Christians. While these Awake events are not Tea Party events, they definitely tout Teavangelical values. And Trombino reminds us that it will be this Awake crowd who will be a big part of the fuel for the Tea Party movement. That political energy will come through prayer. "Unless the Tea Party are on their knees," says Trombino, "it won't make a hill of beans' difference." Spoken like a true Teavangelical.

Sunday School Teavangelicals

If you want to learn about the Bible, then Sunday school is a great place to delve deeper. But Sunday school isn't just for Bible stories anymore. The Teavangelical strikes again!

At Scottsdale Bible Church near Phoenix, Arizona, church members hurry to reserve their seat in a class called "Christian Essentials," taught by Dr. Wayne Grudem, one of the top Protestant theologians in the country. The series of classes is based upon his book *Politics—According to the Bible* and examines how Christians should approach the political issues of the day. For example, one of his classes focuses in on taxes. He suggests that a flat tax may indeed be biblical, arguing that, "The principle of a 10 percent tithe in the Bible would give some support to the idea." In arguing against overtaxation, Grudem also points out that Luke 10:7 says, "The worker deserves his wages."[7] Do you see what churchgoers are learning on Sunday? Yes, they are getting fed spiritual nourishment from their pastor, but they are also getting a Teavangelical plate full of political fruit.

How about what's going on at First Baptist Church of Fort Lauderdale? In the fall of 2011, Pastor Larry Thompson led a ten-week series called "Politics and the Bible." This one takes place at the church on Wednesday night, and you know how the word gets around about the meeting? It's not just through the church bulletin. Libertarian social media sites also spread the word. For example, a member of the Constitution Party of Florida posted the information about Pastor Thompson's classes on one of their Meetup social networking sites.[8] Once again libertarians and evangelicals intersect, partnering on the issues they champion.

Perhaps there's no better illustration of a church-sanctioned Tea Party–type event than what's going on at Calvary Chapel of Fort Lauderdale, one of the largest evangelical megachurches in America, with roughly twenty thousand weekly attendees. On the third Friday of every month, dozens of Christians gather for "Faith Forums" designed to educate church members and get them engaged in political and civil matters. Depending on their expertise, the people who show up are assigned a certain political issue that they then research and report back to the group. Ultimately, it's all about gaining knowledge and then taking action. It's not uncommon for these events to include voter-registration drives. In addition, the group becomes more familiar with the positions of local and state political candidates. At times, these faith forums bring in special Tea Party heroes like Florida Senator Marco Rubio and Florida Congressman Allen West.

The man behind this effort is Scott Spages. Leading these faith forums is a natural fit for him since he's been active in local politics for twenty-five years. But not until 2004 did Spages try to become politically active within the church. That year he went to the pastor of Calvary Chapel and asked to run a monthly faith-forum meeting. The answer? No. Not now. But four years later the situation changed. Residents in the state of Florida found themselves in a heated debate over the protection of traditional marriage as a battle brewed over plans to put a Marriage Protection Amendment on the November 2008 ballot. Scott went back to the pastor, asking him if these faith forums could take place at the church. This time the answer was yes, and the meetings have been taking place ever since.

Spages approaches his important duties in a biblical way. He cites James 2:17 as a guiding verse, which states, "Faith by itself, if it is not accompanied by action, is dead." Those words describe Calvary Chapel's faith forums completely. He also knows something else. If you take faithful Christians out of the Tea Party movement, you have a dead movement. "Fifty percent of it disappears," Spages tells me. He is also well aware that conservative Christians have no plans to abandon the Tea Party, because the country's future lies in the balance. You can count on Spages to be praying for a positive outcome. "One of my prayers is for revival and awakening."

Pastor Power

It is one thing for a pastor to preach a solid sermon on the inerrant Word of God. This person would be called "an evangelical pastor." Yet when a pastor decides to engage in the economic, social, and moral issues of the day, then that pastor turns into "a Teavangelical preacher." In this section, you're about to discover organizational networks that have been set up to unleash a tidal wave of Teavangelical clergy across America.

Now, as you read through this chapter, keep in mind one very important point. Don't think for a minute that these Teavangelical preachers will suddenly start to change their preaching style by concentrating on Tea Party–type issues, like the debt or national healthcare. Some of their sermons may touch on these issues, but that isn't their main goal. The overarching objective here is to equip pastors on political issues so their passion will spread to their congregations. Ideally, the "flock" will take their pastor's cue and want to participate in the political process of restoring our nation to its sound Judeo-Christian principles and a constitutionally limited government. Remember, engaged evangelicals are crucial to the success of the Tea Party, especially at the ballot box, so encouraging pastors to get vocal in this fight is an essential part of a victorious strategy.

Pastor Policy Briefings

When it's time to call a family meeting to discuss important matters in your household, everybody gathers around the kitchen table. When it's time for pastors to gather for a serious "Come to Jesus" talk, these are called Pastor Policy Briefings.

For the past several years, in several states (many of them political battleground states like Iowa, South Carolina, and Nevada), thousands of pastors have gathered for an all-expense-paid, closed-to-the-media two-day event where they hear prominent political and religious speakers on topics such as the roots of America's Christian heritage and the intersection of public policy and the Bible. Additionally, because churches are nonprofit 501c3 organizations, federal tax laws put certain restrictions on what they can and cannot say from the pulpit. What the pastors find out, however, is that they can do and say a lot more than they think without receiving an audit from the Internal Revenue Service.[9]

The American Family Association pays for many of these Pastor Policy Briefings (which are also called "Renewal Projects"). But these briefings can be traced back to the 1990s when a man by the name of David Lane began organizing them in Texas and California. In 2006, under the banner of the Texas Restoration Project, Lane helped organize briefings and mobilized Lone Star State pastors during Texas Governor Rick Perry's reelection effort.[10]

Lane's connection to Rick Perry doesn't stop there. He also was the finance chairman for the huge August 2011 prayer event called "The Response" at Reliant Stadium in Houston, an occasion called for by Rick Perry.

David Lane's influence should not be underestimated. Along with the money provided by AFA, he's a big reason why so many pastors are starting to get engaged in the political issues of the day. Doug Wead, a presidential historian and once an evangelical consultant to President George H. W. Bush, calls these Pastor Policy Briefings "extremely important because they involve large numbers of evangelical leaders from every branch of the evangelical movement." As for Lane, Wead calls him "a great organizer."[11]

Lane likes to keep a low profile, but at a recent Pastor Policy Briefing in Iowa he acknowledged the ultimate purpose of these meetings: "What we're doing with the pastor meetings is spiritual, but the end result is political.... From my perspective, our country is going to hell because pastors won't lead from the pulpits."[12]

This sentiment is at the heart of these meetings. In an email invitation to pastors by Mike Huckabee for the Iowa briefing in March 2011, Lane wrote, "The silence of the church and her pastors have helped to create this mess."[13] That Iowa event in front of hundreds of pastors included speeches by presidential hopefuls like Michele Bachmann, Newt Gingrich, and others.[14] A few weeks later, highlights of the briefing were posted on the American Family Association website and streamed out to hundreds of churchgoers around America.[15]

These pastor briefings have increased with frequency in the last few years because there's a pastoral hunger out there to be more engaged on political issues. Richard Land, the president of the Southern Baptist Convention's Ethics and Religious Liberty Commission, probably put it best when he said, "This is the congregational version of the Tea Party.... Pastors who in the past would dodge my calls are calling me saying, 'How can we be involved?'"[16]

United in Purpose:
Helping Pastors to Get Out the Vote

All this talk about pastors getting together sounds great on paper, but if Christians don't turn up and vote in November 2012, then what's the point? Well, a newly formed organization is ready to use pastors and some logistical muscle in their quest for an increase in evangelical voter turnout.

With the goal of bringing positive biblical change to America, the organization United in Purpose is working to register five million new Christian voters. Why that amount? According to their research, they believe it will take that many new voters to swing an election. Their voter registration program, called "Champion the Vote," provides training and materials to a grassroots army of volunteers.

United in Purpose points out that of the sixty million Christians who are eligible to vote, only half are registered.[17] Therefore, the group has created PowerPoint slides, bulletins, and talking-point memos for pastors so they can explain to their parishioners how to get mobilized and vote.[18] Beyond all the paraphernalia, they also host "One Nation Under God," a two-hour event starring Teavangelical speakers such as David Barton, gifted politicians like Newt Gingrich, and evangelical icons like Dr. James Dobson. The affair is billed as a way to learn "the truth about the biblical foundation of our nation" from top-notch "spiritual, political, and educational leaders."[19] If you miss the event, not to worry. Churches can purchase the DVD for $49.95 and play it for their congregations.[20]

With help from the Liberty Institute (a conservative Christian legal-defense organization), United in Purpose also gives pastors a list of guidelines of what churches are permitted to do under federal tax law. In 1954, an amendment was added to the tax code that forbids pastors of tax-exempt organizations (read: churches) from supporting or opposing candidates from the pulpit. In the decades since, pastors have shied away from pulpit politics for fear of an audit from the IRS. But according to the handout provided by United in Purpose, the only restrictions on churches are that they can't endorse or oppose a political candidate, and they can't provide church resources to one candidate over another (including the always-important church mailing list!). The IRS, however, does not preclude churches from registering their members to vote, passing out voter guides, or speaking candidly about the morality of political issues.[21] In other words, there's plenty of room for evangelical pastors to turn into Teavangelical ones.

Vision America

Dr. Rick Scarborough has a vision of pastors speaking boldly from the pulpit and church members becoming actively involved citizens in rescuing America's Judeo-Christian principles. "I believe pastors are why we've lost this country, and I believe they're the hope of reclaiming this country," Scarborough says.[22] Appropriately, his Vision America organization tackles that formidable challenge.

Rick Scarborough knows all about marshaling the troops. As senior pastor of First Baptist Church in Pearland, Texas, in the 1990s, he was always preaching about active citizenship. As time went by, many church members started running for local office.[23] During that period, he wrote a book called *Enough Is Enough: A Call to Christian Involvement*, which became a bestseller. His penchant for firing up the flock led to establishing Vision America in 1998. Since that time, Scarborough has been assembling pastors on the front lines of America's culture war by getting them involved in issues like judicial overreach, same-sex marriage, abortion, and more.

When the Tea Party began its uprising in 2009, the movement became a perfect fit for Dr. Scarborough. What he found was a movement full of vigorous political libertarians making serious noise about the state of our country. Scarborough became heartened by the passion of the constitutional crusade and knew that weaving in Judeo-Christian principles had to be part of the fabric of the movement. It wasn't hard at all since Scarborough quickly points out that "Jesus is the heart of what drives most of the Tea Parties."[24]

So what happened after the Tea Party came on the scene? Dr. Scarborough became a regular part of the movement. In February 2010, Vision America played an active role at the first National Tea Party Convention. Scarborough spoke to the crowd, led a prayer service, and conducted a breakout session on "Why Pastors and Churches Must Engage in Politics."[25] Later that year, he organized evangelical leaders to sign a petition in support of the Tea Parties, stating that they "stand in solidarity with the Tea Parties' goals of lower taxes, less government, and adherence to the Constitution and vision of the Founding Fathers, as articulated in the Declaration of Independence."[26]

Scarborough is so passionate about merging church activism with the Tea Party that he goes on the road quite often to speak at Tea Party rallies. Fred and Julie McCarty remember how Dr. Scarborough made a direct impact on them. The McCartys lead the NE Tarrant Tea Party located north of Dallas, Texas. After reading *Enough Is Enough*, they asked Scarborough to speak to their Tea Party group. They didn't realize how robust his fee would be, so it didn't look promising ... that is, until the good doctor called them and said because of his love for the Tea Party, he would waive the speaking fee. Excited and relieved, the McCartys gathered up local Tea Party members, and they all soaked up his message. "It's up to the church to save America, and Rick had a plan to do that," Julie McCarty explained. Ever since Scarborough's visit, members of the NE Tarrant Tea Party are now more active in conducting voter-registration drives in their churches.[27]

The New Black-Robed Regiment

Reverend Peter Muhlenberg would have loved the Tea Party. Too bad he's not around today (he'd be pushing 270 years old!). As pastor of a church in Woodstock, Virginia, during the 1770s, Muhlenberg was part of what the British referred to as the "Black Regiment." The term described this collection of pre–Revolutionary War preachers (dressed in their black robes) who spoke out from the pulpit against British rule and for colonial revolution. They never marched in the army as a unit but rather spoke of how this patriotic insurgency was justified in the eyes of God. They were relentless.[28] Remember, in the 1770s, many colonists and especially parishioners were loyal to the British government and weren't sold on this radical concept of revolution, so the Brits were none too happy about this clergy uprising. Guess what? These pastors didn't care.

Most pastors didn't literally take up arms against the British during that time, but Reverend Muhlenberg did. During his farewell sermon to his Virginia church in the winter of 1776, he referred to the book of Ecclesiastes, saying, "There was a time for all things, a time to preach and a time to pray, but those times had passed away; that there was a time to fight, and that time had now come!"[29] That said, Muhlenberg shed his black robe to unveil his full military uniform underneath. He left the church bound for war against the British.

Word of his action spread to other churches, and before the day was over, three hundred men signed up to fight in the Revolutionary Army. A year later he was appointed brigadier general and led the raid on Yorktown. By the end of the war this pastor-turned-military-hero was promoted to major general.

This riveting story of the past begs a question for today: Where are these type of pastors nowadays? Are they out there? Pastor Chuck Baldwin, the state chairman of the Florida Moral Majority in the 1980s and the 2008 presidential candidate for the Constitution Party, has put together an online directory that lists more than eight hundred of them around the country. All you have to do is go online and find the Black Robe Regiment pastors in your area.[30]

Then there is media megastar Glenn Beck. He's on a quest to find some more Peter Muhlenbergs. When the Tea Party started, Beck understood that the movement could not be sustained without the mighty outstretched hand of God. With that mindset, he began to recruit pastors from all over the country and asked them to join forces in a new "Black Robe Brigade." He brought 240 religious leaders from around the country on stage during his Restoring Honor rally on the Washington Mall in August 2010. Many, but not all, were conservative evangelical pastors, and they stood side by side with Beck to make the bold statement that pastors cannot be silent anymore and that it's time for the clergy to lead America back to its religious roots.[31] "The black-robed regiment is back again today," Beck shouted to hundreds of thousands on the mall.[32]

David Barton, president of WallBuilders, was among those on stage. "Why has the church lost its voice to speak out on these issues today? It used to be if something was in the headlines it was in the pulpit to give a biblical perspective," Barton tells me. He has example after example of Revolutionary War–period preachers speaking out on the topics of the day. Whether it was sermons opposing the British Stamp Act imposed on the colonies in 1765 or the horror of the Boston Massacre in 1770, Christian pastors weren't afraid to take to the pulpit to make a stand.[33]

Barton sees a rekindling of that effort beginning in this era of the Tea Party. "I think churches and pastors are starting to recognize that we need to talk about the stuff that's going on, the issues that are out there. They did that with marriage, they did that with abortion. Is it any less biblical to talk about economic stuff when the Bible deals so extensively with economic issues? Certainly not."

The Ayn Rand Controversy

This chapter on the church and Teavangelicals wouldn't be complete without a thorough discussion of the controversy surrounding Ayn Rand (pronounced: Ine Rand). She's an icon among Tea Party libertarians, but should evangelicals be wary of her views that leave God out of the process and disparage him to boot?

Ayn Rand may have died thirty years ago, but her legacy lives on within the Tea Party. The Russian-born philosopher grew up during the early 1900s and witnessed the Bolshevik Revolution, which led to the founding of the Communist state in Russia. Rand deplored these tactics from the outset and even at age twelve began to form her opinion against what would later be called collectivism: the theory that "man must be chained to collective action and collective thought for the sake of what is called 'the common good.'"[34]

In high school, her worldview began to take shape. She came to the conclusion that she was an atheist and valued the power of reason more than anything else. She also began to learn about American history and immediately was drawn to the power of a free society. At twenty-one, she was granted a visa to visit relatives in America. She arrived in Manhattan and fell in love with this country right away. She eventually moved to Hollywood in her quest to become a screenwriter. She married an American actor and never returned to Russia.

While she had a few screenwriting jobs, she ended up writing for a living. Her first best-selling novel, *The Fountainhead*, was published in 1943. It centered on the concept of individualism, that is the ability of man to think for himself as well as a focus on "the moral worth of the individual."[35] This work, along with her most famous novel, *Atlas Shrugged*, published in 1957, also focused on a philosophy she created. It's called Objectivism. Conservative Christians may cringe when they hear the definition, but this is a philosophy that is at the heart of pure libertarian thought. Rand describes it as follows: "My philosophy (Objectivism), in essence, is the concept of man as a heroic being, with his own happiness as the moral purpose of his life, with productive achievement as his noblest activity, and reason as his only absolute."[36] She continues to explain that man "must exist for his own sake, neither sacrificing himself to others nor sacrificing others to himself. The pursuit of his own rational self-interest and of his own happiness is the highest moral purpose of his life."[37] The concept is even deeper than that, but you get the general idea.

Dr. Richard Land, a leading evangelical figure and the president of the Southern Baptist Convention's Ethics and Religious Liberty Commission, begs to differ with a major part of what Rand is saying. "She's right when she talks about that man is selfish. She's wrong when she makes selfishness a virtue," Land tells me. Renowned conservative Christian leader Chuck Colson is dismayed by Rand's *Atlas Shrugged* novel, writing, "It's hard to imagine a world view more antithetical to Christianity."

This theory of Objectivism leads Rand directly to the conclusion that a political system of laissez-faire "capitalism is best because it protects the rights of the individual to operate in a fair and effective way." Basically, it means a system where the government for the most part leaves people alone when it comes to economic transitions. That specific free-market expression by Rand comports with most conservative evangelicals. The problem for conservative Christians is that she leaves God out of the equation, especially when arguing that "there should be (but, historically, has not yet been) a complete separation of state and economics, in the same way and for the same reasons as the separation of state and church."[38]

In the decades that followed, Rand began to write books on Objectivism. Even after her death, all her books are still in print, and hundreds of thousands of them are bought every year, totaling 25 million copies sold.[39] Additionally, it shouldn't come as a surprise that since the financial crisis started to unfold with bank bailouts and stimulus funding starting in 2007, sales of *Atlas Shrugged* spiked significantly.[40] Congressman Paul Ryan of Wisconsin, a Tea Party favorite, summed it up by saying that today in America, "We are living in an Ayn Rand novel."[41] At Tea Party events across the country, her name is invoked and passages from her books are read.[42]

Speaking of her passages and quotes, here's where there is a philosophical divide between libertarians and evangelical Christians over Rand. You see, Rand is an atheist, and therefore she has made quite a few anti-God references throughout her life and in her works. What are some of her greatest hits? Try this one on for size: "The alleged short-cut to knowledge, which is faith, is only a short circuit destroying the mind." Or how about this one? "Faith, as such, is extremely detrimental to human life: it is the negation of reason." Then this whopper: "I would say that man's only moral commandment is: Thou shalt think."[43] Progressive Christians try to create a wedge between the Tea Party and conservative evangelicals, arguing that there is a choice to be made. That is, how can you support the Tea Party when one of their great philosophers spews offensive, anti-God comments? It's a legitimate question worth considering.

To ponder the question, one must first understand that there are two components to consider here. First, there is the reality that most churchgoing conservative Christians probably have never even heard of Ayn Rand. Moreover, as David Barton of WallBuilders pointed out to me, "I will contend that most Christians have not even read *Atlas Shrugged*, and they don't know who she is." If Ayn

Rand (or any Tea Party member) was spewing her anti-God rhetoric on stage today, it would be a direct affront to the sensibilities of evangelicals and downright offensive. If this were happening, there wouldn't be any Teavangelicals because they'd be gone from the movement in a heartbeat. In other words, whether you call it ignorance or lack of research into the philosophical underpinnings of the Tea Party movement, most evangelicals don't even recognize that the movement gets its juice from many of her writings.

Yet there is a second important part here as well and it is philosophical in nature. The very nature of libertarian thought and the Tea Party movement as a whole is derived from her philosophies. Her view on objectivism sees the individual as the primary moral authority and leaves God totally out of the equation. The dirty little secret is that this is indeed a conflict in worldview between Libertarians and Evangelicals. Because Ayn Rand is such an important Tea Party figure, evangelicals must be well informed about both the good and bad in Rand's concepts.

On the positive side, evangelicals would mostly agree with Rand's belief that statism is abhorrent. The idea that an individual's collective efforts belong to the society or state or even nation is deeply troubling. She believed strongly in a constitutionally limited government where the constitution should limit the government, not individuals. Additionally, she loved how the Founding Fathers were able to take ideas from the Revolutionary War period and come up with a way to make them work in a societal context such as the governmental system of checks and balances that provided protection against any sort of dictatorship state. All of these ideas are what the Tea Party is about today, and these are major reasons why evangelicals are present within the movement.

There is a flip side, however. At her core, she was very much an anti-Christian philosopher who, as we have mentioned previously, had plenty of anti-God rhetoric in her background. It can be argued that her objectivism flows out of her atheist beliefs because objectivism leaves God out entirely. When you leave the Almighty behind and make individual man the standard bearer for right and wrong you run into problems. Conservative evangelicals understand that there are biblical moral absolutes. Ayn Rand does not have that same internal compass and therefore believes that man, should "exist for his own sake, neither sacrificing himself to others nor sacrificing others to himself."[44] Since that's the case, then it's no wonder that Rand believes that while prostitution and drugs are indeed immoral, the government doesn't have the right to prohibit them. After all, the way she sees it, if people willingly partake in it, why should they be stopped? And abortion? The pro-choice Rand calls it a "moral right" where only the woman's wish matters. Forget the rights of the little child inside of the woman because, as she says, "An embryo has no rights."[45]

It's important to point out that while Rand's philosophical views are at the core of libertarian belief, it doesn't necessarily represent the Tea Party as a whole. Still, we've laid out some of the good and bad points of Rand's philosophy from a conservative evangelical perspective so that churchgoing Christians will better understand the libertarian mindset and thus decide for themselves if they can break bread with folks who ascribe to Rand's views.

While some evangelicals may want to distance themselves from Rand's works and the Tea Party, there will be many who can separate the good from the bad. Of course 2012 presidential candidate Ron Paul knows all about Ayn Rand. He admires her work, but as a Christian himself he's able to separate the two. In a conversation I had with him during a Faith and Freedom Conference in 2011, he simultaneously defended Ayn Rand while at the same time saying that her works helped him to be *more* of a defender of his Christian faith. "People like to go after me and say he's just a 'Randie' and he's an objectivist and say all the negative things because she was an atheist, but I thought she was very thought provoking. I read her books as a young person, and she was good on the markets and individual liberty and being heroic in defending and standing up for what she believes in. At the same time she was very challenging, so people who might come from a church background and read her might have to stop and think. I actually believe I came out with a much stronger faith after being challenged by her."

I think it's fair to assume Ayn Rand would never be part of a Black Robe Brigade, and she may indeed scoff at the Teavangelicals' injection of faith into the Tea Party discussion. But with all due respect to Ayn Rand, Teavangelicals are alive and well inside the Tea Party movement, because these worshipers understand something very fundamental: Without God, none of this would even be possible.

Chapter 8

TEAVENGELICALS
and the MEDIA

MICHELLE BACHMANN STARED AWKWARDLY INTO SPACE LIKE A strange alien from another planet. The crackerjack team from *Newsweek* magazine (sarcasm dripping) had taken this beautiful fifty-five-year-old candidate for president and turned her into a candidate for "Zombie of the Year." The *Newsweek* cover, unveiled right at the height of Michele Bachmann's presidential nomination run, was unflattering to say the least and downright sinister to say the worst. At least it wasn't as bad as an article in the *New Yorker* where the reporter called her "a religious zealot whose brain is a raging electrical storm of divine visions and paranoid delusions."[1] Classy. But then again, should evangelical candidates who run for the presidency expect anything different from the mainstream media?

We've all heard the classic children's line "Sticks and stones may break my bones, but names will never hurt me," so you may ask, what's the big deal? If you run for president (like Bachmann), you're in the big leagues and you have to take it. But the mainstream media bias against conservative Christians is so blatant as to defy belief. The unfairness against the Tea Party is less evident but nonetheless permeates the mainstream media. Asking whether there is overt bias against evangelical Christians and the Tea Party in the mainstream media is like asking if Lebron James is hated in Cleveland. You bet.

Actually, conservative Christians and the Tea Party are fed up with the subtle and not-so-subtle putdowns, stereotyping, and denigration of their cherished values and have decided to look elsewhere for their news. That's not to say that they don't or won't watch some mainstream media coverage, but the playing field has changed. The major media outlets no longer have a monopoly on the news.

In this chapter, we set out to specifically define examples of Teavangelical bias and why both evangelicals and Tea Party members have decided to turn toward alternative outlets for their news. We then detail what those outlets are and why they matter to the Teavangelical crowd.

The Rise of Media Bias

Believe it or not, media bias against evangelical Christians is relatively new in our nation's history. In *Prodigal Press: The Anti-Christian Bias of the American News Media*, Marvin Olasky explains how up until the mid nineteenth century there were more than one hundred cities in America that had overtly Christian newspapers. The *New York Christian Advocate* was actually the biggest weekly paper in the United States, and even the *New York Times* had a distinct Christian viewpoint, as a Bible-believing Presbyterian founded it.[2] The *New York Times* as a Christian newspaper? Someone grab the smelling salts, quick! Of course, we know how the story ends, don't we? For various reasons, including the fact that American society began to move away from Judeo-Christian principles, so did the *New York Times*.

This shift of values over time shows up quite explicitly when it comes to the ideological makeup of mainstream media reporters. The definitive study on this comes from Robert Lichter and Stanley

Rothman in their groundbreaking book from 1979 called *The Media Elite: America's New Powerbrokers*. They surveyed 240 journalists from major national media outlets across the country and found a group of people with a distinct secular viewpoint. Half didn't claim any religion, and just 8 percent attended church or synagogue.[3] Furthermore, 90 percent of them were pro-choice, only 25 percent of them thought homosexuality was wrong (and that was thirty years ago — imagine today!), and shockingly just 47 percent of reporters thought adultery was wrong.[4] Those attitudes have been shaping journalism for decades.

Over the last twenty-five years, media bias has gotten progressively worse. Only a quarter of people now believe mainstream media outlets (that is, cable networks, major national print publications, and the main television and radio networks) actually gets their facts straight (in 1985 it was 55 percent). Furthermore, more than three-quarters of Americans think the mainstream media tends to favor one side (in 1985 that figure was just 53 percent).[5] A study conducted by UCLA showed that eighteen of the twenty media outlets studied were to the left of center. The CBS Evening News, the *New York Times*, and the *Los Angeles Times* were the major liberal culprits.[6]

To add insult to injury, a liberal press simply cannot grasp the Christian worldview. They are incapable of it based strictly on the fact that it's a world they don't understand, yet they are the ones that typically form the narrative on Christian presidential candidates, politicians, and evangelicals as a whole. In a way, they can't help their ignorance. Just as Christians tend to live in their isolated environment, so do members of the media. They incessantly talk among themselves at events, cocktail parties, and media functions. It becomes an echo chamber. Newt Gingrich once explained to me during an interview in Florida that media elite reporters "reach whatever the snap judgment over a drink that afternoon is."[7]

This leaves both a perplexing and frustrating conundrum: although we live in a country with tens of millions of evangelicals, a small contingent of powerful liberal media elites drives the conversation about evangelical candidates. Because their worldview precludes them from really understanding how these candidates tick in the first place, however, their articles and analyses are full of bias (some intentional, some unintentional). Candidates like Rick Perry, Michele Bachmann, and Rick Santorum who wear their faith on their sleeve have to overcome not only general liberal media bias against conservatives but bias against evangelicals as well. Is it any wonder that evangelicals began to look elsewhere for media coverage that better reflects their worldview and values?

Teavangelical Presidential Campaign Bias

So you want evidence of this media bias against evangelicals? Do you have a few weeks to spare so I can detail all of the examples? I can't lay it all out here, but all you have to do is pick up a newspaper or grab the remote control to figure out that the media bias against evangelicals is everywhere. The 2012 presidential race offers numerous examples of this bias. A Media Research Center study monitored the main three television networks (ABC, NBC, CBS), and their findings revealed that during the first ten months of 2011 the networks were thirteen times more likely to run stories that were critical of Republican candidates' faith as compared to what was run about the Democrats candidates' faith back in 2008. Specifically, Michele Bachmann's faith was criticized in fifteen out of twenty-three stories (that's about two-thirds of the time), while Rick Perry's faith was criticized in 63 percent of the networks' stories.[8] The organization also conducted a five-million-dollar campaign called "Tell the Truth! 2012" in an effort to document and expose the media's liberal bias.[9] It should be noted that Republican candidates are going to get more stories and scrutiny about their faith because many of them readily admit that it informs their views and is central to their campaigns. So while the treatment may be unfair, the media's fascination with the candidate's faith is warranted.

Scrutiny of Rick Perry began shortly before he even entered the presidential race. Perry decided to call a giant prayer meeting at Reliant Stadium down in Houston, Texas. The objective was to publicly seek God's help in the midst of this nation's moral and economic troubles. In a nation where the majority of Americans are Christians this wouldn't be such a big deal, right? Think again. The liberal media went into separation of church and state overdrive mode, questioning whether a governor should be headlining such an event. ABC ran the headline, "Is Perry Going Too Far?" Some critics called it "government-supported evangelism."[10] Yet does anyone blink an eye when liberal politicians show up at the pulpits of African American churches? Of course not, and when evangelicals see this level of vitriol for an evangelical prayer event, they are well aware of the media double standard.

Anita Perry, the wife of presidential candidate Rick Perry, spoke openly about media bias against evangelicals, especially her husband: "It's been a rough month. We have been brutalized and beaten up and chewed up in the press ... I think they look at him, because of his faith."[11] While Rick Perry's failed candidacy cannot be chalked up to media bias (various missteps were the real reason), his faith did receive undue scrutiny from the media.

Meanwhile Karen Santorum, the wife of presidential candidate Rick Santorum, was the target of a *Newsweek* article detailing how, before she met Santorum, she had a six-year romantic relationship with an abortion doctor. Apparently *Newsweek* thought this was newsworthy because the staunchly pro-life Rick Santorum had received the backing of prominent evangelical leaders during the week of the South Carolina Primary.[12] But Media Research Center president Brent Bozell points out the double standard, wondering, "Who was Michelle Obama sleeping with before Barack Obama? If you think that's an outrageous question — and I'd agree — then why did reporters ask it about Mrs. Santorum?"[13]

The media criticized both Rick Perry and Michele Bachmann for their relationships with some members of the New Apostolic Reformation movement. These Christians believe in what is known as Dominion theology, which, in a nutshell, "states that biblical Christianity will rule all areas of society, personal and corporate.... Those who hold these views believe that it is the duty of Christians to create a world-wide kingdom patterned after the Mosaic Law."[14] The *Texas Observer* magazine went with the headline "Rick Perry's Army of God" with the sub headline: "A little-known movement of radical Christians and self-proclaimed prophets wants to infiltrate government, and Rick Perry might be their man."[15] *The Daily Beast* website, read religiously (excuse the pun) by members of the mainstream media, likened Dominionism to other radical ideas. "Think of it like political Islamism, which shapes the activism of a number of antagonistic fundamentalist movements, from Sunni Wahabis in the Arab world to Shiite fundamentalists in Iran," writes Michelle Goldberg of *The Daily Beast*.[16]

Most evangelical Christians do not subscribe to Dominionism, let alone have ever heard of it. While it's legitimate to inquire whether Rick Perry or Michele Bachmann hold these views, neither ever claimed to adhere to this theory, yet that didn't stop the media from running stories asserting that they may be "Dominionists." These stories (and others like them) perpetuate the tired old "evangelicals are strange" stereotype. Not only that, but as religion writer Lisa Miller from the *Washington Post* points out, the media's "echo-chamber effect reignites old anxieties among liberals about evangelical Christians. Some on the left seem suspicious that a firm belief in Jesus equals a desire to take over the world."[17]

Perhaps there is no bigger division between evangelicals and the liberal media than over the issue of homosexuality. Overall, the liberal media sees nothing wrong in it, so you can imagine the hoopla when ABC News did a story about the use of reparative therapy at the Christian clinic owned by Michele and Marcus Bachmann. Reparative therapy is a therapy designed to convert gays back to heterosexuality through prayer and a therapeutic clinical process. ABC used undercover video shot by a gay rights advocacy group[18] and titled their story: "Michele Bachmann Clinic: Where You Can Pray Away the Gay?"

The ABC story comes across as bias on a number of levels. Everyone interviewed by ABC in the piece supported the pro-homosexual viewpoint. In fact, the network interviewed Clinton Anderson, a doctor with the American Psychological Association who concluded that efforts to change someone from gay to straight just can't be successful. The respected APA. Sounds legitimate, right? Well, actually, ABC never mentions that Dr. Anderson's full title is "Director of the Lesbian, Gay, Bisexual, and Transgender Concerns Office"[19] and that his professional biography lists a bunch of pro-homosexual legislation that he has pursued during his career. ABC News left that part out.

Reporter Brian Ross and the ABC crew never even came close to giving the evangelical response in their story. They could have quoted the conservative Christian group Exodus International, which believes that reparative therapy is but one potential tool in the process of getting people to break the bondage of homosexuality. Ultimately, the group says, the conclusion to leave homosexuality has to do with a relationship with Jesus Christ, a belief evangelicals understand, but that the media just doesn't get.[20]

The issue of homosexuality came up yet again, this time at an ABC News Republican presidential debate. But when Newt Gingrich was asked a question about gay rights, he characteristically used it as an opportunity to ridicule the media and defend Judeo-Christian principles. "I just want to raise a point about the news media bias. You don't hear the opposite question asked. Should the Catholic Church be forced to close its adoption services in Massachusetts because it won't accept gay couples?... The bigotry question goes both ways, and there's a lot more anti-Christian bigotry today than there is concerning the other side, and none of it gets covered by the liberal media."[21] Gingrich tapped into the sentiment of conservative evangelicals all across the country, and that's one reason he did well with this group of voters during the 2012 presidential race.

The inherent problem with the media isn't just how they cover certain stories, it's also about the stories they *don't* cover. For example, the Institute for Jewish and Community Research released a major study finding that a whopping 53 percent of college professors and faculty "hold unfavorable views of evangelical Christians." Yet only the *Washington Post* reported the story out of all the major mainstream media outlets in the country.[22] Why is that exactly? The best guess is that members of the mainstream media either don't find the story very interesting (who cares about bias against evangelicals) or they don't consider it newsworthy, since it isn't necessarily shocking that there is a bias against conservative Christians on college campuses in America. But either way, isn't bias against any religion a story? There are plenty of stories in the media about bias against peace-loving Muslims, but conservative Christians feel they are always getting the short end of the stick.

Beware of the Extreme, Violent, and Hostage-Taking Tea Party!

Whereas evangelicals have been dealing with media bias for decades, the Tea Party has only had to deal with the liberal media slant for just a few years since their inception in 2009. But as we lay out below, the media's attitude toward the Tea Party movement has been downright nasty at times.

Both the press corps and liberal politicians are determined to paint a picture of an angry, violent political movement. Headlines scream about "The Tea Party Taliban"[23] and "The Tea Party's Terrorist Tactics."[24] Vice President Joe Biden declared that the Tea Party has "acted like terrorists," and Rep. Mike Doyle of Pennsylvania exclaimed, "We have negotiated with terrorists!"[25] When the debt ceiling crisis was the big talk on Capitol Hill, Senator Robert Menendez came up with this ditty: "For weeks this Congress has been held hostage by a radical few, a band of Tea Party tyrants."[26]

There's no doubt that Tea Party members have not learned the art of compromise, and as the movement moves forward Tea Party congressmen are either going to have to grow their legislative majority so they can call the shots or figure out a way to compromise without sacrificing their principles. That said, the language used by liberal media publications and politicians makes the movement look like they are completely insane, which is utterly fictitious.

There's data to back up the claim that the media loves to play the extreme card when it comes to the Tea Party. In the two months before the 2010 midterm elections, the Media Research Center looked at the big three network evening newscasts (ABC, NBC, and CBS) and found that thirty-five stories labeled the Tea Party candidate running for office as either extreme, fringe, or out of the mainstream. Conversely, during that same period there wasn't a single story labeling Democratic candidates out of the mainstream. Digging deeper, two Tea Party candidates at the time (Christine O'Donnell and Joe Miller) were labeled by the networks as "ultraconservative." However, not one Democrat running for office was described as "ultra-liberal."[27]

If you think about it, it makes sense that liberal media members would consider O'Donnell and Miller ultra-conservatives, because when you hang out with other liberals all the time the two of them probably seem that way. This is a good example of how a media member's worldview creeps into their storytelling. While some in the media may portray conservatives in a negative light on purpose, many of them actually do it out of pure ignorance. Believe me, this is also done on the conservative side too, but it's no wonder Tea Party members have no desire to watch or listen to what they consider a biased approach from people who have no clue about the movement or the people inside of it.

The Tea Party Versus Liberal Groups

When the media is not ridiculing the Tea Party, it's choosing to ignore it. Once again, the Media Research Center painstakingly tracked down every mention of the Tea Party in the big three networks' morning and evening news shows starting from when the Tea Party first began to form (February 2009) through March of 2010. Astonishingly, during 2009 there were only nineteen stories devoted entirely to the Tea Party. Compare that to Louis Farrakhan's 1995 "Million Man March," when the networks ran twenty-one stories on the event in just one evening set of newscasts! The "Million Mom March," held in 2000 to promote tougher gun restrictions, received forty-one reports during a twenty-four hour period.[28] Double standard? Sure.

Think of it this way. As a Tea Party member, would you pay more attention to a Ron Paul event or a Harry Reid event? Exactly. You will give more consideration to something you're familiar with or are excited about. That same mentality exists within the media structure. Of course, that goes both ways. Conservative media outlets will tend to concentrate on conservative issues and causes. Because the mainstream media is extremely liberal, Tea Party members and evangelicals have no choice but to find their interests represented in other media outlets.

Occupy Wall Street Versus The Tea Party

Clearly the best example of media bias against the Tea Party comes in the form of how the mainstream media treated the Occupy Wall Street (OWS) protesters movement. While the Tea Party was painted as extreme, the OWS crowd was seen by the media (at least at first) as fighting a worthy cause.

The Occupy Wall Street protesters began gathering in a New York City park in September 2011 to express their anger and frustration about corporate greed and economic inequality in America. Yet in just the first few weeks of the movement there were clashes with police and arrests, not to mention the fact that the park became a sanitary hazard because protesters pitched their tents and stayed put so the park couldn't be cleaned. In addition, their protest took place on private property, which is not allowed in the first place, but the owners didn't make waves until things got out of control later on.[29]

Despite all of these problems, the media was doing a liberal coronation dance. CBS News correspondent Bigad Shaban called the protest a "self-operating mini-community, with a complimentary breakfast buffet of fresh fruits and bagels."[30] *USA Today* called it a "carnival atmosphere."[31] Not to be outdone, the *New York Times* called the OWS folks "a noble but fractured and airy movement of rightly frustrated young people."[32] My favorite one, though, is from the *Washington Post*, which observed that the events at the park "had the feeling of a street fair, with women in brightly colored wigs playing with hula hoops."[33] Doesn't it all sound so lovely? Makes you want to take the kids down there for an afternoon outing of fun and games, doesn't it?

The problem with this New York City "street fair" was that fresh fruit and bagels weren't the only things being served. Drugs and free love were being dished out too,[34] not to mention raw hatred for America and anti-Jewish rage. My CBN colleague Paul Strand saw both of those firsthand when he ran into self-identified Communists who burned a dollar and then stomped on the American flag. They exclaimed that the American flag "represents true evil for me." Another guy told Strand that the Jews were to blame for the financial crisis. "The Zionists are unscrupulous in their ways, unsavory. They commit more white collar crimes in America than any other ethnic, religious group."[35] Nice street fair. Respected pollster Doug Schoen polled the OWS crowd and concluded that the movement "reflects values that are dangerously out of touch with the broad mass of the American people.... The protesters have a distinct ideology and are bound by a deep commitment to radical left-wing policies."[36]

There's no need to go into the full history of the Occupy Wall Street movement, but it should be noted that these "street fairs" soon spread to other cities, and so did the violent clashes with police, arrests, sexual assaults, drugs, and a whole lot more. As time went on it was also discovered that some in the media were also giving advice to some of the OWS leaders regarding tactics and messages. The conservative *Big Journalism* website found emails from MSNBC Host Dylan Ratigan to OWS organizers, one of which mentioned an upcoming meeting Ratigan was going to have with Senator Richard Durbin about the movement. Ratigan's email states, "Are there grievances you have that I can express to him?"[37] This is from a guy who, when broadcasting on MSNBC from the OWS protest site, exclaimed, "I love what you're doing."[38] I guess the Tea Party shouldn't be surprised at the cheerleading, but it's just another incentive to go find alternative programming.

Perhaps Congressman Lamar Smith sums it up the best. The congressman from Texas, who also founded the Media Fairness

Caucus on Capitol Hill, succinctly states, "During the Tea Party's peak, the media seemed to inflame the rhetoric and acted as if the Tea Party movement was about to toss America into revolutionary violence.... Why have the mainstream media vilified the peaceful Tea Party all the while praising and celebrating Occupy Wall Street.... Our national media should be held accountable for their performance, just like any other institution. We need to remind the media of their profound obligation to provide the American people with the facts, rather than tell them what to think. The Occupy Wall Street and Tea Party movements may both have legitimate grievances with our country, but distorting their images does not move us towards positive solutions."[39]

Teavangelical Media Choices

Now that we've detailed just a small sampling of the bias directed at the Tea Party and evangelicals, you can see why these groups have decided to look elsewhere for a more balanced point of view and one that is more sympathetic to their worldview. Just like liberals gravitate to places like MSNBC, Teavangelicals have mapped out their own media sources across various platforms. Since there are too many media sources to list, we've decided to highlight some of the major ones (in no particular order).

Television

Fox News Channel

It won't come as a shock to you that the Fox News Channel is a magnet for conservatives. That means Tea Party members and evangelicals make watching the network a regular habit. The Pew Research quantitatively confirmed this in a recent study that concluded, "Republican voters, Tea Party supporters, and conservatives are much more likely than Democratic voters, liberals, and those who do not support the Tea Party to get political or campaign news from Fox News Channel."[40] A CBS–*New York Times* poll showed that 63 percent of Tea Party members get their news from Fox compared to just 23 percent of Americans overall.[41]

Fox News had skin in the game early since they started trumpeting the first ever Tea Party rallies six weeks before other media outlets. A week before the April 15, 2009, rallies, hosts Sean Hannity and Glenn Beck were encouraging people to show up at the rallies. Anchors Megyn Kelly and Bill Hemmer directed viewers to the Fox News website to find out the latest Tea Party events. On the actual big day of April 15, Fox News hosts Greta Van Susteren, Neil Cavuto, Sean Hannity, and Glenn Beck all anchored their shows from Tea Party events around the country.[42]

However, a warning note about Fox News. The network's embrace of the Tea Party has scaled back since the 2010 midterm elections. Roger Ailes, the president of the Fox News Channel, has made a deliberate attempt to tone down some of the conservative rhetoric, especially since the shooting of Congresswoman Gabrielle Giffords, which some say was motivated by the gunman's right-wing political philosophy. While the majority of Teavangelicals still tune in to Fox News, at the network itself there seems to be a slow shift away from rabid coverage of the Tea Party. These days CNN is just as likely to cover Tea Party stories, so this television-viewing trend bears watching.

GBTV: Glenn Beck: The Empire Strikes Back

I was soaking wet and I just wanted to get out of the rain. That's what happens when you walk nearly two miles through the streets of Manhattan in a steady rain. At least it was for a good reason. I was on my way to interview media superstar Glenn Beck.

Beck is one of the most important media figures in America.

The bulk of the Tea Party listens intently to his constitutionally based words and agrees with a majority of what he has to say. His highly rated radio show is heard on four hundred stations across America by millions of people, but it is his new venture called GBTV (Glenn Beck TV) that plans to shake up this country and change old media paradigms.[43] Not only does GBTV feature Beck's two-hour daily show, it also provides insightful news documentaries and other original programming ready to be swallowed up by a rabid Teavangelical audience.

Of course, Beck's in-your-face message is not received well by liberals. The hate for him is palpable, so security is tight. When we showed up at his office we were escorted down to what can only be described as one of those secret underground complexes you might see in the television series *Get Smart*. After weaving through a couple of hallways, we made our way to the entrance. As we entered the studio filled with neon lights and Founding Fathers memorabilia, I remember thinking, "Wow, this looks like a constitutional pinball machine!"

Glenn Beck is a hugger, and after my interview with him I got the full treatment. It makes sense once you get to know him because his genuine passion for this country manifests itself in many ways. But while his personality was friendly, his words were sobering. "Where the Tea Party is going I don't know, but what I would warn the Tea Party is you are friendless. You are friendless in the halls of power. You are friendless in the halls of media," Beck told me. It's that mindset in part that led Beck to create an alternative venue where individuals can get informed about the history of America, the problems the country faces, and the solutions that are available.

Beck especially wants to make the viewer get off the couch and become engaged in getting this country back to sacred Judeo-Christian principles. He calls his GBTV Network a "verb." "For people who want to change the world, gather to spread the word.

Let me be an Aaron to your Moses. Please. Please. I built this to be able to have the voice go out. Not my voice ... I have very little to say. Others have done all the work. Let me hold up their arms. Let's mobilize people ... the time for action is now. We live in historic times. God will not hold us blameless. He won't. He won't. I'm going out swinging, man!"

He tried doing his shout-from-the-rooftops message at Fox News, and though the ratings were through the roof it eventually didn't quite work out. During his time there, Beck held his "Restoring Honor" rally on the National Mall in Washington, DC, which was attended by hundreds of thousands of people, but the line between his role as Fox News host and citizen activist became blurred. "Fox didn't cover [the rally] when I was in Washington. That was the network that didn't cover it," Beck explains. "Expected it from CNN, expected it from MSNBC, but Fox was uncomfortable with anybody who was going to be an activist like that."

Ultimately Beck left Fox and GBTV was born. He finally realized that trying to change the media monster from the inside wasn't going to be possible so he had to try something new. "We're sitting here at a time now where the people are waking up, and the media has slowly let us go to sleep and put us to sleep. Those days are over. I started my own network because it's over. It's over. Those titans are going to fall," Beck told me. "I tried both Fox and CNN. I've been around. I've seen them. I've been in radio for thirty-five years. I really had this stupid belief that you could tell the truth and back it with facts. Not your facts, not your opinion, not just words, but video of them saying it, and the media would wake up and say, 'Oh, I hadn't seen that video. I didn't see the video of him saying that very thing.' Doesn't matter to them. They've so disconnected from the truth."

The way Beck sees it, people have to go somewhere to find the truth, and he's ready to be that vessel. In his attempt to help people and save the culture in the process, Beck isn't going to go down without a fight. "I've got all my chips on the table. I'm in. I'm in. Will you join me?"

Radio

Rush Limbaugh

He is known simply as "Rush" or "El Rushbo," but you could easily just call him the king of talk radio. Between fifteen and twenty million people hear Rush Limbaugh's national show every week,[44] and it has been the number-one commercial talk-radio show in the country for twenty-plus years. But Rush's true power lies in the fact that when he speaks, the mainstream media listens. It's not often that liberal elites take their cue from a conservative figure, but Limbaugh's popularity and ability to define the conservative conversation in America have made him unquestionably unique.

Limbaugh often speaks about the Tea Party, describing it as a movement that is trying to positively reshape the Republican Party. "The establishment Republicans are trying to take the Tea Party out," Limbaugh laments.[45] "The Republican Party is hell-bent on making sure that the Tea Party does not conquer this party and end up controlling it or running it."[46] His audience loves this bravado, and Rush's demographics prove it. Seventy-six percent of Tea Party supporters say they listen to Limbaugh, and that 76 percent number is the same for conservative Christians too. In his listening audience Limbaugh has an ideal Teavangelical mix.[47]

Sometimes, however, Limbaugh's bravado can land him in hot water. In February 2012, he called Georgetown law student Sandra Fluke a "slut" and a "prostitute" after her congressional testimony in support of contraceptives becoming mandatory in private health-insurance coverage. Limbaugh apologized for the comments but a handful of companies still pulled their advertising from the show.

Rather than arguing the merits of the contraception issue here, the concern from a media perspective is that sometimes conservative radio hosts can be over the top with their rhetoric. Some Teavangelicals may not care about what Limbaugh said, but if you're trying to win the argument on the substance of an issue and ultimately bring more people in line with your views, the wrong choice of words can hurt your overall argument. The trick for conservative talk-show hosts is to be passionate in their beliefs without diluting their power by giving the mainstream media fodder to pursue controversial comments.

Sean Hannity

Fox News host and radio talk-show host Sean Hannity is fond of saying, "You're a great American!" Well, Teavangelicals feel the same way about him. Hannity rivals Limbaugh's audience, and along with "El Rushbo" he has become a must listen for Teavangelicals.

Sean Hannity regularly has Tea Party newsmakers and leading evangelical figures on his radio show, but one thing that sets Hannity apart is that he wears his Catholic faith on his sleeve and enjoys talking about issues of faith. That makes sense since nearly 80 percent of his audience say they're conservative Christians.[48] Hannity can't stand when liberals try to beat up conservatives Christians. On one show Hannity was frustrated with media reports that Democrats were planning to compare evangelicals to the Taliban. This set Hannity off. "You can't compare mainstream Christian conservatives with the Taliban. You can't make that comparison. It doesn't fit.... There's a level of hatred toward Christian conservatives that I think is at the root of this."[49]

Mark Levin

There are plenty of radio talk-show hosts in broadcasting, but Mark Levin is a radio talk-show host in name only. The fact that his national show is listened to by eight and a half million people a week is a nice feather in his cap, but his true power lies in the fact that he's an idea factory, and those ideas have given increased philosophical lift to the Tea Party movement.

Levin will be the first one to admit that his ideas are not new, but his book *Liberty and Tyranny: A Conservative Manifesto* has sold over 1.3 million copies. Levin is a lawyer by trade and is also president of the Landmark Legal Foundation, which advocates for constitutionally based Judeo-Christian principles. He also served in President Ronald Reagan's administration and was chief of staff for Attorney General Edwin Meese. Those qualifications give him immediate "street cred" with the Tea Party and many evangelicals.

His book *Liberty and Tyranny* pits a titanic battle between the conservative and the statist, who Levin defines as the liberal who wants to control people through an all-powerful central government. Levin lays out the case why this would be disastrous for America and how this was not what the founders intended. He calls on Americans to get heavily involved in public matters and says it "will require a new generation of conservative activists larger in number, shrewder, and more articulate than before, who seek to blunt the statist's counterrevolution — not imitate it — and gradually and steadily reverse course."[50]

The Tea Party has apparently heeded his call. It's not unusual to see members of the movement at town hall meetings and rallies with his book in hand. Sarah Palin has been photographed with the book at certain events,[51] and Tea Party favorite Michele Bachmann has talked about how Levin's book is "providing [the] intellectual balance and foundation" for the Tea Party.[52]

Levin's latest book, *Ameritopia*, is also expected to be a hit with Teavengelicals. Levin traces the history of liberal utopianism, in which powerful individuals see themselves as wiser than regular people. Levin sees President Obama as someone who thinks his way is superior, and if people would just get out of the way then he and his allies could put together a perfect society. Levin thinks Obama and most of the mainstream media are elite utopians. His charge to his radio audience is simple. "You have to view yourselves as the Paul and Paulette Reveres of this nation. The media's not going to do it. Certain politicians aren't going to do it. One election's not going to do it. We have to save ourselves from this utopian tyranny."[53]

Internet

Drudge Report

Simply put, the *Drudge Report* is one of the most trafficked websites in the entire country. For example, on one day in February the site received thirty-one million hits. In the month of January it was over nine hundred million. And for the year? Are you sitting down (I guess most people don't stand and read)? More than ten *billion* paid a visit to Drudge.[54]

With his conservative slant, site creator Matt Drudge has become the Internet fly zapper for Tea Party members since they behave like flies that are attracted to pro–Tea Party headlines. Drudge either draws attention to the movement's happenings or points out how they are under attack. Headlines like "Waitress Fired from Outback Steakhouse for Wearing Tea Party Bracelet" and "Academics Dub Tea Partyers Devout, Racist"[55] provide a deft touch of stirring the pot. It's the Drudge way, and it has been extremely successful. Historian Tim Stanley got it right when he said: "Feeling that they are unable to get a fair hearing on TV, the Tea Party has placed greater and greater faith in Web-based reportage like Drudge's."[56]

Newsmax

If there was ever going to be a quintessential Teavangelical media website, *Newsmax* may indeed be it. Founded in 1998 by Christopher Ruddy, the website and its companion magazine are loaded up with frequent articles centered on the Tea Party and matters of faith. Cover stories like "Tea Party Power"[57] and "Jesus: Will He Return?"[58] go into great detail about issues Teavangelicals care deeply about. This strategy has reaped major dividends for Ruddy and his crew down in their West Palm Beach, Florida, headquarters. In 2010 revenues increased by roughly eighteen million dollars,[59] and in 2011 their web traffic increased 247 percent.[60] Their companion magazine has wider home distribution than the *Weekly Standard* and *National Review*, considered two of the top conservative magazines in the country.[61] But these statistics tell only part of the story.

Teavangelical political figures like Sarah Palin, Michele Bachmann, and many others have made pilgrimages to *Newsmax* headquarters. They understand that Ruddy's audience is an extremely important one for them to reach. Yet there's another political tie-in. *Newsmax* allows political campaigns to rent out their subscriber list. They will drop special messages from the campaigns into a subscriber's inbox, and then they have the choice of whether or not they want to click on it to donate. This system works for both parties involved, because *Newsmax* collects a fee, and political campaigns have a much better chance of collecting new donors. After all, *Newsmax*'s subscriber list is more than three million strong.[62]

RedState

If you are a politically astute conservative then you know all about *RedState*. The Tea Party–leaning blog has been around since 2004 and has turned into a grassroots powerhouse in the conservative world. Its managing editor is Erick Erickson. His daily "Morning Briefing" email, sent to tens of thousands of conservative activists around the country, often defines the conversation on the Internet and other media outlets. The *Washington Post* writes, "The ability of a single email to shape a message illustrates the power of the conservative network—loosely affiliated blogs, radio hosts, 'tea-party' organizers and DC institutions that are binding together to fuel opposition to President Obama and sometimes, to Republicans."[63]

These emails by Erickson are sort of like a trifecta in that many times they rile up an audience that doesn't care too much for Obama while at the same time hitting both fiscal and social issues. This is a major draw for Teavangelicals. A good example of this is when he called out the president for misusing Scripture to defend a tax increase on the rich and for forcing Catholic hospitals and universities to provide contraception services. Erickson concludes, "Barack Obama has gone to war with Christians' consciences, and he is perverting God's word in the process to get his way on public policy."[64]

This is a good illustration of *RedState*'s dual purpose. Because the blog weaves fiscal and social issues together, it's able to spread the Teavangelical message. In addition, it is very active in bringing both Tea Party members and evangelicals into the fold with grassroots organizing. Their annual "Red State Gatherings" feature Tea Party–backed speakers, but they also focus on training conservative grassroots activists to effect political change in their local communities. The goal is to make a serious difference at the ballot box in November of 2012 and beyond.[65] As *RedState* likes to proclaim, "We are conservatives in primaries and Republican in general elections, and we aim to win."[66]

Townhall.com

Similar to *RedState*, *Townhall.com* is a regular stop for Teavangelicals looking for conservative political commentary. A couple million people check out the site every month.[67] Not only does it feature more than a hundred top columnists from around the country, it also functions as a web community for conservatives. Teavangelicals can now arm themselves for battle by getting a one-stop shop of conservative blogs, podcasts, and links to the top radio talk-show hosts, including Bill Bennett, Mike Gallagher, Hugh Hewitt, Michael Medved, and Dennis Prager. All of these men talk extensively about both fiscal and social issues.

The *Townhall* network is vast. It started in 1995 as part of the Heritage Foundation, a conservative think tank based in Washington, DC. Ten years later it split off and was acquired by Salem Communications in 2006. In case you didn't know, Salem just happens to be one of the biggest media organizations focused on Christian content and conservative values.

FoxNews.com

Teavangelicals enjoy watching the Fox News Channel, but their website is just as potent. It's estimated that *FoxNews.com* brings in thirty-two million unique monthly visitors.[68] Web surfers find not only the normal hodgepodge of videos and articles there, but also a section of the site devoted to the Tea Party.[69]

Its power speaks for itself since it is linked with the Fox News Channel, but one interesting event may shed some light on how much of a threat the website really is to liberals. In the fall of 2011, anonymous hackers threatened to disrupt *FoxNews.com*. The threat was made because of the "continued propaganda" against the Occupy Wall Street protesters. The hackers said, "Since they will not stop ridiculing the occupiers, we will simply shut them down."[70] It never happened, and the popular conservative website keeps on humming along.

The Daily Caller

Relatively new to the scene, *The Daily Caller* is a 24-hour online news site cofounded by conservative commentator Tucker Carlson and Neil Patel, a former policy advisor to Vice President Dick Cheney. The site, which debuted in January of 2010, is chockfull of original reporting, and while it usually takes on a more conservative flavor, Carlson is quick to point out that when applying to *The Daily Caller*, potential employees are not asked about their political beliefs.

The site is known to run quite a few stinging articles about President Obama, however, and that's a major draw for the Tea Party. Opinion headlines like "What Does Obama Do All Day?"[71] or "Obama: Above the Fray or Above the Law?"[72] tickle the Tea Party pink (or maybe red is a better color). Carlson admits that this new venture was cooked up over a dinner conversation with Patel because they saw the media tripping over themselves with praise for President Obama. They wanted to change that, and after three million dollars in venture capital money, their dream became a reality. The Tea Party is forever thankful.[73]

As for what evangelicals get out of *The Daily Caller*, you'll see plenty of articles highlighting how conservative Christians are treated in society. It's not uncommon to see headlines like "Evangelicals Excluded from Washington National Cathedral's 9/11 commemoration."[74] *The Daily Caller* provides a nice mix for Teavangelicals to get their media fix.

Other Notables

We should mention that there are plenty of other news sources that Teavangelicals turn to, including biggies like Breitbart TV (run by the late conservative renegade Andrew Breitbart), Michelle Malkin's popular blog, *The Blaze* (part of Glenn Beck's empire), my own *CBNNews.com* (Christian Broadcasting Network), *The Jordan Sekulow Show* (where the host mentions Teavangelicals frequently), and *HotAir.com* (affiliated with the *Townhall* network).

The New Media Maze

One thing should be clear when it comes to Teavangelicals and the media: There is a new media maze out there now in which Teavangelicals have plenty of outlets to choose from. The maze has interconnectivity in that many of the Internet sites link to the radio shows and vice versa. The websites of all Teavangelical media have linkable ways to connect with other grassroots conservatives who are interested in political activism. In a way, it's one big happy (some might say dysfunctional) family. The history of liberal media bias has driven Teavangelicals to an insular community, and while critics might suggest a narrow world lends itself to narrow viewpoints, Teavangelicals (and the broader conservative community) don't really care. They're tired of latte-sipping media elites driving the conversation, so they're tuning out the old media and turning on the new media outlets — and loving every minute of it.

Chapter 9

WHERE DO TEAVANGELICALS GO *from* HERE?

A METEOR CRASH-LANDS IN PHOENIXVILLE, PENNSYLVANIA. AN older gentleman notices that it landed by his house and goes searching for it. He finds it and begins to poke around. But then all of a sudden a jellylike substance oozes out of the meteor and attacks him. Soon the whole town is under attack! Sometimes this substance lies low and doesn't reveal itself publicly, but sometimes it quietly makes its way under someone's door or completely engulfs people.

Scary, right? Well, not to worry. It's just a scenario from the 1958 science fiction horror movie called *The Blob*. But it illustrates a point as it relates to the future of the Teavangelical movement. As Tea Party favorite and Congressman Allen West told me, the Tea Party exhibits many of the same qualities.[1] "Just because you don't see it does not mean that it does not exist," Allen West explained to me. "It's kind of like the old Steve McQueen movie, *The Blob*. It can show up wherever it wants, it can generate energy, momentum, and then it can dissipate as quickly as it appeared." I'm sure liberals see this blob as a terrorizing force. Teavangelicals see it as a force to be reckoned with.

West nicely sums up what the Tea Party may indeed look like in the near future. Because it's such a new movement, evangelicals and Tea Party Libertarians are in the process of figuring out how to be most effective. For example, in case you hadn't noticed, you don't see big Tea Party rallies anymore, do you? This is part of the protean nature of the movement. "What we've seen is that people are working on a local and state level," Tea Party Express Chairwoman Amy Kremer told me. "People are engaged ... and we're going to come back together, and we're going to have sweeping victories in 2012."

But how do they get there? What are the challenges ahead for not just the Tea Party movement as a whole but specifically the Teavangelicals? How does the movement stay relevant and work to effect serious, long-lasting change? The birth of the Tea Party was fascinating to watch, but just as a baby grows, the Tea Party must do the same. It must mature and morph into a different state to survive. Below we list the five main challenges facing Teavangelicals that, if navigated effectively, will give them a great shot at transforming the political landscape in America for years to come.

Challenge #1: Making the Message Mainstream

Tea Party Libertarians and evangelicals face an immediate challenge: both these groups have an image problem among independent voters. And that's an issue considering the fact that 40 percent of voters now identify themselves as independent.[2] Now, there are two options here. Teavangelicals can insist they are right and not worry about how they come across to independents. Or they can put on their working boots and do their best to convince independent voters that the Tea Party message is actually mainstream and, more importantly, good for the country.

There's definitely some work to do with this group and the trend is not encouraging. In February 2010, 24 percent of independents viewed the Tea Party unfavorably. A year and a half later (August 2011), that unfavorable number was up to 41 percent.[3] Part of the problem is that the Tea Party, whether they like to hear it or not, has a reputation for being uncompromising. The Tea Party would say they are being principled, but independents don't see it that way.

Take the fight over the debt ceiling. Sixty-one percent of Independents thought the GOP should agree to raise taxes as part of the debt ceiling agreement. Nearly 60 percent of Tea Party supporters, however, said the Republicans shouldn't give in.[4] This is a wide disconnect and accounts for some of the unfavorable feelings among independents toward the Tea Party. The more the Tea Party digs in its heels, the less independents seem to like their act. Therefore, the Tea Party must do one of two things: either compromise on their principles during legislative fights (which does not seem likely), or find a way to convince independents that their way is best and rally public opinion to their side. There is no better legislative weapon than having the public behind you on an issue.

As a bridge to independents, the Tea Party might need to concentrate on racking up legislative victories in areas where independents agree with them. How about term limits for congressmen? Seventy-four percent of independents are in favor of them.[5] Or what about cutting spending except in defense, Medicare, or Social Security? Sixty percent of independents are for that.[6] What about pushing for a balanced budget amendment? It's not an easy process, but 68 percent of independents support doing it.[7] By achieving consensus and legislative victories, the Tea Party will be seen as a movement that can actually get laws passed, instead of just a gang of congressional gridlockers. That's a key part of the messaging.

Of course there are significant hurdles to overcome in reaching independents, but you have to start somewhere. Independents are there for the taking. Survey after survey shows that a majority of them are dissatisfied with the size of the federal government[8] and federal spending.[9] It's incumbent upon Teavangelicals, however, to not only explain these issues in a very straightforward, coherent way, but also break bread on some common ground issues so the messaging is one of positive bridge building rather than of uncompromising, ideological individuals.

Until then, though, the mainstream media will control the messaging of the Tea Party, and we all know how that will likely turn out. That's why Senator Rand Paul, a Tea Party favorite, believes that eventually it's going to take a multitude of grassroots groups to actually buy advertising to compete with the liberal media. "There has been a concerted effort since the Tea Party began to rise, since my victory, to paint us as something we are not. Until we buy advertising, the message is controlled by the other side."[10]

Challenge #2: The Extreme Makeover of Congress

Talk of courting independent voters and achieving legislative victories on Capitol Hill sounds all hunky dory, but I'm sure you're thinking, *Is this guy crazy? There's no way that's going to happen. Haven't you ever heard of congressional gridlock?* Ah, yes. Excellent point, and that is why another serious challenge for the Tea Party is to actually change the makeup of Capitol Hill. It's called strength in numbers. The Tea Party needs to give the Republican Party an extreme makeover, shifting it into a more constitutional conservative party. The task is large to say the least.

The midterm election in 2010 was definitely a good start. Eighty-seven Tea Party–backed lawmakers, many of whom were conservative Christians, joined the ranks of both the House and Senate. But right now the influence of the Tea Party is limited. They have begun to change the conversation in America and have increased pressure on GOP leadership to plot legislative strategy to cater to their demands. Those are great accomplishments, but legislative goals aren't being achieved yet.

The debt-ceiling vote is a perfect illustration. Boehner and his leadership team were reluctant to cut a deal unless they got support from the bulk of the Tea Party members. Concessions were made, but it wasn't what the Tea Party had in mind at all. So in the future if the Tea Party really wants to achieve legislative victories (rather than just receive a few concessions), they're going to have to change the numerical pie. Put another way, they're going to have to elect many more constitutional conservative Republicans. Eighty-seven was a nice start, but that's still only one-third of the party. The Tea Party claimed it's first House Republican victim of the 2012 race when veteran GOP Congresswoman Jeanne Schmidt of Ohio was defeated in the Republican primary by a Tea Party–backed candidate by the name of Brad Wenstrup. Schmidt voted for the debt ceiling, and Wenstrup pounced on that with backing from the Tea Party.

Despite this victory, there's no guarantee that new Tea Party members will actually stick together on votes. Not all the Tea Party freshmen stuck together, which simply complicates matters. Some actually voted for the debt ceiling increase, leaving some to question their cohesiveness. "We cannot have another experience like we've had in my freshman class, of people saying one thing and doing another," said Congressman Mick Mulvaney.[11]

As you can see, the challenge is twofold. Elect more constitutional conservatives, and then make sure they don't go off the reservation. There's a third element to this challenge too. Finding the right candidates. In 2010, the Tea Party got attention when Sharron Angle and Christine O'Donnell won primary contests in Nevada and Delaware by beating their more established moderate GOP counterparts. But they ultimately proved to be weak general-election candidates, unlike Senators Rand Paul and Marco Rubio, who were a notch above. That's the next step for the Tea Party. Finding the "notch above" candidates who can not only pull off a GOP primary victory but actually win the seat in the fall.

Of course, if you think powerful Teavangelical politicians and groups can agree on who the best candidate is, think again. Just have a look at the roadmap of the US Senate in the 2012 cycle. In the Texas Senate race, Senator Jim DeMint and the Tea Party Express are backing Ted Cruz in the Republican primary while Mike Huckabee is backing David Dewhurst. In Nebraska, the Tea Party Express and Mike Huckabee are backing Republican Jon Bruning while DeMint is backing Don Stenberg. This is not uncommon. When there are a couple Tea Party–leaning candidates you'll get discrepancies, but in the end it's all about getting the right (excuse the pun) legislator in place who will not sell out his or her Tea Party principles.

Challenge #3: Libertarians Versus Social Conservatives

Here is what we know for a fact: The Tea Party is made up of Americans who consider themselves either Libertarians or social conservatives. The split is roughly 60 percent social conservatives and 40 percent Libertarian.[12] Obviously these two groups disagree on the role the government should play in supporting traditional family values. Libertarians pretty much want government to stay out of the way on everything including social issues (drugs, abortion, gay marriage, prostitution, drugs, gambling, and so on). Social conservatives see the federal government's role as a more active one when it comes to defending traditional biblical values.

Let's take marriage, for example. Recently, a couple states have ruled that the Defense of Marriage Act (DOMA) is unconstitutional. DOMA was approved by Congress and signed into law by

President Clinton in 1996. It states that under federal law, marriage is defined as a legal union between one man and one woman. In addition, states don't need to recognize same-sex marriages from another state. A US District Judge in California ruled that DOMA violated the equal protection clause of the Constitution because health benefits were denied to the spouse of a same-sex couple. In addition, the Obama administration has refused to uphold DOMA and is working to get it repealed. It appears that ultimately the Supreme Court is going to have to weigh in on the constitutionality of DOMA.

Here's where it gets tricky for the Tea Party. Most pure Libertarians are against DOMA in the first place because they believe the federal government shouldn't be involved in defining relationships.[13] Polls also show that 71 percent of Libertarians believe homosexuality should be accepted by society.[14] So there will be a part of the Tea Party who not only disagree with DOMA to begin with but have no desire to make a big stink out of it. Conversely, with a Supreme Court fight over marriage on the horizon, you have the larger social-conservative contingent of the Tea Party who will most likely begin to clamor for a constitutional amendment defining marriage as between one man and one woman.

How are those social issues going to play with the Libertarians in the Tea Party, not to mention those who want to keep the movement's mission laser focused on fiscal issues and limited government? Will a potential rift like this tear the movement apart? The underlying question is this: When is it proper to call for an amendment to the US Constitution? And when does protecting the sanctity of marriage trump a Libertarian federalist approach? David Boaz, a Libertarian and executive vice president of the Cato Institute, believes that Tea Party Libertarians would push for a balanced budget amendment but *not* one on marriage. "I don't think there's likely to be a lot of social activism coming out of them," he said.[15]

So how do you preserve the integrity of the Tea Party's mission to pursue fiscal discipline while at the same time not abandon the marriage constitutionality fight? Well, we're soon to find out. Since this is a bottom-up movement, will social conservatives simply become so passionate about this that they will use the Tea Party platform to push their goals? Or will social conservatives use other avenues and socially conservative organizations to do this? We just don't know at this point. With a solid majority of social conservatives in the movement, it may just morph into a fight against DOMA on constitutional grounds despite what national Tea Party leaders want. Remember, the belief in Judeo-Christian principles is extremely strong within the Tea Party. The obvious route is for the DOMA fight to be separate from the Tea Party, but with a movement so young you can't predict how it will proceed on certain topics that have both a strong social component and a constitutional one too.

That is the challenge for evangelicals, but there is one for national Tea Party leaders too. While they recognize that the movement cannot be controlled by any one group or set of leaders, they also need to realize that they set the tone for the movement when they have an adverse reaction to any topic that may be construed as a social issue. The attempt to defund the pro-choice Planned Parenthood is a good example. National Tea Party leaders didn't want to touch that topic with a ten-foot pole despite the fact that it was tied in with the deficit and the budget. So the question is this: Can national Tea Party leaders—who began this movement talking about the country's debt and fidelity to the constitution— branch out a little and accommodate *some* issues with a social component? Will it really kill the movement just to speak out against the Planned Parenthood cuts?

Some leaders may be starting to get the message. Look at what happened with the controversy over President Obama's birth-control mandate. Originally the president announced that under his new health care plan even religious-affiliated universities and hospitals would be required to provide contraception coverage. Catholic bishops vehemently objected, and Obama modified it so that these religious institutions wouldn't have to directly finance the contraception coverage but their insurance companies would have to. That didn't leave many Catholic leaders satisfied. Complaints ranged from how this was another example of President Obama's government overreach to the fact that this was a constitutional infringement on Catholics' religious freedom.

Here's a perfect illustration of an issue that clearly has the appearance of a social issue yet goes to the underlying issue of constitutionality. Is this an issue the Tea Party can embrace despite the dreaded word *contraception?* Well, actually, some national Tea Party leaders are saying yes. Mark Meckler, who cofounded the Tea Party Patriots, says this issue will "invigorate the Tea Party" in 2012. "One of the fundamental tenets of the Tea Party is constitutionally limited government, and really they're intruding on the Constitution in the most fundamental way, they're intruding on the right to religious freedom," he said.[16] Meckler seems to get it. Imagine if the Tea Party championed this issue under their banner of adherence to the constitution? Their ranks would swell with even more evangelicals and Catholics too. Sometimes there are simply issues that transcend the divide. The contraception issue is one of those. It should be noted, however, that this debate got diluted when influential conservatives (like Rush Limbaugh and others) suggested that this issue is also about how liberals want taxpayers footing the bill for contraception coverage. While an argument can be made on both sides of this issue, it is the overreaching mandate by the Obama administration that has the cohesion to bring the Tea Party and evangelicals together. Sticking solely to a constitutional argument would be more effective in bringing both libertarians and social conservatives together. Think about this for a moment. If the Tea Party actually started embracing some select social issues (as long as they had a major constitutional component), they could become even more powerful. They might dilute the message slightly, but they potentially open up the movement to a wider array of concerned social conservatives. Will Libertarians jettison the movement because the Tea Party is now protesting over defunding Planned Parenthood or the constitutionality of President Obama's overreach on his original birth-control mandate? Don't Libertarians want the government to stay out of people's personal lives? If that's the case, then the federal government's payout to Planned Parenthood or encroaching on someone's religious liberty are doing exactly that, so why should issues like that be a problem in the first place?

It's true that the Tea Party can't be all things to all people. Too much dilution is bad for the movement. But if you think of the Tea Party as a glass of cold sweet tea, the fiscal issues are the main beverage, but the social conservative issues are the lemon perched on the side of the glass. They don't dominate the flavor of the beverage, but they give it some added zest to keep people coming back to drink more.

Challenge #4: Becoming One Big Happy Family

Here's a simple question: Who's plotting strategy for the Tea Party? The answer: Who knows? Sure, the national Tea Party groups work as a clearinghouse of sorts to help keep the trains running, and many local Tea Party groups are well organized. But ultimately there's just no way you can get a grassroots movement to walk in lockstep at all times. It's impossible.

We saw this during the 2012 presidential campaign. The Tea Party and evangelicals were split about whom to support. Most of them seemed to know that Romney wasn't their cup of tea, but even that assumption was up for debate. At one event in Concord,

New Hampshire, the Tea Party Express invited Romney to address supporters as part of their "Reclaiming America" bus tour. Supporters of FreedomWorks, however, another major Tea Party group who helped organize the tour, decided to protest the speech and pull out of the tour, citing blemishes in Romney's past conservative record. "If every political opportunist claiming to be a tea partier is accepted unconditionally, then the tea party brand loses all meaning," FreedomWorks leader Matt Kibbe declared.[17] Tea Party Express didn't take kindly to FreedomWorks's protest move and shot back, "It's just silly to protest a tea party where Governor Romney is speaking.... Narrow-mindedness is not the way to strengthen the tea party movement.... We view this move by FreedomWorks at best as a misguided press stunt and are disappointed at the disingenuous approach."[18] Sarah Palin warned both sides about the potential division within the movement. "We don't have time to be bogged down in internal conflicts."[19]

In the case of the Tea Party Patriots, there were some serious internal conflicts between Jenny Beth Martin and Mark Meckler, the two cofounders of the organization. In February 2012, Meckler resigned, citing how he had lost "influence in the leadership of the organization, and it has been that way for quite some time." He went on to say that he and Martin had been having disagreements since November 2011, "in which I was complaining about the direction, operation (top-down), and finances of the organization."[20] The whole situation is ironic considering the two of them had just coauthored a book together and were in the middle of a publicity tour!

Having disputes within organizations is nothing new, but it gives you an idea of the challenges the Tea Party faces within its own ranks. As the Tea Party grows and becomes more powerful, serious disputes will likely arise about philosophical direction and allocation of money. If these national Tea Party groups start to squabble more often and end up splintering rather than working together toward their commonly defined purpose, then the movement will come across as divided and unfocused. This is part of the problem of being a leaderless movement. You don't really have any firm structure in any one place.

In a way, the Tea Party movement wouldn't be a movement at all if it were run out of one central clearinghouse, but you do need some sense of unity to move forward. The purpose of the Tea Party has been well defined, but the mechanisms and strategies to get there haven't been ironed out yet. It's a work in progress. You can be sure the mainstream media will run with the leaderless, disorganization storyline above the fold in the *New York Times* and elsewhere for a long time. Any internal conflicts will be magnified, making excellent fodder for the 24/7 cable news shows. It's up to evangelicals and Tea Party Libertarians to change the narrative.

Challenge #5: Staying Visible with Victories

To stay relevant you need media attention. It's really that simple. The Tea Party received plenty of it when their national rallies attracted hundreds of thousands of people all over the country. Local television stations also covered many of the city and state rallies. But getting media attention requires victories. The 2010 midterm elections were a big start, but that is now history and so are the rallies. While there may be big rallies in the future (watch out for Herman Cain in this area, he is cooking up some ideas), for the most part Teavangelicals are intent on making their mark in their own states, cities, and local communities. Trying to get on the same page backing a presidential candidate has proven difficult, so victories will be more attainable by finding suitable candidates to run for the US Senate and House. But it goes deeper than that. The true power of the Tea Party may rest in its ability to effect systematic change within its own communities.

Let's look around the country for a moment. This is just a small sampling of what's taking place. In Texas, they are already pretty well organized at the statehouse in Austin with a vibrant Tea Party caucus. The chairman is Senator Dan Patrick from Houston, and guess what? He's a Teavangelical! He calls himself "a Christian first, a conservative second, and a Republican third" and has even written a book encouraging people to read the Bible.[21] As leader of the Tea Party caucus in the state legislature, he helps pass legislation that is recommended from an advisory board made up of Tea Party citizens. So far the success rate has been pretty good. Their victories included a much-sought-after voter-identification bill and preventing Republican lawmakers from using money from the Rainy Day Fund. Instead deeper budget cuts were made.[22]

In Kentucky, Tea Party activists helped convince lawmakers in the state senate to pass a bill that would set a limit on the state's debt.[23] The sponsor of the bill was senator Joe Bowen, who also helped sponsored a bill that would make sure Bible classes were part of the curriculum in public schools.[24] That's a Teavangelical two-step by Mr. Bowen.

In Florida, the Tea Party notched a big win when Governor Rick Scott decided not to accept two billion dollars in federal money to pay for a high-speed rail project that would have linked Tampa and Orlando. Some local Tea Party leaders met with Scott and explained to him that the project's defeat was their top priority.[25] In the Jacksonville, Florida, area the Peoples Tea Party made lots of noise and was able to convince the county school board to reject a nearly two-million-dollar teachers' contract that was just not affordable.[26]

How about Pennsylvania, where the York 9–12 Patriots group had a dozen members run for the local school board.[27] Or Wisconsin, where the Tea Party is mobilized and ready to fight the recall of Wisconsin Governor Scott Walker. Then there's the Tea Party group in Lockport, Illinois, who prevented the mayor from raising property taxes.[28] Shall I go on? You get the idea. Even the *New York Times* acknowledges the Tea Party's local emphasis. "They are showing up at planning meetings to denounce bike lanes on public streets and smart meters on home appliances—efforts they equate to a big-government blueprint against individual rights," the *Times* writes.[29]

If evangelicals and Tea Party Libertarians continue to rack up victories on the local and state level as well as get a solid majority in state houses, school boards, and on the board of county commissioners, then what you have is a serious ground game that will not only influence state issues and elections but national races too. It will probably also influence people's opinions of the Tea Party. Since the height of the midterm elections, multiple polls have shown how the Tea Party's favorability ratings have declined.[30] Part of the reason for that is the perception that the Tea Party is an uncompromising force at the national level, but a steady stream of local victories should produce more good will among Americans who may begin to see a Tea Party that affects positive change rather than just an uncompromising bunch bent on opposing everything under the sun. Tea Party members hope the ultimate result will be controlling the agenda and comprising the makeup of many of the state Republican parties. Nobody is saying it's going to be easy, but that's part of the plan. Change the game from within, and reap the political rewards.

Whatever the future holds for the Teavangelicals, we do know that they've already had success because they've steered the nation's conversation to that of fiscal restraint and constitutional responsibility. But that triumph is temporary. The Teavangelicals' ultimate accomplishment is an America where the federal government is minimized and Judeo-Christian principles are maximized. The outcome depends on confronting the five challenges listed in this chapter. Conquering just one or two won't cut it. But this is a process that will take time, measured not in months but years … many years. In the meantime, Teavangelicals will soldier on in their long, arduous task of fighting the problems of out-of-control spending, entrenched Beltway establishment protocol, and a liberal mainstream media who will do them no favors in championing their cause. But that's okay. Because Teavangelicals have their study Bibles, pocket constitutions, and most importantly, an Almighty God who has it all under control. And Teavangelicals wouldn't have it any other way.

Epilogue

A TEAVANGELICAL
UTOPIA:
MYTH *or* REALITY?

TAKE A WALK WITH ME, WON'T YOU? WE'RE GOING TO TRAVEL INTO the future and have a look at what a perfect Teavangelical world would look like. It takes quite a bit of imagination, but bear with me here for a moment. Let's have a little fun. What would it be like if Teavangelicals could snap their fingers and have their way? Close your eyes now ... you're getting sleepy ... very sleepy!

November 6, 2012: Barack Obama is defeated in the general election. He is sent packing, and his new mailing address is somewhere in Chicago, Illinois. The US House stays in Republican control and the Senate flips narrowly to the GOP side.

November 4, 2014: After working hard the previous two years to try and recruit constitutionally conservative candidates, Teavangelicals are able to increase their numbers slightly in both the US House and the Senate. They try and replace Republican Senate Majority Leader Mitch McConnell because he's part of the stuffy old GOP establishment, but he is barely reelected. Still, McConnell's close race leads to calls for a new Senate Majority Leader, and lo and behold, look who is elected: Teavangelical Jim DeMint.

November 8, 2016: After the successful repeal of Obamacare, the incumbent Republican president wins reelection and the number of constitutionally conservative members of the Senate and House continues to inch along. Liberal Michael Moore moves to Cuba to access their health care system. Congressman Paul Ryan is named Treasury Secretary. The Environmental Protection Agency and the Department of Education are eliminated. Local control now rests with individual states. A Tea Party candidate in the Alaska Primary defeats moderate Senate Republican Lisa Murkowski. That person goes on to win the general election seat. Senate *Minority* Leader Harry Reid, despite being in his mid-seventies, decides to run for office again but is defeated by a Tea Party candidate in the general election. Senate Majority Leader Jim DeMint holds true to his term limits promise and resigns from the Senate but is replaced by Senator Rand Paul, who has just finished winning his race for a second Senate term.

November 6, 2018: Teavangelicals continue to increase their majorities in the Senate and House. They are buoyed by the fact that during the last two years under the leadership of Rand Paul in the Senate and House Majority Whip Allen West, Congress passed a bill called the "You Need to Read the Constitution Act." It requires that each bill passed by both chambers must cite the provision in the Constitution that allows the bill to become the law of the land in the first place! Meanwhile, outside the beltway, Rick Perry and Sarah Palin establish a new national organization called "Teavangelical Central." (Maybe their motto could be "Shootin' straight from the hip.") It is a national think tank and resource center that helps fund local Tea Party groups for legislative battles in their home states, counties, and cities. Mike Huckabee is the group's national spokesman. Democratic Senator John Kerry decides not to seek reelection in 2020 and moves to Switzerland to start a windsurfing clinic for underprivileged Swiss children.

November 3, 2020: Powered by conservative Christians, the Tea Party, and a common sense Reaganesque message that appeals to independent voters, Indiana Governor Mike Pence becomes the president of the United States. He is sixty-one years old. His vice president is Marco Rubio. A major breakthrough takes place in Congress. Because of the vision and communication of the Pence/Rubio ticket, the down-ballot effect is tremendous, and the GOP now has close to a supermajority in both the House and Senate, which means they are very close to passing legislation without the help of the Democratic Party. On election night, MSNBC host Chris Matthews says, "I felt this thrill going up my leg, but I'm now in a lot of pain!"

November 1, 2022: The Teavangelicals finally get there. After adding a few more constitutional conservatives they now have their much-sought-after supermajority in both chambers of Congress. That Teavangelical congress goes on to pass a law that puts a cap on the growth of total federal spending. The Congress also abolishes the IRS with a new simpler, fairer tax system. Child tax credits are increased, and the "death tax" is killed for good. A new push begins to pass a Federal Marriage Amendment.

November 5, 2024: President Pence wins reelection in a landslide. Among his legislative priorities is a school-choice bill that allows parents to select the educational institutions that are best for their child. He also seeks to once and for all end federal funding for Planned Parenthood. Both bills become law, and MSNBC calls it quits.

November 3, 2026: House member Tim Scott, a Tea Party favorite, is elected by his peers to become the first African-American Speaker of the House in US history.

November 7 2028: Vice President Marco Rubio wins the presidency. He is fifty-seven years old. In his first year in office, with a supermajority of constitutional conservatives by his side, Congress passes a balanced budget amendment and it is sent to the states for ratification. It passes after forty of the fifty states approve it. Liberals around the country hold candlelight vigils mourning the America they once knew under President Obama, but George Soros becomes a Teavangelical!

Whew! My imagination really ran wild, didn't it? Let me do a quick disclaimer. Go ahead and substitute Sarah Palin, Chris Christie, or whomever you like in the presidential and vice presidential slots. What you see above is just some fun projections, but you get the idea. Plus, for all you naysayers who think I've gone batty, remember, it's a Teavangelical utopia! Anything is possible in that realm, but it will require a unique ability by all involved to make the message mainstream.

ACKNOWLEDGMENTS

I COULD PROBABLY WRITE AN ENTIRE BOOK OF ACKNOWLEDGMENTS when it comes to this project. There are simply so many people to thank, and paragraph upon paragraph could be written about each one of them, but let me try and sum it up as best I can.

My family has given new meaning to the word *sacrifice*. My wife, Lisette, has graciously run our household as I spent months either traveling around the country or at home sequestered in a room writing this book. She and my son Lance also came up with the initial concept for the cover! I'm so thankful for Lance's creativity and for his desire to see this book a success. My son Drew has been a great prayer warrior for me during this time, and my beautiful daughter, Arielle, has foregone quite a few play dates with Daddy during this process; yet she has been my biggest cheerleader. Her smile lifts me up every day. I want to also thank Titi Lissia for always giving me constant encouragement, especially after those long trips on the road. And to my extended family, a big thank you to Marina Wilson, whose cheerful demeanor always brightened up my day and to Inés Cardenas for all of her wonderful work on putting together the countless endnotes for this project.

To my mother, Annette Brody, I just want to say how much I appreciate your confidence in me and your active interest in this project from start to finish. Thanks for dealing with all the missed phone calls I should have returned sooner! My sister, Karen Brody, is an accomplished author and playwright herself, and her valuable advice about the business was extremely helpful. Love ya, KB! To my best friend, Ty—how did I go from those late-nights talks on the roof in NYC to here? Thanks for your steadfast support and unconditional love. Let me also just say a special word about the Mstowski family. This wonderful Christian family is a gift from God, and their constant curiosity and interest about this project showed just how special they are. I do want to give a special note of thanks to Michael Mstowski, a devoted Christian man and the main person who encouraged me to write this book and who wouldn't let go of his eagerness to see me get it done. I appreciate it more than you'll ever know.

To my coworkers, let me start by thanking my News Director at CBN, Rob Allman, who has always given me latitude to pursue my passions and the wings to fly; and our DC Bureau Chief, Robin Mazyck, has been extraordinarily helpful throughout this process as she gave me the flexibility to work at home when I needed to. She always did it with a smile on her face. I am forever indebted to her. She's a great friend and a magnificent woman of God; to my partner-in-crime on the road and utterly fabulous producer, Dana Ritter, who kept encouraging me and kept me smiling with her quick wit and a sparkling personality! The amount of time she spent transcribing newsmaker interviews were an enormous help to me, not to mention keeping me organized and focused on the road and in the DC Bureau. She's a godsend; to my great friend and colleague Erick Stakelbeck who has provided a steady stream of amazing advice and information along the way since he is an accomplished author himself. He helped me navigate the book industry, but more than that he took time out of his busy life to make sure I stayed on track. I'm proud to call him a colleague and even prouder to call him one of my best friends. Let me also say how much I appreciate the constant backing and phenomenal talents of reporters Jennifer Wishon, John Jessup, and Paul Strand, all of whom took a keen interest in this project. Let me also not forget the wonderful photojournalists who accompanied me on the road for so many of the newsmaker trips: Steve Jacobi, Royce Sallstrom, Tyler James, Jerome Young, Ian Rushing, Mark Bautista, David Page, Jacob Moore, and Matt Keedy. Also a big thank you to office secretary Tamatha Papadeas, whose organizational skills led to so many less headaches on my end. Thanks to all of you!

As for the outstanding team at Zondervan, what can I say? If there was a picture next to the words *professional* and *kind* in the dictionary all of your photos would appear. Thanks to my editors Sandra Vander Zicht and Bob Hudson who challenged me throughout the writing of this book. I now understand why they have such outstanding reputations. I am a better author because of them. A big thank you to Don Gates and Heather Adams along with the rest of the marketing team who were gracious and full of phenomenal ideas from the very beginning of this project. Thank you to publicist Sandy Schulz, who impeccably navigated me through the media maze. I really appreciate it Sandy! Thank you to Cindy Lambert, Julie Kemme, and Madeleine Hart for all their hard work and dedication in seeing this project through. But let me say a separate word about Verne Kenney. Simply put, it was Verne who originally saw the value in this book and brought it to the attention of Zondervan. I will always and forever be grateful to him for taking a chance on a first-time author. Verne, a sincere and heartfelt thank you!

Let me also acknowledge all of the wonderful people who helped shape the information and stories detailed in this book. So many of them gave up some of their precious time to see this project done well and accurately: so thank you to Ralph Reed, Gary Marx, Billy Kirkland, Tony Perkins, J. P. Duffy, Peter Waldren, Mark DeMoss,

Mark Rogers, John Brabender, Hogan Gidley, Rob Johnson, Mark Block, Rick Tyler, Penny Nance, David Barton, Jesse Benton, Sydney Hay, Doug Wead, Danita Kilcullen, Josh Kimbrell, Janne Myrdal, Bobbi Radeck, Luke Livingston, Colleen O'Boyle, Carrie Stoelting, Stacie Stoelting, Alex Conant, Kellen Giuda, David Lane, Jim Garlow, Gary Bauer, Herman Cain, Scott Spages, Bob Heckman, Sue Trombino, Mike Huckabee, Amy Kremer, Jenny Beth Martin, Keith Nahigian, Glenn Beck, Joel Cheatwood, and Bob Vander Plaats.

Finally, let me just say that the biggest thank you of all goes to the Lord Jesus Christ. He is my personal Savior, and not only did he save me spiritually in 1988 when I gave my life over to him, but I couldn't have written this book without him by my side. During the busyness of this election season, and with a tight deadline to turn this book out, there were so many times when I threw my hands up in the air and said, "Lord, I'm overwhelmed. I'm not sure how I'm going to do this—so please figure this out since I sure can't!" Lord, thank You for being a God who keeps his promises and loves me unconditionally. I am eternally grateful.

NOTES

A Note from the Author

1. Scott Clement and John C. Green, "The Tea Party, Religion and Social Issues." *Pew Research Center Publications:* pewresearch.org/pubs/1903/tea-party-movement-religion-social-issues-conservative-christian.

CHAPTER 1: The DNA of a Teavangelical

1. The Barna Group, LTD, "Survey Explores Who Qualifies as an Evangelical." *The Barna Group:* barna.org/barna-update/article/13-culture/111-survey-explores-who-qualifies-as-an-evangelical.

2. Tea Party Patriots, "Tea Party Patriots Mission Statement and Core Values." *Tea Party Patriots:* teapartypatriots.org/mission.aspx.

3. Scott Clement, "The Tea Party and Religion." *The Pew Forum on Religion and Public Life:* pewforum.org/Politics-and-Elections/Tea-Party-and-Religion.aspx.

4. Robert P. Jones and Daniel Cox, "Survey Religion and the Tea Party in the 2010 Elections." *Public Religion Research Institute:* publicreligion.org/site/wp-content/uploads/2010/05/Religion-and-the-Tea-Party-in-the-2010-Election-American-Values-Survey.pdf.

5. David Gibson, "Tea Party Is Much Like the Religious Right—Only More So, Survey Finds." *Politics Daily:* politicsdaily.com/2010/10/05/tea-party-is-much-like-the-religious-right-only-moreso-surve/.

6. Audrey Mullen and Dave Mohel, "Evangelical, Social Conservative Turnout Highest Ever Recorded in Mid-Term Election." *Christian News Wire:* christiannewswire.com/news/1660315402.html.

7. Pew Research Center for the People and the Press, "Beyond Red vs. Blue: The Political Typology." *Pew Research Center:* people-press.org/2011/05/04/beyond-red-vs-blue-the-political-typology/.

8. Pew Research Center, "Political Typology: Analyze Groups and Issues." *Pew Research Center:* people-press.org/typology/quiz/?pass&src=typologyreport.

9. Christian Talk Radio, "Christian Talk Radio/Contact Us." *Christian Talk:* christiantalk660.com/page/contact-us.

10. Administrator, "Santorum Blames 'Abortion Culture.'" *The Hill:* thehill.com/blogs/ballot-box/gop-presidential-primary/152441-santorum-says-abortion-culture-to-blame-for-problems-with-social-security.

11. Colby Itzkowitz, "Santorum Links Abortion to Social Security." *The Morning Call:* articles.mcall.com/2011-03-29/news/mc-santorum-abortion-social-security-0110329_1_randall-k-o-bannon-social-security-abortion.

12. The Pew Forum on Religion and Public Life, "Growing Number of Americans Say Obama is a Muslim." *Pew Research Center:* pewforum.org/uploadedFiles/Topics/Issues/Politics_and_Elections/growingnumber-full-report.pdf.

13. David E. Campbell, "Crashing the Tea Party." *New York Times:* nytimes.com/2011/08/17/opinion/crashing-the-tea-party.html?_r=1.

14. David Brody, "Tea Party's Scott: I'm Not 'The Black Republican.'" *CBN:* cbn.com/cbnnews/politics/2010/September/Tea-Partys-Tim-Scott-Im-Not-The-Black-Republican/.

15. Al and Tammy Roesch, "The Narrow Way Ministries/About Us." *The Narrow Way Ministries:* thenarrowwayministries.org/About.asp.

16. David Brody, "Fed Up Citizens 'GOOOH' for Capitol Hill." *CBN:* cbn.com/cbnnews/us/2010/March/Fed-Up-Citizens-GOOOH-for-Capitol-Hill/.

CHAPTER 2: Fast and Furious:
The Rise of the Tea Party

1. AFP News Wires, "Bush Says Sacrificed Free-Market Principles to Save Economy." *Breitbart:* breitbart.com/article.php?id=081216215816.8g97981o.

2. Web User, "Mail A Tea Bag To Congress & To Senate!" *Ticker Forums:* tickerforum.org/cgi-ticker/akcs-www?post=79282&page=1.

3. Assorted, "The Economic Crisis." *FedupUSA:* fedupusa.org/OldSite .html.

4. Ed Pilkington, "How the Tea Party Movement Began." *The Guardian:* guardian.co.uk/world/2010/oct/05/us-midterm-elections-2010-tea-party-movement/print.

5. Kate Zernike, "Unlikely Activist Who Got to the Tea Party Early." *New York Times:* nytimes.com/2010/02/28/us/politics/28keli.html.

6. Fox News, "Home Buyer Helper." *Fox News:* video.foxnews.com/v/ 3923712/homebuyer-helper.

7. Rick Santelli, "Rick Santelli: Tea Party." *Freedom Eden:* freedomeden .blogspot.com/2009/02/rick-santelli-tea-party.html.

8. Glenn Beck, "We Surround Them." *Glenn Beck:* glennbeck.com/content/ articles/article/198/21018/.

9. Liz Robbins, "Tax Day Is Met with Tea Parties." *New York Times:* nytimes .com/2009/04/16/us/politics/16taxday.html.

10. Herman Cain, "In Defense of American Exceptionalism." *The American Spectator:* spectator.org/archives/2011/03/03/in-defense-of-american-excepti#.

11. Paul Johnson, "The Capitalism & Morality Debate." *First Things:* firstthings.com/article/2007/08/003-the-capitalism--morality-debate--1.

12. Donald B. Billings, "The Moral Case for Competitive Capitalism." *The Freeman Ideas On Liberty:* thefreemanonline.org/columns/the-moral-case-for-competitive-capitalism/.

13. Kim Hart, "Netflix Streaming to Washington." *Politico:* politico.com/ index.html.

14. Greene Tea Patriot Members, "Tea Party Declaration." *Greene Tea Patriots:* greeneteapatriots.org/Editorials/Declaration.htm.

15. David Waters, "Will Christian Right Join the Tea Party?" *The Washington Post:* newsweek.washingtonpost.com/onfaith/undergod/2010/02/will_christian_right_join_the_tea_party.html.

16. Libertarian Party Members, "Platform." *Libertarian Party:* lp.org/ platform.

17. Jess Henig, "Czar Search." *FactCheck.org:* factcheck.org/2009/09/czar-search/.

18. Neil King Jr., "Role of White House Czars Sparks Battle." *The Wall Street Journal:* online.wsj.com/article/SB125261851127501015.html.

19. 3 Mike Dorning, "Barack Obama Administration's Czars: How Many Are There?" *Chicago Tribune:* chicagotribune.com/news/nationworld/chi-talk-czarsjun14,0,5035131.story.

20. Cindy Roberts, "AFA Calls for Resignation of Kevin Jennings, 'Safe and Drug Free Schools' Head." *American Family Association:* afa.net/Media/PressRelease.aspx?id=2147487137.

21. Bob Barr, "America Needs 'Surge' in Fiscal Responsibility, Says Bob Barr." *Libertarian Party:* lp.org/news/press-releases/america-needs-"surge"-in-fiscal-responsibility-says-bob-barr.

22. Rick Santorum, "Rick Santorum's New Radio Ad 'Courage to Fight for America.'" *Rick Santorum:* ricksantorum.com/news/2011/06/rick-santorums-new-radio-ad-courage-fight-america.

23. David Brody, "The Brody File." *Christian Broadcasting Network:* blogs.cbn.com/thebrodyfile/archive/2011/02/27/speaker-boehner-to-brody-file-americas-debt-is-moral-hazard.better.aspx.

24. Brian Riedl, "Federal Spending by the Numbers 2010." *The Heritage Foundation:* heritage.org/research/reports/2010/06/federal-spending-by-the-numbers-2010.

25. William Voegeli, "Paul Ryan's Roadmap." *The Claremont Institute:* claremont.org/publications/crb/id.1749/article_detail.asp.

26. Paul Ryan, "Congress of the United States." *Budget House:* budget.house.gov/UploadedFiles/RyanLetterToDolan4292011.pdf.

27. Rob Moll, "Scrooge Lives." *Christianity Today:* christianitytoday.com/ct/2008/december/10.24.html.

28. Devin Dwyer, "Planned Parenthood at Center of Budget Shutdown Threat." *ABC News:* abcnews.go.com/Politics/planned-parenthood-center-budget-shutdown-threat/story?id=13328750.

29. Jonathan Weisman, "Wealthy Face Tax Increase." *The Wall Street Journal:* online.wsj.com/article/SB10001424052748704107204575038733246595218.html.

30. Philip Klein, "Obama's Big Government Gamble." *The American Spectator:* spectator.org/archives/2009/04/17/obamas-big-government-gamble.

31. Americans for Tax Reform, "Comprehensive List of Tax Hikes in Obamacare." *Americans for Tax Reform:* atr.org/comprehensive-list-tax-hikes-obamacare-a5758.

32. Major Garrett, "Boehner Seeks to Close Tax-Hike Window That Norquist Opened." *National Journal:* nationaljournal.com/congress/boehner-seeks-to-close-tax-hike-window-that-norquist-opened-20110721.

33. Chuck Donovan and Patrick Fagan, "Taxes in the Stimulus Package and the New Congress." *Family Research Council:* frc.org/get.cfm?i=IS09A03.

34. Libertarian Party Members, "Libertarian Party 2010 Platform." *Libertarian Party:* lp.org/platform.

35. Robin Klay and John Lunn, "The Relationship of God's Providence to Market Economies and Economic Theory." *Journal of Markets & Morality:* homepage.univie.ac.at/charlotte.annerl/texte/smith8.pdf.

36. Paul Oslington, "Adam Smith, Economics and Christian Hope." *Religion and Ethics:* www.abc.net.au/religion/articles/2011/06/10/3240643.htm.

37. Mark Oppenheimer, "Christian Economics Meets the Antiunion Movement." *New York Times:* nytimes.com/2011/04/30/us/30beliefs.html?_r=1.

38. Gary North, "An Introduction to Christian Economics." *Gary North's Specific Answers:* garynorth.com/public/1033.cfm.

CHAPTER 3: Teavangelical Organizations and Leaders

1. Faith and Freedom Coalition, "See How Your Representative Scored." *Faith and Freedom Coalition:* ffcoalition.com/scorecard/.

2. Faith and Freedom Coalition, "Evangelicals Hit Record Voter Turn-Out." *Faith Report:* oregonfaithreport.com/2010/11/evangelicals-hit-record-voter-turn-out/.

3. Faith and Freedom Coalition, "Afternoon Breakout Sessions." *Faith and Freedom Coalition:* ffcoalition.com/wp-content/uploads/2011/05/breakout-schedule.pdf.

4. American Family Association, "Who Is AFA?" *American Family Association:* afa.net/Detail.aspx?id=31.

5. Liz Robbins, "Tax Day Is Met With Tea Parties." *New York Times:* nytimes.com/2009/04/16/us/politics/16taxday.html.

6. Nate Silver, "How Many Attended The Tea Parties?" *Five Thirty Eight:* fivethirtyeight.com/2009/04/how-many-attended-tea-parties.html.

7. American Family Association, "Obama's Budget Out of Control."

AFANET: web.archive.org/web/20090401134531/http://www.afa.net/alert_
teaparty4_20090323.html.

8. American Family Association, "Tell Us About Your Tea Party." *TeaPar-
tyDay:* web.archive.org/web/20090415224756/http://www.teapartyday.com/.

9. American Family Association, "Tell Us About Your Tea Party." *TeaPar-
tyDay:* web.archive.org/web/20090415224756/http://www.teapartyday.com/.

10. Benjamin Scafidi, "The Taxpayer Costs of Divorce and Unwed Child-
bearing." *American Values:* americanvalues.org/coff/executive_summary.pdf.

11. Family Research Council, "Tell Congress We Need to Be Serious
about Reducing the Debt." *FRC Action:* capwiz.com/frc/issues/alert/?alertid=
46719501.

12. Family Research Council, "Taxman Cometh: Stopping the Obama
Tax Hikes." *FRC Action:* frcaction.org/taxman.

13. Family Research Council, "Cut, Cap, Balance Webcast." *FRC Action:*
frcaction.org/cutcapbalance.

14. George Zornick, "How the Right-Wing Is Pushing the U.S. to the
Brink." *CBS News:* cbsnews.com/stories/2011/07/28/opinion/main20084965
.shtml.

15. Ken Blackwell, "Mike Gerson Gets the Tea Party Wrong." *Family
Research Council:* frc.org/op-eds/mike-gerson-gets-the-tea-party-wrong.

16. Tony Perkins, "A Tale of Two Tea Parties." *Family Research Council:*
frc.org/op-eds/a-tale-of-two-tea-parties.

17. Family Research Council, "Vote Scorecard — Full 110th Congress."
FRC Action: frcaction.org/get.cfm?i=VR08I01.

18. Russell Shorto, "How Christian Were the Founders?" *New York Times:*
nytimes.com/2010/02/14/magazine/14texbooks-t.html?pagewanted=print.

19. David Barton, "The Bible and Taxes." *WallBuilders:* wallbuilders.com/
LIBissuesArticles.asp?id=119.

20. Dr. Janice Shaw Crouse, "The 4.4 Trillion Dollar Man." *Concerned
Women for America:* cwalac.org/cwblog/?p=356.

21. AFP, "Spending Revolt Tour Coming to Florida." *Americans For Prosperity:* americansforprosperity.org/091710-spending-revolt-tour-coming-florida.

22. Values Voter Summit, "Schedule of Events." *Values Voter Summit:*
ncaabbs.com/showthread.php?tid=453231.

23. Ken Blackwell, "Have the Republicans Learned Their Lesson?" *Find Articles:* findarticles.com/p/articles/mi_hb3465/is_201007/ai_n54717140/pg_3/.

24. Tea Party Patriots, "About Tea Party Patriots." *Tea Party Patriots:* teaparty patriots.org/AboutUs.aspx.

25. Faith and Freedom Coalition, "2011 Faith & Freedom Conference and Strategy Briefing." *Faith and Freedom Coalition:* ffcoalition.com/wp-content/uploads/2011/05/Website-Agenda-v5.pdf.

26. Ralph Reed, "Ralph Reed at 2011 Tea Party Patriots Summit." *YouTube:* youtube.com/watch?v=Ju5RaoCEN7Y.

27. President Obama, "Remarks by the President at a DNC Finance Event in Austin, Texas." *The White House:* whitehouse.gov/the-press-office/2010/08/09/remarks-president-a-dnc-finance-event-austin-texas.

28. Felicia Sonmez, "Who Is 'Americans for Prosperity'?" *The Washington Post:* voices.washingtonpost.com/thefix/senate/who-is-americans-for-prosperit.html.

29. Americans for Prosperity, "About Americans for Prosperity." *Americans For Prosperity:* americansforprosperity.org/about.

30. Americans for Prosperity, "Tim Phillips." *Americans for Prosperity:* americansforprosperity.org/about/staff/tim-phillips.

31. Greg Keller, "Defending the American Dream Summit a Success." *Faith and Freedom Coalition:* ffcoalition.com/2010/04/03/defending-the-american-dream-summit-a-success/#.

32. Family Research Council, "Government Takeover of Healthcare: Counting the Cost." *FRC Action:* frcaction.org/events/government-takeover-of-healthcare-counting-the-costs.

33. David Weigel, "Tea Party Boot Camp." *Slate:* slate.com/id/2263422/.

34. FreedomWorks, "Matt Kibbe Biography." *FreedomWorks:* freedomworks.org/matt-kibbe-biography.

35. Michael Duncan, "Saturday: Policy and Media Training." *FreedomWorks:* freedomworks.org/blog/mduncan/saturday-policy-and-media-training.

36. FreedomWorks, "Connect with Activists." *FreedomWorks:* connect.freedomworks.org/node/22653.

CHAPTER 4: Teavangelical Rallies

1. *Cherokee Chronicle Times*, "Stoeltings Appear on 'Fox & Friends.'" *Chronicle Times*: chronicletimes.com/story/1760006.html.

2. "Tea Party Distinguished by Racial Views and Fear of the Future." *University of Arkansas*: uark.edu/rd_arsc/blairrockefellerpoll/5295.php3.

3. Adelle M. Banks, "Values Voters See Common Cause, If Not Agenda, with Tea Party." *Cross Walk*: crosswalk.com/news/values-voters-see-common-cause-if-not-agenda-with-tea-party-11638467.html.

4. Kerry Basinger, "Kerry Basinger Tea Party Prayer 2011." *YouTube*: youtube.com/watch?v=ltNBelcw9ko.

5. John Onstad, "Santa Fe NM, Tea Party Tax Day Rally 4-16-11 Prayer." *YouTube*: youtube.com/watch?v=J3idT0fgCCM.

6. David Brody, "The Brody File." *CBN*: blogs.cbn.com/thebrodyfile/archive/2010/04/21/senator-demint-to-brody-file-tea-party-movement-will-bring.aspx.

7. "The Texas Tea Party." *The Texas Tea Party*: texasteaparty.org/christian heritage.html.

8. Barbara Bradley Hagerty, "The Tea Party's Tension: Religion's Role in Politics." *NPR*: npr.org/templates/story/story.php?storyId=130238835.

9. blogs.denverpost.com/thespot/files/2010/04/IMG_2018.jpg.

10. talkingpointsmemo.com/assets_c/2010/09/teaparty-constitution-cropped-proto-custom_6.jpg.

11. images.politico.com/global/news/100730_teaparty_bible_ap_289.jpg.

12. o.aolcdn.com/photo-hub/news_gallery/6/8/686331/1284753127464 .JPEG.

13. Melinda Warner, "My Tea-Stained Weekend: An Evangelical Conservative Turned Progressive Goes to the Tea Party Convention." *Huff Post Politics*: huffingtonpost.com/melinda-warner/my-tea-stained-weekend-an_b_ 455810.html.

14. William and Selena Owens, "William and Selena Owens Inspire Many Tea Party Express Pat." *YouTube*: youtube.com/watch?v=L4-_O6OsAwY.

15. David Brody, "The Real Tea Party Housewives of Atlanta." *CBN*: http://www.cbn.com/cbnnews/politics/2011/June/The-Real-Tea-Party-Housewives-of-Atlanta-/.

16. "Tea Party Distinguished by Racial Views and Fear of the Future." *University Of Arkansas:* uark.edu/rd_arsc/blairrockefellerpoll/5295.php.

17. Brian Montopoli, "Poll: Most Tea Partiers Believe Too Much Made of Problems Facing Blacks." *CBS News:* cbsnews.com/8301-503544_162-20002538-503544.html.

18. Devin Burghart and Leonard Zeskind, "Tea Parties—Racism, Anti-Semitism and the Militia Impulse." *Institute For Research and Education On Human Rights:* irehr.org/issue-areas/tea-party-nationalism/the-report/tea-parties-racism-anti-semitism-and-the-militia-impulse.

19. David Holthouse, "'Fertile Ground': White Nationalists Organize Within Tea Party." *Media Matters For America:* mediamatters.org/blog/201108030016.

20. Krissah Thompson, "Some Black Conservatives Question Tea Party's Inclusiveness." *The Washington Post:* washingtonpost.com/wp-dyn/content/article/2010/04/07/AR2010040703402.html.

21. Devin Burghart and Leonard Zeskind, "Introduction." *Institute For Research & Education On Human Rights:* irehr.org/the-report/introduction.

22. Paul Strand, "Blacks Defend Tea Party against Racist Claims." *CBN:* cbn.com/cbnnews/politics/2011/June/Blacks-Defend-Tea-Party-Against-Racist-Claims-/.

23. Mary C. Curtis, "Glenn Beck 'Restoring Honor' Rally Draws Vast Crowd to National Mall." *Politics Daily:* politicsdaily.com/2010/08/28/glenn-beck-restoring-honor-rally-draws-tens-of-thousands-to-na/.

24. Adelle M. Banks, "RNS: Values Voters See Common Cause, If Not Agenda, with Tea Party." *The Pew Forum:* pewforum.org/Religion-News/RNS-Values-voters-see-common-cause-if-not-agenda-with-tea-party.aspx.

25. "Some Evangelicals on Defensive over Partnering with Glenn Beck, a Mormon." *CNN:* religion.blogs.cnn.com/2010/08/27/some-evangelicals-on-defensive-over-partnering-with-glenn-beck-a-mormon/.

26. Dan Barton, "Beck a Good Christian, but Not Dems." *TFN Insider:* tfninsider.org/2010/08/22/barton-beck-a-good-christian-but-not-democrats/.

27. Barbara Bradley Hagerty, "The Tea Party's Tension: Religion's Role in Politics." *NPR:* npr.org/templates/story/story.php?storyId=130238835.

28. "Adlai Stevenson Quotes." *Search Quotes:* searchquotes.com/quotation/Patriotism_is_not_a_short_and_frenzied_outburst_of_emotion_but_the_tranquil_and_steady_dedication_of/204506/.

CHAPTER 5: The Teavangelical Flavor of the Month

1. David Brody, "Michele Bachmann Tells Brody File She's a 'Teavangelical.'" *CBN*: blogs.cbn.com/thebrodyfile/archive/2011/09/22/michele-bachmann-tells-brody-file-shes-a-teavangelical.aspx.

2. Throughout this chapter, quotations from Keith Nahigian, Bob Heckman, Peter Waldron, and others are all from my personal interviews and conversations with them.

3. Ben Smith and Jonathan Martin, "Rick Perry Schools Michele Bachmann in Waterloo." *Politico*: politico.com/news/stories/0811/61366.html#ixzz1mXtiQnQd.

4. Michael D. Shear, "Perry's Immigration Problem." *The New York Times*: thecaucus.blogs.nytimes.com/2011/09/23/perrys-immigration-problem/.

5. Alex Pappas, "Rivals Criticize Rick Perry over HPV Vaccine Order During Debate." *The Daily Caller*: dailycaller.com/2011/09/12/rivals-criticize-rick-perry-over-hpv-vaccine-order-during-debate/.

6. John Hayward, "Herman Cain Leads Republican Field in Zogby Poll." *Human Events*: humanevents.com/article.php?id=46473.

7. Matthew Jaffe, "Herman Cain: 'They Are Trying to Do Character Assassination on Me.'" *ABC News*: abcnews.go.com/blogs/politics/2011/11/herman-cain-they-are-trying-to-do-character-assassination-on-me/.

8. David Brody, "Herman Cain's Story of God's Healing Power." *CBN*: blogs.cbn.com/thebrodyfile/archive/2011/03/22/herman-cains-story-of-gods-healing-power.aspx.

9. "Romney's Mormon Faith Likely a Factor in Primaries, Not in a General Election." *The Pew Forum*: pewforum.org/Politics-and-Elections/Romneys-Mormon-Faith-religion-and-campaign–2012.aspx.

10. Karla Dial, "Herman Cain's Evangelical Star Loses Some Luster." *Citizen Link*: citizenlink.com/2011/10/20/herman-cain's-evangelical-star-loses-some-luster/.

11. Don Walker and Craig Gilbert, "Cain Stumbles on Libya Question." *JSOnline*: jsonline.com/news/statepolitics/cain-backs-collective-bargaining-for-public-employees-l931tg4–133828808.html.

12. Howard Kurtz, "Newt Gingrich Rips GOP Establishment at CPAC Conference." *The Daily Beast*: thedailybeast.com/articles/2012/02/10/rick-santorum-slams-mitt-romney-at-cpac-conference.html.

13. Sarah Palin, "Cannibals in GOP Establishment Employ Tactics of the Left." *Facebook*: facebook.com/note.php?note_id=10150516734848435.

14. "South Carolina Exit Polls: How Different Groups Voted." *The New York Times*: elections.nytimes.com/2012/primaries/states/south-carolina/exit-polls.

15. "300 Tea Party Groups Endorse Newt Gingrich." *Political Arena*: politicalarena.org/2012/01/30/300-tea-party-groups-endorse-newt-gingrich/.

16. Newsmax Wires, "Gingrich Wins Tea Party Patriots Straw Poll in Florida." *Newsmax*: newsmax.com/InsideCover/Gingrich-Tea-Party-Florida/2012/01/30/id/425987.

17. Dan Kotman, "Newt Gingrich's American Solutions Comes to the Tea Party." *Western Front America*: westernfrontamerica.com/2009/03/18/newt-gingrichs-american-solutions-tea-party/.

18. Marjorie Connelly, "Exit Poll Tells Story Behind Gingrich Win." *The New York Times*: nytimes.com/2012/01/22/us/politics/exit-poll-tells-story-behind-gingrich-win.html?_r=2.

19. David Brody, "Newt Gingrich Tells the Brody File He 'Felt Compelled to Seek God's Forgiveness.'" *CBN*: blogs.cbn.com/thebrodyfile/archive/2011/03/08/newt-gingrich-tells-brody-file-he-felt-compelled-to-seek.aspx.

20. David Brody, "Exclusive: Newt Gingrich Says Media Doesn't Get Evangelicals." *CBN*: blogs.cbn.com/thebrodyfile/archive/2012/01/24/exclusive-gingrich-says-media-doesnt-get-evangelicals.aspx.

21. Grace Wyler, "10 Evangelical Powerbrokers Behind Rick Perry's Prayer Rally to Save America." *Business Insider*: businessinsider.com/here-are-the-masterminds-behind-rick-perrys-prayer-rally-to-save-america – 2011 – 8#david-lane-the-mastermind – 3.

22. Erik Eckholm, "An Iowa Stop in a Broad Effort to Revitalize the Religious Right." *The New York Times*: query.nytimes.com/gst/fullpage.html?res=9806E5DF1E30F930A35757C0A9679D8B63&pagewanted=1.

23. ABC News, "Iowa Conservative Leader Mired in Controversy After Rick Santorum Endorsement." *ABC News*: abcnews.go.com/blogs/politics/2011/12/iowa-conservative-leader-mired-in-controversy-after-rick-santorum-endorsement/.

24. Rachel Weiner, "Bob Vander Plaats Endorses Santorum. Does It Matter?" *The Washington Post*: washingtonpost.com/blogs/the-fix/post/bob-

vander-plaats-endorses-santorum-does-it-matter/2011/12/20/gIQAKvSK7O_blog.html.

25. "Definitive Proof: Santorum Does Not Have Concerns about the Tea Party." *therightscoop.com*: therightscoop.com/definitive-proof-santorum-does-not-have-concerns-about-the-tea-party/.

26. David Lightman and William Douglas, "Santorum Scores High with Tea Party," *stltoday.com*: stltoday.com/news/national/santorum-scores-high-with-tea-party/article_9925d1d2-fa13–5bc4-ae58–0a1003b0f6fa.html.

27. Emily Ekins, "Is Half the Tea Party Libertarian?" *Reason.com*: reason.com/poll/weekly/2011–09–25.

28. "Santorum Catches Romney in GOP Race." *Pew Research Center*: people-press.org/2012/02/13/santorum-catches-romney-in-gop-race/?src=prc-headline.

29. Sarah Wheaton, "Santorum Calls Morality Crucial to Economic Success." *The New York Times*: thecaucus.blogs.nytimes.com/2011/10/07/santorum-calls-morality-crucial-to-economic-success/.

30. Andrew Rafferty, "Santorum Hits on Religious Tones in Pre-Debate Speech." *msnbc.com*: firstread.msnbc.msn.com/_news/2012/02/22/10480280-santorum-hits-on-religious-tones-in-pre-debate-speech.

31. "Rick Santorum Defends Satan Comments." *The Huffington Post*: huffingtonpost.com/2012/02/22/rick-santorum-satan-_n_1293658.html.

32. "Glenn Beck: Rick Santorum 'Is The Next George Washington.'" *RickSantorum.com*: ricksantorum.com/blog/2011/11/glenn-beck-rick-santorum-next-george-washington.

33. "Santorum Catches Romney in GOP Race." *Pew Research Center*: people-press.org/2012/02/13/santorum-catches-romney-in-gop-race/.

34. "Romney's Mormon Faith Likely a Factor in Primaries, Not in a General Election." *The Pew Forum*: pewforum.org/Politics-and-Elections/Romneys-Mormon-Faith-Likely-a-Factor-in-Primaries-Not-in-a-General-Election.aspx.

35. Baptist Press, "Rick Santorum Easily Won Evangelical Vote in Iowa." *Opposing Views*: opposingviews.com/i/religion/santorum-wins-evangelical-voters-iowa-caucuses.

36. "Tea Party on Foreign Policy: Strong on Defense and Israel, Tough on China." *Pew Research Center*: pewresearch.org/pubs/2114/tea-party-foreign-policy-nation-security-israel-defense-china-immigration.

37. Tom McLaughlin, "Tea Party: Romney Most Electable; Paul Best President." *Re TEA Party:* reteaparty.com/2012/01/26/tea-party-romney-most-electable-paul-best-president/.

CHAPTER 6: Teavangelical
Political Powerhouses

1. Felicia Sonmez, "A Mixed Bag for Sarah Palin's Endorsed Candidates in 2010 Election." *The Washington Post:* voices.washingtonpost.com/thefix/governors/a-mixed-bag-for-sarah-palins-e.html.

2. Luke Johnson, "Jim DeMint Compares Sarah Palin to Ronald Reagan: 'She's Done as Much to Change the Political Landscape.'" *The Huffington Post:* huffingtonpost.com/2011/10/06/jim-demint-sarah-palin-2012_n_998015.html.

3. Amy Gardner, "Sarah Palin Issues a Call to Action to 'Mama Grizzlies.'" *The Washington Post:* washingtonpost.com/wp-dyn/content/article/2010/05/14/AR2010051402271.html.

4. "Susan B. Anthony List's Pro-Life Leadership Presidential Pledge." *P2012:* p2012.org/interestg/sbapledge.html.

5. Christopher Lee, "Putting a New Face on Conservatism." *The Washington Post:* washingtonpost.com/wp-dyn/articles/A54940-2005Mar21.html.

6. Kathy Kiely, "Conservatives Urge Pence to Aim for the White House." *National Journal:* nationaljournal.com/politics/conservatives-urge-pence-to-aim-for-the-white-house-20110116.

7. Steven Ertelt, "Mike Pence Not Running for President, Governor Bid Likely." *Life News:* lifenews.com/2011/01/27/mike-pence-not-running-for-president-governor-bid-likely/.

8. David Brody, "Senator Jim DeMint: 'I Need Some New Republicans.'" *CBN:* blogs.cbn.com/thebrodyfile/archive/2010/07/29/mike-pence-talks-2012-with-brody-file.aspx.

9. Evan McMorris-Santoro, "Dick Armey: Mike Pence Is the Second Coming of Reagan." *TPM:* tpmdc.talkingpointsmemo.com/2011/01/dick-armey-mike-pence-is-the-second-coming-of-reagan-video.php.

10. FRC, "Mike Pence Wins Values Voter Summit Straw Poll." *FRC Action:* frcaction.org/action/mike-pence-wins-values-voter-summit-straw-poll.

11. Penny Starr, "Tea Party Movement Shouldn't Focus Only on Fiscal

Conservatism, It's Also About Traditional Morality, Congressman Says." *CNS News:* cnsnews.com/news/article/tea-party-movement-shouldnt-focus-only-fiscal-conservatism-it-s-also-about-traditional.

12. Michael Foust, "Election '08: Dallas Paper Backs Huckabee." *Baptist Press:* bpnews.net/bpnews.asp?id=27538.

13. Huck PAC, "Issues." *Huck PAC:* huckpac.com/?Fuseaction=Issues .Home.

14. "Huck PAC." *Open Secrets:* opensecrets.org/pacs/lookup2.php?strID =C00448373&cycle=2010.

15. "SarahPAC." *Open Secrets:* opensecrets.org/pacs/lookup2.php?strID =C00458588&cycle=2010.

16. David Brody, "Exclusive Interview: Backstage with Mike Huckabee." *CBN:* blogs.cbn.com/thebrodyfile/archive/2010/09/17/exclusive-interview backstage-with-mike-huckabee.aspx.

17. Dick Armey, "Marco Rubio in Give Us Liberty: A Tea Party Manifesto." *On The Issues:* ontheissues.org/Archive/Give_Us_Liberty_Marco_Rubio.htm.

18. Beth Reinhard and Miami Herald, "Rubio's Income Grew with His Political Clout, Tax Records Show." *Tampa Bay:* tampabay.com/news/ politics/national/rubios-income-grew-with-his-political-clout-tax-records-show/1096766.

19. Brian Friel and Richard E. Cohen, "A Congressional Coalition Is Harder to Puzzle Out." *National Journal:* nationaljournal.com/2008voterati ngs?person=400105.

20. Alexander Bolton, "Sen. DeMint Relishes Role as Kingmaker." *The Hill:* thehill.com/homenews/senate/119115-sen-demint-relishes-role-as-kingmaker.

21. David Brody, "Senator Jim DeMint: I Need Some New Republicans." *CBN:* blogs.cbn.com/thebrodyfile/archive/2009/12/10/senator-jim-demint-i-need-some-new-republicans.aspx.

22. "Senate Conservatives Fund." *Open Secrets:* opensecrets.org/pacs/ lookup2.php?cycle=2010&strID=C00448696.

23. David Brody, "Senator DeMint: 'The Problem in the Republican Party Is That the Leadership Has Gone to the Left.'" *CBN:* blogs.cbn.com/the-brodyfile/archive/2009/12/10/senator-demint-the-problem-in-the-republican-party-is-that.aspx.

24. Michael O'Brien, "Mitt Romney Will Sign DeMint's 'Cut, Cap and

Balance' Pledge." *The Hill:* thehill.com/homenews/campaign/169065-romney-joins-demint-backed-cut-cap-and-balance-pledge.

25. Peter Hamby, "5 GOP Candidates Compete at South Carolina Forum." *CNN:* articles.cnn.com/2011–09–05/politics/demint.forum_1_mitt-romney-tea-party-health-care?_s=PM:POLITICS.

26. David Brody, "Senator DeMint to Brody File: Tea Party Movement Will Bring on 'Spiritual Revival.'" *CBN:* blogs.cbn.com/thebrodyfile/archive/2010/04/21/senator-demint-to-brody-file-tea-party-movement-will-bring.aspx.

27. "Go West U.S. Congress." *Allen West for Congress:* allenwestforcongress.com/about.

28. "U.S. Officer Fined for Harsh Interrogation Tactics." *CNN:* web.archive.org/web/20071211102752/http://www.cnn.com/2003/US/12/12/sprj.nirq.west.ruling/index.html.

29. Jamie Weinstein, "The Second Battle of Boca Raton." *The Weekly Standard:* weeklystandard.com/Content/Public/Articles/000/000/017/341xlrau.asp?pg=1.

30. Marc Caputo, "Spat between Wasserman Schultz and Allen West Is Political—and Personal." *The Miami Herald:* miamiherald.com/2011/07/20/v-fullstory/2323481/spat-between-wasserman-schultz.html#ixzz1asLjqTHP.

31. William Gibson, "Florida Reps. Allen West, Debbie Wasserman Schultz Clash." *Los Angeles Times:* articles.latimes.com/2011/jul/20/news/la-pn-west-wasserman-schultz-clash–20110720.

32. "Allen West Unloads on Debbie Wasserman Schultz Again." *The Huffington Post:* huffingtonpost.com/2011/09/29/allen-west-unloads-on-debbie-wasserman-schultz-again_n_987720.html.

33. Alex Leary, "Tea Party Favorite Allen West Gunning for Ron Klein's Seat." *Tampabay.com:* tampabay.com/news/military/war/tea-party-favorite-allen-west-gunning-for-ron-kleins-seat/1124337.

34. Allen West, "Congressional Candidate LTC Allen West At The Revolution / American Freedom Tour." *YouTube:* youtube.com/watch?v=VP2p91dvm6M.

35. Anthony Man, "Ron Klein Attempts to Fend off Challenge from Tea Party Favorite Allen West." *Sun Sentinel:* weblogs.sun-sentinel.com/news/politics/broward/blog/2010/09/ron_klein_attempts_to_fend_off.html.

36. Meena Rupani, "Rep. Allen West to CAIR Director: 'Don't Try to

Blow Sunshine Up My Butt.'" *TalkingPointsMemo.com*: tpmdc.talkingpoints memo.com/2011/02/rep-allen-west-to-cair-director-don't-try-to-blow-sunshine-up-my-butt.php.

37. Allen West, "CPAC 2010." *Conservative.org*: conservative.org/cpac/ archives/archivescpac – 2010-allen-west/.

38. Allen West, "Allen West at Ebenezer Baptist Church (Part 2)." *You-Tube*: youtube.com/watch?v=pSTE21GMqnc&feature=related.

CHAPTER 7: Spreading the Good News: Teavangelicals and the Church

1. "History of Our Tea Party." *Tea Party Fort Lauderdale*: teapartyfort lauderdale.com/contact.html.

2. "Our Pastor." *The Worldwide Christian Center*: twwcc.org/about/pastors-corner/.

3. Dr. O'Neal Dozier, "Dr. O'Neal Dozier, Pastor, 'God Is Not a Socialist, He Is Not a Robin Hood.'" *YouTube*: youtube.com/watch?v=8SOQMwbMhwU.

4. "About the Freedom Federation." *Freedom Federation*: freedomfedera-tion.org/content/about.

5. "The Awakening 2011 Video Presentations." *Freedom Federation*: freedomfederation.org/content/awakening.

6. Liberty Counsel, "Liberty Counsel Hosts Florida Awake! Events with Several Thousand Activists." *The Moral Liberal*: themoralliberal.com/2010/09/14/ liberty-counsel-hosts-florida-awake-events-with-several-thousand-activists/.

7. "Online Audio Messages." *Christian Essentials*: christianessentialssbc. com/messages/.

8. "The Constitution Party of Florida." *Meetup*: meetup.com/Constitution PartyBroward/.

9. Erik Eckholm, "An Iowa Stop in a Broad Effort to Revitalize the Religious Right." *New York Times*: nytimes.com/2011/04/03/us/politics/03pastor .html?pagewanted=all.

10. Wayne Slater, "Kansas Gov. Brownback Will Attend Rick Perry's Day of 'Prayer and Fasting' for Troubled Nation." *Dallas News*: trailblazersblog .dallasnews.com/archives/2011/06/kansas-gov-brownback-will-atte.html.

11. Grace Wyler, "The Christian Right Is Back and Ready to Dominate

the 2012 Campaign." *Business Insider:* businessinsider.com/rick-perry-and-the-return-of-the-christian-right-2012-campaign-2011-8#ixzz1ZpUZ8RUS.

12. Erik Eckholm, "An Iowa Stop in a Broad Effort to Revitalize the Religious Right." *New York Times:* nytimes.com/2011/04/03/us/politics/03pastor.html?pagewanted=all.

13. Lynda Waddington, "Iowa 'Pastors' Policy Briefing' to Host Bachmann, Other 2012 Hopefuls." *The Minnesota Independent:* minnesota independent.com/78361/iowa-.

14. "Amazing Grace — GOP Frontrunners Recruit Pastors for Front Lines Bachmann, Gingrich, Huckabee, Urge Preachers to Renew Their Presence in Politics." *TCU Nation:* tcunation.com/profiles/blogs/amazing-gracegop-frontrunners.

15. Erik Eckholm, "An Iowa Stop in a Broad Effort to Revitalize the Religious Right." *New York Times:* nytimes.com/2011/04/03/us/politics/03pastor.html?pagewanted=all.

16. Tom Hamburger and Matea Gold, "Evangelical Pastors Heed a Political Calling for 2012." *Los Angeles Times:* latimes.com/news/nationworld/nation/la-na-adv-christian-right-20110911.

17. championthevote.com/images/CTV-Insert.pdf.

18. championthevote.com/services.html.

19. "One Nation Under God Event." *One Nation Under God:* onenation undergodevent.com/.

20. championthevote.com/headquarters.html.

21. championthevote.com/downloads/ChurchesandElections.pdf.

22. "Scarborough 1 of 3." *YouTube:* youtube.com/watch?feature=player_embedded&v=iV50CVXUxCw.

23. "About Dr. Scarborough." *Vision America:* visionamerica.us/about-us/about-dr-scarborough/.

24. "Scarborough 1 of 3." *YouTube:* youtube.com/watch?feature=player_embedded&v=iV50CVXUxCw.

25. "Success Stories." *Vision America:* visionamerica.us/success-stories/.

26. "Petition in Support of the Tea Parties and Against Defamation." *Vision America:* visionamericaaction.us/cmedia/tea-party-petition.pdf.

27. visionamerica.us/.

28. "Black-Robed Regiment." *Teaching History.org* teachinghistory.org/history-content/ask-a-historian/24635.

29. Steve Williams, "John Peter Muhlenberg." *American Founding Fathers:* americasfoundingfathers.com/index.php/blacklist.

30. "The 'Black Regiment.'" *Chuck Baldwin Live:* chuckbaldwinlive.com/blackregiment.php.

31. Glenn Beck, "The Black Robe Brigade-Restoring Honor." *YouTube:* youtube.com/watch?v=JfOCfNuNF00.

32. Robert Parham, "Glenn Beck's Generic God." *The Washington Post:* newsweek.washingtonpost.com/onfaith/panelists/robert_parham/2010/08/glenn_becks_generic_god.html.

33. David Barton, "A Brief History." *Black Robed Regiment:* brr.wallbuilders.com/the-original-brr/what-is-the-black-robed-regiment.aspx?utm_source=WallBuilders+Mailings&utm_campaign=09bde20a83-Black+Robe+Regiment&utm_medium=email.

34. aynrandlexicon.com/lexicon/collectivism.html.

35. Steven M. Lukes, "Individualism." *Britannica:* britannica.com/EBchecked/topic/286303/individualism.

36. William R. Thomas, "What Is Objectivism." *The Atlas Society:* atlassociety.org/what_is_objectivism.

37. Ayn Rand, "Introducing Objectivism." *ARI:* aynrand.org/site/PageServer?pagename=objectivism_intro.

38. Ayn Rand, "Introducing Objectivism," *Los Angeles Times* (June 17, 1962), 3–6.

39. Ayn Rand, "Sales of Ayn Rand Books Reach 25 Million Copies." *ARI:* aynrand.org/site/News2?page=NewsArticle&id=17345&news_iv_ctrl=2682.

40. Ayn Rand, "Atlas Felt a Sense of Déjà Vu." *The Economist:* economist.com/node/13185404.

41. Paul Ryan, "Paul Ryan's Videos." *Facebook:* facebook.com/video/video.php?v=1191939045695.

42. Noah Kristula-Green, "Tea Party Embraces Ayn Rand." *Frum Forum:* frumforum.com/conservatives-make-room-for-ayn-rand.

43. Ayn Rand, "Quotations on Freethought and Religions." *About:* atheism.about.com/library/quotes/bl_q_ARand.htm.

44. Ayn Rand, "Introducing Objectivism." *Ayn Rand Institute:* aynrand
.org/site/PageServer?pagename=objectivism_intro.

45. Harry Binswanger, "Abortion" *The Ayn Rand Lexicon: Objectivism from A to Z:*aynrandlexicon.com/lexicon/abortion.html.

CHAPTER 8: **Teavangelicals and the Media**

1. Matt Taibbi, "Michele Bachmann's Holy War." *Rolling Stone:* rollingstone
.com/politics/news/michele-bachmanns-holy-war-20110622?print=true.

2. Marvin Olasky, "The Decline of American Journalism." *WORLDmag:* worldmag.com/world/olasky/Prodigal/c1.html.

3. S. Robert Lichter and Stanley Rothman and Linda S. Lichter, *The Media Elite: America's New Powerbrokers* (New York: Hastings House, 1990), 22.

4. Lichter, Rothman, and Lichter, *The Media Elite,* 29.

5. "Press Widely Criticized, But Trusted More than Other Information Sources." *Pew Research Center:* people-press.org/2011/09/22/press-widely-criticized-but-trusted-more-than-other-institutions/

6. Meg Sullivan, "Media Bias Is Real, Finds UCLA Political Scientist." *UCLA Newsroom:* http://newsroom.ucla.edu/portal/ucla/Media-Bias-Is-Real-Finds-UCLA-6664.aspx.

7. David Brody, "Newt Gingrich to Brody File: Media's Two-Man Race Storyline Smacks of 'Arrogance and Stupidity.'" *CBN:* blogs.cbn.com/thebrodyfile/archive/2011/09/24/newt-gingrich-to-brody-file-medias-two-man-race-storyline-smacks.aspx.

8. Matt Philbin, "Baptism by Fire." *Media Research Center:* mrc.org/cmi/reports/2011/Baptism_by_Fire.html.

9. "Media Research Center Announces $5 Million Campaign Exposing Media Bias." *Media Research Center:* mediaresearch.org/press/releases/2012/20120126120414.aspx.

10. Nicola Menzie, "Rick Perry's Prayer Rally — Church-State Problem or American Tradition?" *The Christian Post:* christianpost.com/news/christian-group-perrys-event-is-government-sponsored-evangelism-53468/.

11. David Brody, "Rick Perry's Wife Says Husband Under Attack Because of His Evangelical Faith." *CBN:* blogs.cbn.com/thebrodyfile/archive/2011/10/13/rick-perrys-wife-says-husband-under-attack-because-of-his.aspx.

12. Nancy Hass, "Before Karen Met Rick." *The Daily Beast:* thedailybeast .com/newsweek/2012/01/15/mrs-santorum-s-abortion-doctor-boyfriend.html.

13. "Media Research Center Announces $5 Million Campaign Exposing Media Bias." *Media Research Center:* mediaresearch.org/press/releases/2012/20120126120414.aspx.

14. "What is dominion theology / theonomy / Christian reconstructionism?" *Got Questions.org:* gotquestions.org/dominion-theology.html.

15. Forrest Wilder, "Rick Perry's Army of God." *Texas Observer:* http://www.texasobserver.org/cover-story/rick-perrys-army-of-god.

16. Michelle Goldberg, "A Christian Plot for Domination?" *The Daily Beast:* http://www.thedailybeast.com/articles/2011/08/14/dominionism-michele-bachmann-and-rick-perry-s-dangerous-religious-bond.print.html.

17. Lisa Miller, "Be Not Afraid of Evangelicals." *The Washington Post:* washingtonpost.com/national/on-faith/dominionism-beliefs-among-conservative-christians-overblown/2011/08/17/gIQAb5eaNJ_story.html.

18. Brian Ross, "Michele Bachmann Clinic: Where You Can Pray Away the Gay?" *ABC News:* abcnews.go.com/Blotter/michele-bachmann-exclusive-pray-gay-candidates-clinic/story?id=14048691&singlePage=true# .TyWYAWDDF5l.

19. "About the Lesbian, Gay, Bisexual and Transgender Concerns Office." *American Psychological Association:* apa.org/pi/lgbt/about/index.aspx.

20. exodusinternational.org/about-us/policy-statements/#Homosexuality.

21. Brad Wilmouth, "Gingrich Calls Out Media's Liberal Bias on Gay Rights." *News Busters:* newsbusters.org/blogs/brad-wilmouth/2012/01/07/gingrich-calls-out-medias-liberal-bias-gay-rights#ixzz1kWJpSDj1.

22. Colleen Raezler, "Media Ignores Study Revealing Anti-Evangelical Bias." *Media Research Center:* mrc.org/cmi/articles/2007/Media_Ignores_ Study_Revealing_AntiEvangelical_Bias.html.

23. Martin Frost, "The Tea Party Taliban." *Politico:* politico.com/news/ stories/0711/60251.html.

24. William Yeomans, "The Tea Party's Terrorist Tactics." *Politico:* politico .com/news/stories/0711/60202.html.

25. Jonathan Allen and John Bresnahan, "Sources: Joe Biden Likened Tea Partiers to Terrorists." *Politico:* politico.com/news/stories/0811/60421.html.

26. "Sen. Menendez: Congress Held Hostage by 'Tea Party Tyrants.'" *Real*

Clear Politics: realclearpolitics.com/video/2011/08/01/sen_menendez_congress
_held_hostage_by_tea_party_tyrants.html.

27. Rich Noyes, "Worst of the Week: MRC Study: 'News' Media Aid
Democrats' Tea Party Trashing." *Media Research Center:* mrc.org/realitycheck/
realitycheck/2010/20101026080909.aspx.

28. "TV's Tea Party Travesty: How ABC, CBS and NBC Have Dismissed
and Disparaged the Tea Party Movement." *Media Research Center:* mrc.org/
specialreports/2010/TeaParty/ExecSumm.aspx.

29. Laura Batchelor, "Occupy Wall Street Lands on Private Property." *CNN
Money:* money.cnn.com/2011/10/06/news/companies/occupy_wall_street_
park/.

30. cbsnews.com/stories/2011/10/11/earlyshow/main20118475.shtml.

31. Laura Bly, "New York's Newest Tourist Attraction? Wall Street
Protests." *USA Today Travel:* travel.usatoday.com/destinations/dispatches/
post/2011/10/new-yorks-newest-tourist-attraction-wall-street-protests/550164/1.

32. Ginia Bellafante, "Gunning for Wall Street, with Faulty Aim." *New
York Times:* nytimes.com/2011/09/25/nyregion/protesters-are-gunning-for-
wall-street-with-faulty-aim.html.

33. "'Occupy Wall Street' Protests Spread to D.C., Boston, L.A. and Chicago." *The Washington Post:* washingtonpost.com/business/occupy-wall-street-
protests-spread-to-dc-boston-la-and-chicago/2011/10/04/gIQA9IOOLL_story
.html.

34. Billy Hallowell, "'Increasingly Debauched': Are Sex, Drugs & Poor
Sanitation Eclipsing Occupy Wall Street?" *The Blaze:* theblaze.com/stories/
increasingly-debauched-are-sex-drugs-poor-sanitation-eclipsing-occupy-wall-
street/.

35. Paul Strand, "Occupy Wall Street Attracting 'Political Fringe.'"
CBN: cbn.com/cbnnews/finance/2011/October/Occupy-Wall-Streets-Political
Fringe/.

36. Douglas Schoen, "Polling the Occupy Wall Street Crowd." *Wall Street
Journal:* online.wsj.com/article/SB10001424052970204479504576637082965745362.html.

37. Dana Loesch, "Journalist 2.0: Occupy Wall Street Emails Show MSM,
Dylan Ratigan, Working with Protesters to Craft Message." *Big Journalism:*

bigjournalism.com/dloesch/2011/10/16/journolist-2-0-occupydc-emails-show-msm-dylan-ratigan-working-with-protesters-to-craft-message/.

38. P. J. Salvatore, "MSNBC's Dylan Ratigan Leads Protest During Broadcast, Shouts at Protesters: 'I Love What You're Doing.'" *Big Journalism*: bigjournalism.com/pjsalvatore/2011/10/03/msnbcs-dylan-ratigan-leads-protest-during-broadcast-shouts-at-protesters-i-love-what-youre-doing/.

39. Lamar Smith, "Such a Double Standard." *Newsbusters*: newsbusters .org/blogs/lamar-smith/2011/12/16/such-double-standard-tea-party-was-extremist-ows-protester-person-year.

40. Aaron Smith, "The Internet and Campaign 2010." *Pew Research Center*: pewinternet.org/~/media//Files/Reports/2011/Internet%20and%20 Campaign%202010.pdf.

41. "CBS News/New York Times Poll." *CBS News*: cbsnews.com/htdocs/ pdf/poll_tea_party_who_they_are_041410.pdf?tag=contentMain;content Body.

42. Theda Skocpol and Vanessa Williamson, *The Tea Party and the Remaking of Republican Conservatism* (New York: Oxford University Press, 2012), 130–31.

43. "The Glenn Beck Program." *Glenn Beck*: glennbeck.com/content/ radio/.

44. "The Top Talk Radio Audiences." *Talkers*: talkers.com/top-talk-radio-audiences/.

45. Paul Scicchitano, "Limbaugh: GOP Establishment Wants to Erase Tea Party." *News Max*: newsmax.com/InsideCover/Limbaugh-Romney-Gingrich-Republican/2012/01/30/id/426029.

46. Rush Limbaugh, "The Republican Establishment Only Wants Conservatives on Election Day." *RushLimbaugh.com*: rushlimbaugh.com/daily/2012/01/31/ the_republican_establishment_only_wants_conservatives_on_election_day.

47. "Americans Spending More Time Following the News Ideological News Sources: Who Watches and Why." *Pew Research Center*: people-press .org/2010/09/12/section-4-who-is-listening-watching-reading-and-why/.

48. Ibid.

49. "Sean Hannity Confronted On the Air." seanhannityconfronted .blogspot.com/.

50. Mark R. Levin, *Liberty and Tyranny: A Conservative Manifesto* (New York: Threshold Editions, 2009), 195.

51. marklevinshow.com/goout.asp?u=http://i25.tinypic.com/vfbekl.jpg.

52. Jeffrey Lord, "Mark Levin and the Book That Changed America." *The American Spectator:* spectator.org/archives/2010/11/09/mark-levin-and-the-book-that-c.

53. Noel Sheppard, "Mark Levin Talks to NewsBusters About 'Ameritopia' and Media's Role in Advancing Utopianism." *News Busters:* newsbusters.org/blogs/noel-sheppard/2012/01/25/mark-levin-talks-newsbusters-about-ameritopia#ixzz1lcle6Iax.

54. "Drudge Report Network" *Quantcast:* quantcast.com/drudgereport.com#traffic.

55. "Drudge Report Archive Stories about 'Tea Party.'" *Drudge Report:* drudgereportarchive.com/drudge-report-topic/tea%20party/.

56. Tim Stanley, "Rumours of Drudge Bias Are Unfounded: The Report Can't Pretend Newt Gingrich Isn't Flawed." *The Telegraph:* blogs.telegraph.co.uk/news/timstanley/100133792/despite-the-rumours-of-romney-bias-drudge-report-remains-the-king-of-conservative-websites/.

57. "The Tea Party Revolution." *Newsmax.com:* w3.newsmax.com/a/jun10/?promo_code=A274-1.

58. David E. Patten, "Will He Return?" *NewsMax.com:* w3.newsmax.com/a/apr09/jesus/.

59. Jeremy W. Peters, "A Compass for Conservative Politics." *The New York Times:* nytimes.com/2011/07/11/business/media/newsmax-a-compass-for-conservative-politics.html?_r=1&pagewanted=print.

60. Josh Peterson, "As Political Season Heats Up, Politico's Web Traffic Cools Down." *The Daily Caller:* dailycaller.com/2011/12/22/as-political-season-heats-up-politicos-web-traffic-cools-down/.

61. Jeremy W. Peters, "A Compass for Conservative Politics." *New York Times:* nytimes.com/2011/07/11/business/media/newsmax-a-compass-for-conservative-politics.html?_r=1&pagewanted=print.

62. Ibid.

63. Jerry Markon, "New Media Help Conservatives Get Their Anti-Obama Message Out." *Washington Post:* washingtonpost.com/wp-dyn/content/article/2010/01/31/AR2010013102860_pf.html.

64. Erick Erickson, "The Perversion of the Words of Our Lord Jesus Christ by the Sinner Barack H. Obama." *Red State:* redstate.com/erick/2012/02/05/the-perversion-of-the-words-of-our-lord-jesus-christ-by-the-sinner-barack-h-obama/.

65. Nikitas3, "2011 in Review: RedState Gathering was Exceptional," *Red State:* redstate.com/nikitas3/2011/12/30/2011-in-review-redstate-gathering-was-exceptional/.

66. "About." *RedState:* redstate.com/about/.

67. "Townhall.com." *Quantcast:* quantcast.com/townhall.com.

68. "Top 15 Most Popular News Websites." *ebizmba:* ebizmba.com/articles/news-websites.

69. "Tea Partiers Reject Beck's Claim That Support of Gingrich Is Racial." *Fox News:* foxnews.com/topics/politics/tea-party.htm.

70. Stephen C. Webster, "'Anonymous' vows to 'destroy' Fox News website on Nov. 5th." *The Raw Story:* rawstory.com/rs/2011/10/24/anonymous-vows-to-destroy-fox-news-website-on-nov-5th/.

71. Mickey Kaus, "Kaus Files." *Daily Caller:* dailycaller.com/2012/02/02/what-does-obama-do-all-day/.

72. Logan Albright, "Obama: Above the Fray or Above the Law?" *Daily Caller:* dailycaller.com/2012/01/31/obama-above-the-fray-or-above-the-law/

73. Michael Calderone, "Tucker: 'Conventional Journalism Is No Safer than a Start-up.'" *Politico:* politico.com/blogs/michaelcalderone/0110/Tucker_Conventional_journalism_is_no_safer_than_a_startup.html.

74. Caroline May, "Evangelicals excluded from Washington National Cathedral's 9/11 commemoration." *The Daily Caller:* dailycaller.com/2011/09/07/evangelicals-excluded-from-washington-national-cathedrals-911-commemoration/.

CHAPTER 9: Where Do Teavangelicals Go from Here?

1. As in previous chapters, some of the unsourced quotations from people like Allen West and others are from my private conversations and interviews with them.

2. Jeffrey M. Jones, "Record-High 40% of Americans Identify as Independents in '11." *Gallup Politics:* gallup.com/poll/151943/Record-High-Americans-Identify-Independents.aspx.

3. Bruce Drake, "Poll: Tea Party Movement Loses Popularity as It Gets Better Known." *Poll Watch Daily:* pollwatchdaily.com/2011/09/02/poll-tea-party-movement-loses-popularity-as-it-gets-better-known/.

4. "NBC/WSJ poll: Tea party isolating themselves from independents." *Daily Kos:* dailykos.com/story/2011/07/19/996397/-NBC-WSJ-poll-Tea-party-isolating-themselves-from-independents.

5. Dana Blanton, "Fox News Poll: 78 Percent Favor Term Limits on Congress." *Fox News:* foxnews.com/politics/2010/09/03/fox-news-poll-percent-favor-term-limits-congress/.

6. Frank Newport, "Americans Want New Debt Supercommittee to Compromise." *Gallup Politics:* gallup.com/poll/148919/Americans-New-Debt-Supercommittee-Compromise.aspx.

7. Jonathan Strong, "Poll: Large majority support balanced budget amendment to Constitution." *Daily Caller:* dailycaller.com/2011/05/27/poll-large-majority-support-balanced-budget-amendment-to-constitution/.

8. Frank Newport, "Americans Anti-Big Business, Big Gov't." *Gallup Politics:* gallup.com/poll/152096/Americans-Anti-Big-Business-Big-Gov.aspx.

9. Lydia Saad, "Americans' Worries about Economy, Budget Top Other Issues." *Gallup Politics:* gallup.com/poll/146708/americans-worries-economy-budget-top-issues.aspx.

10. Garance Franke-Ruta, "Rand Paul Defends Tea Party as 'Mainstream.'" *The Washington Post:* voices.washingtonpost.com/44/2010/07/rand-paul-defends-tea-party-as.html.

11. Jake Sherman, "Freshman 'Embarrassed' by Fellow Rookies," *Politico:* politico.com/news/stories/0112/71292.html#ixzz1n2loZloU.

12. Emily Ekins, "Is Half the Tea Party Libertarian?" *reason.com:* reason.com/poll/2011/09/26/is-half-the-tea-part-libertart.

13. "Libertarians Say Marriage Equality Only One Step Toward Ending Legal Discrimination." lp.org/news/press-releases/libertarians-say-marriage-equality-only-one-step-toward-ending-legal-discriminat.

14. "Most Say Homosexuality Should Be Accepted by Society." *Pew Research Center:* people-press.org/2011/05/13/most-say-homosexuality-should-be-accepted-by-society/.

15. Michael M. Phillips, "Social Conservatives Line Up to Get a Seat at

the Tea Party." *The Wall Street Journal*: online.wsj.com/article/SB1000142405
2748704858304575498090795879052.html?mod=googlenews_wsj.

16. Justin Sink, "Tea Party Leader: Birth-control Fight Will 'Invigorate' Base." *The Hill*: thehill.com/blogs/blog-briefing-room/news/210223-tea-party-leader-says-contraceptive-fight-could-invigorate-conservatives-.

17. "Ouch! Holier Than Thou?" *Radio Patriot*: radiopatriot.wordpress.com/tag/matt-kibbe/.

18. "Statement from Tea Party Express on FreedomWorks." *Tea Party Express*: teapartyexpress.org/2467/statement-from-tea-party-express-on-freedomworks.

19. Susan Page, "Sarah Palin Warns Against Tea Party Infighting." *USA Today*: content.usatoday.com/communities/onpolitics/post/2011/09/sarah-palin-new-hampshire-tea-party-urges-unity/1#.T0qmI2DDF5k.

20. Alex Pappas, "Exclusive: Co-founder Mark Meckler Resigns from Tea Party Patriots." *The Daily Caller*: dailycaller.com/2012/02/24/exclusive-co-founder-mark-meckler-resigns-from-tea-party-patriots/#ixzz1nJdgL3OR.

21. "Dan's Faith Foundation." *Senate District 7 Dan Patrick*: danpatrick.org/faith-foundation.

22. Brandi Grissom, "For Tea Party, a Successful Legislative Session." *The Texas Tribune*: texastribune.org/texas-politics/tea-party/for-tea-party-a-successful-legislative-session/.

23. Jack Brammer, "After Tea Party Rally, Senate Votes to Set Limit on State Debt." *Kentucky.com*: kentucky.com/2012/02/22/2079315/after-tea-party-rally-senate-panel.html.

24. Lawrence D. Jones, "Ky. Senate Passes Bill to Teach Bible in Public Schools." *The Christian Post*: global.christianpost.com/news/ky-senate-passes-bill-to-teach-bible-in-public-schools−48932/.

25. Mary Ellen Klas, "Scott's Rejection of High Speed Rail Hands Win to Tea Party and Defeat to Some GOP Allies." *The Miami Herald*: miamiherald.typepad.com/nakedpolitics/2011/02/in-a-major-victory-for-the-tea-party-movement-govrickscott-will-reject-the-federal-government-money-to-pay-for-nearly-all-o.html#storylink=cpy.

26. "Clay School Board Rejects Teacher Pay Raise." *WOKV.com*: wokv.com/news/news/clay_school_board_rejects_teac/nrrq/.

27. Jennifer Levitz, "Tea Party Heads to School." *The Wall Street Jour-*

nal: online.wsj.com/article/SB10001424052748704336504576259543303853376.html.

28. "Tax Increase Stopped." *Homer/Lockport Tea Party:* homerlockport illinoisteaparty.org/2011/12/26/tax-increase-stopped/.

29. Leslie Kaufman and Kate Zernike, "Activists Fight Green Projects, Seeing U.N. Plot." *The New York Times:* nytimes.com/2012/02/04/us/activists-fight-green-projects-seeing-un-plot.html?_r=1.

30. http://www.people-press.org/2011/11/29/more-now-disagree-with-tea-party-even-in-tea-party-districts/?src=prc-headline.

INDEX

Share Your Thoughts

With the Author: Your comments will be forwarded to
the author when you send them to *zauthor@zondervan.com*.

With Zondervan: Submit your review of this book
by writing to *zreview@zondervan.com*.

Free Online Resources at

www.zondervan.com

Zondervan AuthorTracker: Be notified whenever your favorite
authors publish new books, go on tour, or post an update
about what's happening in their lives at www.zondervan.com/
authortracker.

Daily Bible Verses and Devotions: Enrich your life with daily
Bible verses or devotions that help you start every morning
focused on God. Visit www.zondervan.com/newsletters.

Free Email Publications: Sign up for newsletters on Christian
living, academic resources, church ministry, fiction, children's
resources, and more. Visit www.zondervan.com/newsletters.

Zondervan Bible Search: Find and compare Bible passages in
a variety of translations at www.zondervanbiblesearch.com.

Other Benefits: Register to receive online benefits like
coupons and special offers, or to participate in research.

■ ZONDERVAN®

ZONDERVAN.com/
AUTHORTRACKER
follow your favorite authors